THE PARADISE TREE

THE
PARADISE
TREE

On Living the Symbols of the Church

By

GERALD VANN, O.P.

SHEED & WARD · NEW YORK

MANUFACTURED IN THE UNITED STATES OF AMERICA

A tree hath hope: if it be cut it groweth green again and the boughs thereof sprout. If its root be old in the earth and its stock be dead in the dust, at the scent of water it shall spring, and bring forth leaves, as when it was first planted.

THE BOOK OF JOB

Impleta sunt quae concinit
David fideli carmine
dicens: In nationibus
regnavit a ligno Deus.

Arbor decora et fulgida,
ornata Regis purpura,
electa digno stipite
tam sancta membra tangere.

VENANTIUS FORTUNATUS

O truly sacred mysteries! O pure light! The Lord reveals the sacred signs, for he himself is the hierophant. And thou shalt dance with angels around the unbegotten and imperishable and only true God, and God's Word shall join with us in hymns of praise.

CLEMENT OF ALEXANDRIA

CONTENTS

PART ONE

THE MYSTERY

I

The Pattern

'IN THE BEGINNING was the Word, and the Word was with God, and the Word was God. . . . All things were made by him: and without him was made nothing that was made.'[1] This is the creative Word, in whom all things are ' summed up '[2], revealing himself, revealing the living God, through the total cosmological process, the travail of creation, but above all through the central point of that process, his own life and work in the world; for ' the Word was made flesh, and dwelt among us, and we saw his glory '[3].

In Hebrew, ' word ' means not only words but deeds, events, as well; and events are not arbitrary, they form a pattern, and the pattern reveals the Word because the Word too is the pattern, the definition, the expression, of the Godhead. Just as, in the last resort, law means not arbitrary precepts but a pattern, deriving from that eternal law which is the Godhead expressed in terms of patterns of being and thence of doing, so divine revelation is essentially a question not of textbook definitions or theological tags or dogmatic formularies but of a personal communication demanding a personal response in terms of living. *Abyssus abyssum invocat:* deep calls to deep: it is the Word calling for a responding word, which is faith, which again is essentially a question not just of an intellectual assent to propositions about the nature of God and man but of a pattern of living, and the clue to the pattern is love.

[1] *John*, i, 1–4 (Douai).　　[2] *Ephes.* i, 10 (Knox).　　[3] *John*, i, 14 (Douai).

' I am come that they may have life,' our Lord said; but they will not have life unless they learn and live the pattern.

We live in an age which is marked, psychologically, by an appalling hypertrophy of the masculine over the feminine aspects of living: of action over contemplation, of scientific, commercial, go-getting activities over poetry and prayer and the pursuit of wisdom.[1] As Guardini has said, we have lost our ' living contact with real things ', and can see them now only as ' objects of pursuit and possession, of commerce or research '[2]. Or, as Dr Buber would say, our relationships with things and with people tend to be I–It, not I–Thou, relationships: a matter of utilization, not of meeting.[3] Concupiscence, commercialism, the lust for power, rob us both of the earth and its fullness and of God. ' God is Pure Good in himself,' says Meister Eckhart, ' therefore will he dwell nowhere but in a pure soul.' But what is purity? ' It is that a man should have turned himself away from all creatures and have set his heart so entirely on the Pure Good that no creature is to him a comfort, that he has no desire for aught creaturely, save so far as he may apprehend therein the Pure Good, which is God. And as little as the bright eye can endure aught foreign in it, so little can the pure soul bear anything in it, any stain on it, that comes between it and God. To it all creatures are pure to enjoy; for it enjoyeth all creatures in God, and God in all creatures.'[4] ' " Whoso knows and loves the nobleness of my Freedom," said the voice of God to Mechtild of Magdeburg, " cannot bear to love Me alone, he must love also Me in the creatures." '[5]

All this we have lost, or are in danger of losing, and so are in danger of becoming the most impoverished of all historical civilizations. And this is true not only in the context of culture, of education, of natural living, but in that of religion as well. We have our doctrinal formularies, our catechisms, our creeds, our dogmatic textbooks; but these, though essential, are no substitute for a ' living contact with real things '; they are no substitute for

[1] For a fuller discussion of this theme cf. *The Water and the Fire.* [2] Romano Guardini: *L'Esprit de la Liturgie*, p. 66. [3] Martin Buber: *I and Thou.* [4] Cf. Evelyn Underhill: *Mysticism*, pp. 205-6. [5] *ibid*, p. 206.

the learning and living of the pattern, no substitute for contemplation, no substitute for symbol.

Prof. Mircéa Eliade has pointed out how the contemporary recovery, in the western world, of symbol as part of the psychic life is in fact recovery and not discovery: recovery of something ' which was general in Europe up to the eighteenth century and which is moreover connatural to the extra-European cultures whether " historical " (for example, those of Asia or central America) or archaic and " primitive " '; he goes on to show how providential it is that this recovery should take place at the historical moment when the non-European world, including ethnic groups which hitherto had hardly impinged on the ' making of history ', is now inextricably mingling with the west in that making : for how indeed, as he says, could the positivist, materialist Europe of the nineteenth century have engaged in a ' spiritual dialogue ' with cultures which ' all without exception make use of ways of thought other than those of empiricism and positivism ' [1].

What we are in fact coming belatedly to recognize is that symbol-thinking is both irreplaceable and inescapable. Inescapable: ' we are coming today to understand something of which the nineteenth century could have had no idea: that symbol, myth, image belong to the very substance of the psychic life; that you can camouflage them, mutilate or degrade them, but never extirpate them ': they will live on, in a kind of ' underground ' existence, as through the nineteenth century the idea of the Earthly Paradise lived on in literature in the form of the paradisal South Sea Island where (though the reality was in fact very different) every happiness was to be found, where man was free, ' where there was no need to work for a living, where the women were beautiful and forever young, where love was untrammelled by any " law " and nakedness found again its metaphysical meaning as condition of perfect humanity, of Adam before the Fall'[2].

But if symbolic thinking is inescapable it is because it is a necessity: ' it is consubstantial with the human being, preceding language

[1] *Images et Symboles*, p. 10.   [2] Eliade: *op. cit.* p. 13.

and discursive reason. The symbol reveals certain aspects of reality —the deepest aspects—which defy all other modes of knowledge. Images, symbols, myths are not irresponsible creations of the psyche: they meet a need and fulfil a function, to unveil the most secret modalities of being. . . . If the mind makes use of images to grasp the ultimate reality of things this is precisely because that reality manifests itself in a contradictory fashion and so cannot be expressed in concepts. (One thinks of the desperate efforts of various theologies and metaphysical systems, of east and west alike, to express conceptually the *coincidentia oppositorum*, a mode of being which is easily—and, moreover, abundantly—expressed in images and symbols) '. Modern man ' may despise mythologies and theologies if he will: that will not prevent him from continuing to feed on degraded forms of myth and image ', as in the trenches of Stalingrad or the German or Russian concentration camps ' men and women sang romantic ballads or listened to stories ' which expressed their nostalgia for the lost paradise and rehearsed again for them the age-old myths. ' Time and again the wisdom of the people has expressed the importance of the imagination for the health of the individual, the richness and balance of his inner life '; and psychologists have shown ' the extent to which the dramas of the modern world spring from a deep disequilibrium of the psyche, individual and collective, due in great part to a growing sterilization of the imagination '—for the imagination is the home of images, and ' to have imagination is to see the world in its totality, for it is images that have the power and function of showing forth all that eludes conceptual thinking ' [1].

Hence the supreme importance for the christian of learning and living the symbols of the Church. Creeds and catechisms are essential but they are not enough. Fr Jungmann has pointed out how, in the early Church, ' the religious knowledge which was derived from the Sunday Mass was, as someone strikingly expressed it, a by-product of simply living with the Church. Just as a child, by living with its mother day by day, picks up its mother's speech

[1] Eliade, *op. cit.* pp. 13–24.

and grows into its mother's outlook, so did the faithful grow up in the speech and thought and mind of the Church by uttering her prayers together and celebrating her divine Service ' [1]. And what is true above all of the Mass is true in degree of all the other christian symbols.

Dr Jung points out how our Lord tries to ' purify the sensuous cast of Nicodemus' mind by rousing it from its dense materialistic slumbers ', re-stating what Nicodemus has said, not in realistic terms but in terms of symbol. ' Do not think carnally ', he says to him in effect, ' or you will be flesh; but think symbolically, and then you will be spirit '. ' When we see how much trouble Jesus took to make the symbolical view of things acceptable to Nicodemus . . . and how important it was—and still is—for the history of civilization that people should think in this way, then one is at a loss to understand why the concern of modern psychology with symbolism has met with such violent disapprobation in many quarters. It is as necessary today as ever it was to lead the libido away from the cult of rationalism and realism—not indeed because these things have gained the upper hand (quite the contrary), but because the guardians and custodians of symbolical truth, namely the religions, have been robbed of their efficacy by science. Even intelligent people no longer understand the value and purpose of symbolical truth, and the spokesmen of religion have failed to deliver an apologetic suited to the spirit of the age. Insistence on the bare concretism of dogma, or ethics for ethics' sake, or even a humanization of the Christ-figure coupled with inadequate attempts to write his biography, are singularly unimpressive. Symbolical truth is exposed undefended to the attacks of scientific thought, which can never do justice to such a subject, and in face of this competition has been unable to hold its ground. Exclusive appeals to faith are a hopeless *petitio principii*, for it is the manifest improbability of symbolical truth that prevents people from believing in it. Instead of insisting so glibly on the necessity of faith, the theologians, it seems to me, should see what can be done to

[1] *The Sacrifice of the Church*, p. 40.

make this faith possible. But that means placing symbolical truth on a new foundation—a foundation which appeals not only to sentiment, but to reason. And this can only be achieved by reflecting how it came about in the first place that humanity needed the improbability of religious statements, and what it signifies when a totally different spiritual reality is superimposed on the sensuous and tangible actuality of this world.'[1]

A symbol is a thing with a double life. A beautiful marble statue, a table or tall-boy of well-chosen wood, a goblet of Venetian glass: these have in them the beauty both of material and of form. So a symbol has its own intrinsic nature and beauty—water, wood, wine, fire—but also points beyond itself to a thing or things greater and more beautiful. A *sign* ' always has a fixed meaning, because it is a conventional abbreviation for, or a commonly accepted indication of, something known '. A *symbol* on the other hand ' is an indefinite expression with many meanings, pointing to something not easily defined and therefore not fully known '; it therefore has ' a large number of analogous variants, and the more of these variants it has at its disposal, the more complete and clear-cut will be the image it projects of its object '[2]. And the Church tries to teach us through symbols as well as through doctrine; but we are slow to see and to hear, and much that is of immense value to us, and necessary for us, passes us by. Without a living contact with christian symbols dogma can very easily become stale and sterile, the meaning rubbed away as from a worn penny; more than that, as Dr Austin Farrer has pointed out, the ' purpose of scientific statement is the elimination of ambiguity, the purpose of symbol the inclusion of it ': and we decisively need that ambiguity, that ambivalence, if we are to understand the realities of God, of the soul, of the christian life. So Christ spoke to them in parable, in paradox: you will not truly apprehend the nature of God unless you see him as both just and merciful; you will not understand life unless you see it in terms of both losing

---

[1] Jung: *Symbols of Transformation*, pp. 225-6. [2] Cf. Jung: *Symbols of Transformation* p. 124.

and finding; you will not understand purgatory, or the earthly process which the mystics call the dark nights, unless you see them as both losing and finding, as both pain and joy.

' It lies in the very nature of the symbolic word and the symbolic action,' writes Fr Rahner, ' that a spiritual meaning can never be fully and exhaustively expressed in sensuous terms. The symbol always retains its mysterious background: it is a garment that reveals and at the same time masks the form of the body. . . . The divine word of Scripture is a mystery, and behind the audible meaning of its words and images, of its whole historical narrative, are concealed unknown realms of the spirit and unsuspected possibilities of ascent to the imageless truth. For those endowed with an eye for this, that which is perceptible to the senses is only a kind of extension, jutting into this dark world, of a more real, transcendent realm, a miniature sketch of the vast divine ideas that are the source and ultimate goal of all created thought. . . . Christianity is never a religion of the naked word, of mere reason and ethical law, but of the veiled word, of loving wisdom, of grace concealed in sacramental symbols—and hence also the religion of mysticism, in which the infinite depths of God are disclosed hidden behind simple words and rituals.' And ' God alone is the mystagogue and hierophant of these mysteries: only when his spirit confers the power of vision does man become an epoptes[1] of the christian mystery '[2].

Mr Joseph Campbell, in his *The Hero with a Thousand Faces*, points out how we modern occidentals are ' not disposed to assign to comedy the high rank of tragedy ' because of our ' total misunderstanding of the realities depicted in the fairy tale, the myth, and the divine comedies of redemption. These, in the ancient world, were regarded as of a higher rank than tragedy, of a deeper truth, of a more difficult realization, of a sounder structure, and of a revelation more complete '. The ' happy ending ', he goes on, is to be read, ' not as a contradiction, but as a transcendence, of the

[1] i.e. an initiate. [2] Rahner: *The Christian Mystery and the Pagan Mysteries*, in ' The Mysteries ', Papers from the Eranos Yearbooks, pp. 365-7.

universal tragedy of man'. 'It is the business of mythology proper, and of the fairy tale, to reveal the specific dangers and techniques of the dark interior way from tragedy to comedy.'[1] The same author goes on to show how, through the ages, humanity has learnt its deepest lessons from a myth which, though it assumes a great variety of forms in detail among different peoples, is nevertheless essentially the same myth, the same pattern, so much so that we are entitled to speak of it as the monomyth. It is the story of the hero and his dark journey. The hero leaves his home and adventures forth into the dark kingdom, often the dark waters; there he encounters an adversary, often a dragon or serpent, and there is a stuggle between them ending in death, often that of the hero himself. In any case having arrived at the nadir of the mythological round and undergone his supreme ordeal he gains his reward; his triumph may be represented as a *hierosgamos* or sacred marriage with the goddess-mother of the world, or as his recognition by and at-one-ment with the father-creator, or as his own divinization or apotheosis: intrinsically it is an expansion of consciousness and therewith of being (illumination, transfiguration, freedom). The final work is the return (resurrection); the hero brings back with him the elixir which restores the world.[2]

All this expresses something which lies very deep in human nature: humanity's longing for life, immortal or divine; and the pattern is so universal that one is entitled to speak of it as the pattern of created reality as a whole. You find it in nature, in the cycle of day and night, the sun dying and going back to his mother the sea to be reborn the next day at dawn; and in the cycle of the year, high summer followed by the ' fall ' of autumn and the death of winter and then the rebirth of spring. You find it in myth and folklore and fairy tale and poetry; you find it in dreams; you find it in the teachings of the mystics, in ascetical theology, in the catholic doctrine of purgatory; you find it in the words of Christ when he speaks of the grain of wheat dying or tells Nicodemus that a man

[1] Bollingen Series, Pantheon Books, N.Y., pp. 28-9.   [2] Campbell, *op. cit.* pp. 245-6.

must be reborn of water and the Spirit and that if he would find life he must first lose it. Above all, you find it in the life of Christ himself: for the Word was made flesh and came to dwell among us that he might himself live out the pattern, that thenceforward the pattern should no longer be the expression of an unfulfilled yearning but something that men would be able to live out, effectively, in their turn.

It seems unnecessary today to argue against the once fashionable but extremely superficial view that if the christian story follows so exactly the pattern of humanity's myths we are entitled to regard it as no more ' real ' than they: the similarities are indeed striking, but less so than the differences; for whereas all the myths, profoundly true as they are psychologically, are quite obviously in the realm of fantasy, not of history, the story of Christ is inescapably real and matter of fact, pegged down to precise dates and places and human agencies. The pattern is there, indeed, but at long last made flesh; the struggle is a very real one; the ordeal is brought about by human greed, cowardice, hate, cruelty; the boon, the elixir, is offered here and now and day by day.

Prof. Eliade has pointed out how, for example, the Fathers of the Church, in their treatment of the christian ritual of baptism, ' did not fail to utilize ' certain elements in pre-christian, universal water-symbolism, while at the same time ' enriching them with quite new significance, relating to the historical drama of Christ '; the symbolism of baptism is in fact ' saturated with biblical allusions ' —from Christ in the Jordan back to Noah and the deluge, to the sea-dragon Behemoth, finally to Adam and to the nakedness, the innocence, of paradise—so that in fact it can be said of the early Fathers that their preoccupation was almost entirely typological, ' finding correspondences between Old and New Testaments '. And, as the same author goes on to show, modern writers have tended to follow this example: ' instead of re-setting christian symbolism in the framework of the " general " symbolism to which all the religions of the non-christian world give universal witness, they persist in referring it back solely to the Old Testament'. This is readily explicable in terms of a reaction against 'the tendency to explain christianity in terms of the mystery-religions and gnostic syncretisms, and against the *confusionnisme* of certain schools of comparative religion. Christian liturgy and symbol are directly linked with judaism: christianity is an historical religion, deeply rooted in another historical religion, that of the Jews'. For the christian, 'revelation has had a *history*; the primitive revelation, given at the dawn of time, survives still among the nations but in a half-forgotten, mutilated, corrupt state; the only way of approach is through the history of Israel, the revelation is fully preserved only in the sacred books of the Old Testament'[1].

For the early Church the rigorous exclusion of everything pagan could well be a necessity if ' the *history* which was at the same time a *revelation*' was not to be confused with pagan 'mysteries' and if ' the message of Christ was to triumph'; but, as Prof. Eliade goes on to show, the same is not necessarily true today. The fact is clear: that ' the judæo-christian symbolism of baptism in no way contradicts the universal water-symbol': flood, waters of death, monsters of the abyss, ritual nakedness, all these are to be found in innumerable traditions throughout the world. It is not that 'judaism or christianity " borrowed " such myths and symbols from neighbouring races: that was not necessary; judaism inherited a pre-history and a long religious history in which all these things already existed'[2]; and some of the early Fathers were in fact at pains to point out to the unbeliever the close relationship between the old universal symbols and the new christian dogmas. The former point the way to the latter; form a natural, perhaps unconscious, prolegomenon to the acceptance of the latter. How, asks Fr Beirnaert, ' could the candidate for baptism understand the symbolic images proposed to him if these did not correspond to his own obscurely-sensed expectations'[3]? The Fathers indeed use this correspondence to convince the unbeliever, they appeal to the universal pattern by way of preparing the ground for the christian

---

[1] Eliade: *op. cit.* pp. 202-7.   [2] *ibid.* pp. 207-9.   [3] *The Mythic Dimension in Christian Sacramentalism*, quoted Eliade, *op. cit.* p. 210.

revelation. ' See ', writes Minutius Felix for example, ' how all nature suggests a future resurrection for our consolation. The sun sets and rises again; the stars sink down and return; the flowers die and come to life again; the vines spend themselves and are renewed; the seeds do not renew life unless they first know corruption.' [1] True, these are but vague indices; the symbols of which christianity makes use ' do not relate primarily to myths and to immanent archetypes but to the intervention of divine power in history. But the new meaning should not lead us to misunderstand the permanence of the old meaning. In taking up again the great figures and symbolizations of the natural religious man, christianity has also adopted their virtues and their powers over the depths of the psyche. . . . The christian has renounced seeking his spiritual salvation in myths and in the sole experience of immanent archetypes, but he has not therefore renounced all that the myths and symbolizations signify and effect for psychic man—for the microcosm. It is through the mediation of the myths that the salvation inaugurated in the fine point of the soul penetrates even to the depths of the psyche. The revival by Christ and by the Church of the great images such as the sun, the moon, the wood, water, mother, etc., signifies an evangelization of the affective powers designated by the images. It is not necessary to reduce the Incarnation to simply the taking on of flesh. God has intervened even in the collective unconscious in order to save it and fulfil it. Christ descended into hell. How then will this salvation reach our unconscious unless it speaks its language, unless it revives its categories? To the extent that a sacramentalism (or, more generally, any religious representation) neglects to make use of archetypal figures, and reduces its ritual to a schematic unfolding, it loses its efficacy over the pagan man which slumbers in each of us—it fails to evangelize the depths ' [2]. But all this must not cause us to lose sight of the one essential fact, that christianity itself is not essentially concerned with immanent archetypes, that ' the great originality of

---

[1] Cf. Beirnaert, *op. cit.* (*Cross Currents*, Fall, 1951, p. 79; cf. Selection I, ed. Cecily Hastings and Donald Nichol, Sheed & Ward, 1953.)   [2] Beirnaert, *op. cit.* p. 84.

judæo-christianity lies in the transforming of history into theology'[1]. Prof. Eliade suggests that the ' accessibility '—perhaps one might say the ' acceptability '—of christianity lies in great part in its symbolism: that the ' universal images which it in its turn resumes have considerably facilitated the diffusion of its message '; for the question which might trouble a non-christian—' how can a " local " history claim to be the model for every divine manifestation in concrete, historical time? '—is answered by the fact that the sacred history, ' though it be, in the eyes of a non-christian observer, a local history, is equally an exemplar since it resumes and perfects trans-temporal images '; but he goes on to ask ' whence comes the irresistible impression, felt especially by the non-christians, that christianity has been an *innovator* in respect of anterior religions? For a Hindoo sympathetic to christianity the most striking innovation (apart from the message of the divinity of Christ) consists in the *valorisation* of time, and in the last resort in the *salvation* of time and of history. The reversibility of cyclic time is replaced by time which is irreversible because the sacred manifestations, the hierophanies, included in it are no longer repeatable: it is once and for all that Christ lived, was crucified, rose again. . . . How could time be vain and empty when it has seen Christ being born, suffering, dying and rising again? How could it be reversible and repeatable *ad infinitum*? From the point of view of the history of religions, judæo-christianity presents us with the supreme hierophany: *the transfiguration of historical events themselves into hierophany*. . . . It is not merely that God intervenes in history, as was the case with judaism, but that he becomes incarnate in an historical being to live a life which is historically " conditioned ": in appearance Jesus of Nazareth is in no way different from his contemporaries in Palestine; . . . [he] eats food and digests it, he suffers from thirst or heat, just like any other Palestinian Jew. But in reality this " his-

---

[1] Eliade, *op. cit.* p. 217. It should be pointed out that Fr Beirnaert's contention is that in baptism the neophyte enters the font, with Christ, precisely to renounce, overcome and annul the archetypes; and that this is what faith does. It may be questioned whether in fact it is the archetypes themselves that faith annuls, or whether (as other experts would prefer to say) it is domination *by* the archetypes; but this is not the place, nor is the present writer in any way competent, to embark on a discussion of this problem.

torical event" which constitutes the life of Jesus is a total theophany '[1].

There is thus an essential difference—in one sense a complete cleavage—between the christian *mysterion* and the pagan ' mysteries '. This has been forcefully stated by Fr Rahner in the paper already quoted. ' *Mysterion* ', he writes, ' is the stupendous drama of human redemption, which issues from the depths of God, is manifested in Christ and the Church, and returns to the depths of God.' It is always both a manifesting and a concealment: ' manifest in the communication of the truth through the promised Christ; concealed in the unfathomable nature of the divine utterance, which even after its communication cannot be fully understood but is apprehended only by faith. For this *mysterion* is a supernatural drama transcending all human nature and all human thought, the drama of man's acceptance as the son of God '; it is secret inasmuch as ' here on earth it appeals only to faith and once taken in faith permits only a slow ascent to understanding, to a holy gnosis '; it is revealed because ' it is " proclaimed from the rooftops ", addressed to all mankind, free from all esotericism and occultism '.

Fr Rahner goes on to show how the great drama of God's self-revealing in Christ—especially the ' Old Testament story of salvation conceived as a single parable finding its key and explanation in Christ ', and then Christ's own acts and Passion, and the Church, and within the Church the sacraments and the formulas of divine truth—how all this is the *mysterion*; so that it is ludicrous to identify that *mysterion* with the ' mysteries ' of the pagan religions, and still more to attempt to derive it from them. ' Recent research has indeed shown that the New Testament *mysterion* cannot be interpreted in the cultic sense that it possesses in the pagan religions of antiquity. . . . It is and remains a riddle how in the period of unrestricted " comparative religion " scholars should even have ventured a comparison, not to speak of trying to derive the basic doctrines of Christ from the mystery religions.'[2] ' Christian revelation is not myth but history, and its deposit is the visible

op. cit. pp. 222-4.   [2] Rahner, *op. cit.* pp. 358-9.

Church, the concrete language of the New Testament, the precisely ascertainable apostolic tradition, the set forms of the sacraments. The God of the christian mystery is no intellectual construction or embodiment of yearning, however sublime, such as grew from the religious searchings of hellenistic man; ' he is the ' " God who is found only in the ways taught by the Gospel ". That is why the christian mystery is " foolishness " to every mere Greek (I *Cor.* i, 23). For it is the incarnation and human death of God. . . . Mystery religion at best is man's earthbound, tragic attempt to purge and raise himself morally (and sometimes only ritually) by his own resources—while in christianity it is not man who raises himself up but *God* who descends, conferring upon man the divine grace that makes possible his moral regeneration in the love of Christ '[1]. Thus we can talk of the ' cosmic mystery of the Cross ' since it explains, sums up, is expressed in and fulfils the whole cosmological process: it is the ' epitome of the structural law of the universe; for the whole cosmos the Cross is the *"mechane"* (as Ignatius of Antioch once called it) of the return to heaven, and its mystical sign can be seen in the whole cosmos . . . everywhere . . . [for] all things are implicitly a *mysterion tou staurou* or mystery of the Cross '[2]. ' The early christian's mystic belief in the significance of the Cross was so profound that it elucidated the Old Testament and the cosmos alike as by a stroke of magic '; and everything that God revealed ' was uttered only with a view to the future act of salvation ' in which incarnate Wisdom would be crucified.[3]

So St Paul, writing in the ' fullness of time ', tells us: ' When all this happened to them, it was a symbol; the record of it was written as a warning to us, in whom history has reached its fulfilment '[4].

Now if it is absurd to think of the christian *mysterion* as derived from the pagan mystery religions, it would be equally absurd to refuse to see any common ground between them: what were at

---

[1] Rahner, *op. cit.* pp. 357-61.   [2] *ibid.* pp. 375-7.   [3] *ibid.* p. 380.   [4] I *Cor.* x. 11 (Knox).

one time thought to be ' " borrowings " of christianity from the mysteries, grew to life in the early Church from a root that has indeed no bearing on a historical-genetic dependence, but that did spring from the universal depths of man, from the psycho-physical nature common to heathen and christian alike. . . . Every religion forms sensory images of spiritual truths: we call them symbols. The revealed religion of the God-man could speak only in images intelligible to man: " And without parable he did not speak unto them " (*Mark*, iv, 34). And the transcendent content of his message was cloaked in primordial human images of the father, the king, of light and darkness, of the living water and the burning fire, of the pearl and the seed of grain. The same is true of the cult rites that he instituted with a view to intimating and inducing transcendent grace: the cleansing, the supper, the anointing, the judgement ' [1].

Now all these things, water, wood, fire, bread, wine, oil and so on, the Church puts vividly before us both in the life of Christ and in the sacramental life of the Church itself. But we have become very blind to and remote from all these things, and so it is that we all too easily miss their meaning and in consequence creeds and doctrinal terms and formulas may easily lose their vitality for us and come to seem very unreal. For both ways of knowledge are necessary: we need dogma to prevent us from straying, in our apprehension of symbol, into strange paths—and the history of mysticism shows how strange such paths can be; on the other hand we need the vitality of symbol to prevent us from coming to find that doctrine and dogma have become for us dead things, dry bones. ' No man has ever seen God; but now his only-begotten Son, who abides in the bosom of the Father, has himself brought us a clear message .' [2] It is that message, as revealed in the life of Christ himself and then in the way of life he fashioned for his Church, that the following pages will be concerned to study.

---

[1] Rahner, *op. cit.* p. 363.   [2] *John*, i. 18 (Knox).

2

The Pattern in the Christ-Life

THE UNIVERSAL MYTH begins with the hero leaving his home and setting forth on his journey into the darkness; the Christ-life begins with the Word leaving, in a sense, his eternal home—emptying himself and taking on the form of a servant—and being born into darkness. (At Christmas we sing the antiphon, ' While all things were held in quiet silence and night was in the midst of its course, then thy almighty Word leapt down from his eternal throne'. And in the Gospel we read that it was while the shepherds were keeping their night watches that Christ was born.) He was born in a stable, and traditionally the stable is thought of as fashioned out of a cave, thus underlining the idea of a descent into the dark, into the earth. For ' the descent into the earth is a piece of womb-symbolism and was widespread in the form of cave-worship. Plutarch says that the Magi offered sacrifices to Ahriman " in a sunless place ". In Lucian, the magician Mithrobarzanes descends into the bowels of the earth " at a desolate spot, marshy and sunless ". According to the testimony of Moses of Chorene, the Armenians worshipped " Sister Fire " and " Brother Spring " in a cave. Julian records the Attis legend of a "descent into the cave ", from which Cybele brings back her son-lover. The cave where Christ was born in Bethlehem (" The House of Bread ") is said to have been an Attis *spelæum* ' [1].

[1] Cf. Jung, *Symbols of Transformation*, pp. 341-2.

The cave-motif thus sets the earthly life of the Word in its general framework of death and life, darkness and light. ' The mysteria begin for the mystes when, as sufferer of the event (*myou-menos*), he closes his eyes, falls back as it were into his own darkness, enters into the darkness. The Romans use the term " going-into ", " *in-itia* " (in the plural), not only for this initiating action, the act of closing the eyes, the *myesis*, which is exactly rendered as *initiatio*, but for the mysteria themselves. A festival of entering into the darkness, regardless of what issue and ascent this initiation may lead to: that is what the mysteria were, in the original sense of the word. . . . [They] took the initiate back to the very beginning of life, its natural genesis. . . . And it is not by accident that they were enacted at night. The nocturnal element was not limited to the covering of the mystes in the first moment of initiation. The mysteria were so essentially nocturnal that in them every aspect of the night was experienced, even that power residing solely in the night, the power to engender the light as it were, to help it come forth. They were not merely a nocturnal festival, they actually—or at least it seems so—solemnized the feeling of being shut in by the night, culminating in a sudden great radiance.'[1]

Christ's entry into the world of men in darkness underlines his ' self-emptying '; at the same time it underlines his homelessness: later on he will remark that ' the foxes have holes and the birds of the air their nests but the Son of Man hath not where to lay his head '. There was no room for him in the inn, among the company of men, for his journey must be made in loneliness; and perhaps we should compare the traditional placing of the ox and the ass in the crib with St Mark's phrase that in the desert he was ' with beasts ', bereft of all human companionship. True, as a child he had the love and care of his parents and as a man he had friends and followers, just as in the myth the hero has his helpers; the journey is not all darkness; his human experience must have included joy of an intensity beyond our imagining; his joy in the beauty of Nature, for instance, must have been not only infinitely more

---

[1] Rahner, *op. cit.* pp. 39-40.

intense, as an æsthetic experience, than any we could know, but also of a *kind* that only he could know, since it included the joy of the artist in his art-work, for ' all things were made by him '; but it is darkness and loneliness which preponderate; he knew the loneliness caused by a lack of understanding, for we read that first his parents, despite their love, and then his followers, again and again failed to understand; and though as a child he knew the shelter of home he would have to leave it and go alone to meet his adversary.

The divine infancy itself is overshadowed by sorrow and tragedy: the malignity of Herod, the flight into Egypt, the massacre of the innocents; and the story of the childhood ends on a note of anguish, that ' anguish of mind ' which his parents knew when they thought, as they returned home from the Temple, that the child was lost. But there was also, before the tragedy and the anguish, a moment of glory, the Epiphany, just as later on before the agony in the garden there would be the moment of glorious transfiguration on the mountain.

The history of the Epiphany—of the actual events themselves and of the christian feast which celebrates them—is complicated; and the picture with which we are now so familiar, the three kings, one of them a negro, representing the three races descended from Noah, coming from the east to adore the divine child, is based largely on legend. But psychologically speaking, legend which is the gradual, mysterious product of popular belief and cultus is as important as history—is indeed part of history—and we are well-advised to study it carefully. In the Gospel we are told simply that ' certain wise men came out of the east to Jerusalem, who asked, Where is he that has been born, the king of the Jews? We have seen his star out in the east, and we have come to worship him ': and that when they were told, 'At Bethlehem in Juda ', they went thither, the star they had seen before now re-appearing and guiding them ' till at last it stood still over the place where the child was '; and so they found the child, and ' fell down to worship him ', and

' opening their store of treasures, they offered him gifts, of gold and frankincense and myrrh ' [1].

St Matthew calls the wise men Magi. This might mean that they were members of the Persian priestly caste; or that they were sorcerers; or again that they were simply learned astronomers, and indeed astrologers but without the pejorative overtones conveyed by the word ' sorcerer '. Lagrange, who favoured this third view, held that they came from Arabia, partly because the gifts they brought were such as visitors from that land would in fact bring with them to do homage to a king. He thought it probable too that the ' star ' was in fact a comet, and noted that the behaviour of Halley's comet in 1910, as observed by him in Jerusalem, matched the description given in the Gospel, and that comets do sometimes give the impression of hovering over a place. [2] The idea that the Magi were kings is post-patristic in origin, though Tertullian speaks of them as *fere reges*, all but kings; as time went by their kingship came to be generally assumed and, in the west, where their number ended by becoming fixed at three (in the east it was generally put at twelve) they came to be referred to by name as Gaspar, Melchior and Balthasar. The gifts they offered suggested, *post factum*, an obvious symbolism: if, taken together, they suggest simply an image of the glory of an eastern king such as the royal young bridegroom of *Psalm* xliv, his garments ' scented with myrrh and aloes and cassia ', taken separately—and, for the myrrh, having the account of our Lord's burial in *John* xix, 39 in mind—they suggest at once human mortality, kingly glory, and godhead, as in the lines of Juvencus:

> *Thus, aurum, myrrham, regique, hominique, Deoque,*
> *Dona ferunt;*[3]

while in the breviary-office of the feast one of the responsories speaks of the gifts as containing within themselves ' divine mysteries ', for ' in the gold is made manifest the power of the King,

---

[1] *Matth.* ii, 1–12 (Knox).   [2] *Evangile selon S. Matthieu*, ii, 2, 9.   [3] Cf. Lagrange, *op. cit.* ii, 11.

in the incense you see the great Priest, and in the myrrh, the burial of the Lord '. There is no reason whatever to suppose that the Magi had any idea of the divinity of the Child to whom they had come to do homage; but in fact they come, these priest-kings, and bow down before the Child who is priest and king and God, and they lay before him the symbols of power and of glory but also of that mortality he has chosen and will later on deliberately choose again when Satan would have him choose power and glory alone; and we can see them as representing humanity as a whole, whether we think of them as three in number (the three races descended from Noah) or as twelve (the twelve tribes, the twelve signs of the zodiac about the central sun); but especially we can see them in their kingly-priestly character, high priests of humanity—and one of the traditional names, Melchior (' king of light') suggests the Old Testament figure of the ' pagan ' priest-king Melchizedech whose sacrifice is recalled, as we shall see, every day in the Canon of the Mass, a sacrifice which was greater than that of Abel and even of Abraham—humanity therefore laying down, so to speak, its pretence of being able to offer sacrifice of itself and saluting instead him who alone could and would offer in and through his own flesh the one true sacrifice and in so doing would institute the sacrifice that would be humanity's as well as his.

Our instinct is to try to escape from pain, struggle, responsibility; to project our guilt on to something other than ourselves, to find a scape-goat. But the pattern cannot be lived out for us; while we cannot achieve it *by* ourselves, it has to be achieved *in* ourselves or it avails us nothing. So the myrrh reminds us of death and darkness and burial; and in the traditional telling of the story it is in a grotto or cave that the kings find the Child, reminding us of the symbolism of the *spelæum*. We have to go down into the darkness, and we have to go naked into the darkness: sacrifice means a total self-giving, the ' self-naughting ' of the mystics, so that just as all kingship and all priesthood can come only from God, so all power and all glory must be given back, consecrated, to God if the power is not to corrupt and the glory be illusory. But the word 'Magi' emphasizes for us the fact that these men were not only kings and priests, they were men of wisdom, that wisdom which is humanity's greatest natural glory and which therefore more than all else has to be laid at the feet of Christ. And that perhaps is why all this takes place when the Child is in fact still a baby. History is obscure here: it is impossible to fix the exact time of the coming of the kings; but at least it seems certain that our Lord must have been less than two years old or Herod's massacre of all the male children of two years old and less in and around Bethlehem would have been pointless. The contrast then is clear: the kings represent the wisdom of this world; indeed as Magi they represent that wisdom at its most esoteric, wisdom as it has appeared at its most godlike in the dreams and ambitions of men; but all this is to be laid at the feet of the Child who is indeed the *Logos* but who also has yet to learn to shape his lips and tongue to his native language. Isaiah had written, long ago: 'I will confound the wisdom of wise men, disappoint the calculations of the prudent'[1]; and St Paul, quoting him, was to write later on: 'What has become of the wise men, the scribes, the philosophers of this age we live in? Must we not say that God has turned our worldly wisdom to folly?.... Here are the Jews asking for signs and wonders; here are the Greeks intent on their philosophy; but what we preach is Christ crucified; to the Jews, a discouragement, to the Gentiles, mere folly; but to us who have been called, Jew and Gentile alike, Christ the power of God, Christ the wisdom of God. So much wiser than men is God's foolishness; so much stronger than men is God's weakness'[2].

There is, then, to be a new priesthood; there is to be a new concept of kingship; there is also to be a new wisdom. 'There is, to be sure, a wisdom which we make known among those who are fully grounded, but it is not the wisdom of this world, or of this world's rulers, whose power is to be abrogated. What we make known is the wisdom of God, his secret, kept hidden till now....

[1] *Isaiah*, xxix, 14 (as quoted in I *Cor.* i, 19, Knox).   [2] I *Cor.* i, 20-6 (Knox).

31

[For] what we have received is no worldly wisdom; it is the Spirit of God, to make us understand God's gifts to us. '[1]

The Magi thus submit, consecrate, sacrifice the wisdom of the world to the folly of God's infancy, the folly of the Cross: they plunge the illusory light of merely human brilliance into the darkness of the cave. The scene thus stands out in sharp contrast to the later moment of temptation when Satan, he too a monarch, brilliant, beautiful, filled with a knowledge older than the world, will offer Christ all power and all glory if falling down he will adore him. And how much more closely Christ would thus resemble the royal young bridegroom of the forty-fourth psalm— girt with all his majesty and all his beauty, riding on triumphant, subduing nations to his will, his garments scented with myrrh and aloes and cassia, daughters of kings coming out to meet him, harps sounding from ivory palaces in his honour [2]—than if he took the other way, the way of the Man of Sorrows! But no; God had already chosen what the world holds weak and foolish, God had already ' chosen what the world holds base and contemptible, nay, ... what is nothing, so as to bring to nothing what is now in being; no human creature was to have any ground for boasting, in the presence of God '; and St Paul goes on to quote the words of Jeremiah: ' If anyone boasts, let him make his boast in the Lord ' [3].

But the new wisdom does not mean the destruction of the old: it means the destruction of the arrogant self-sufficiency, and therefore the falsehood, of the old. Plato and Aristotle are not foolishness; but to think that Plato and Aristotle are enough is foolishness. They are not enough, and all the wisdom of the world is not enough, unless wedded to the folly of the Cross. We think of the feast of the Epiphany as celebrating simply the coming of the Magi, but its history is a complex one, and still today in the breviary-office this history is reflected in the commemoration of other events as well. So, at Lauds, the *Benedictus* antiphon tells us: 'Today the Church

---

[1] I *Cor.* ii, 6–13 (Knox).   [2] Cf. *Ps.* xliv, 4–10 (Knox).   [3] I *Cor.* i, 28–31 (Knox).

is made one with her heavenly bridegroom, because Christ has washed away her sins in the waters of Jordah;[1] the Wise Men hasten with their gifts to the royal nuptials; and those who have been called to the feast are made glad with the water-turned-into-wine '. Bethlehem, Jordan, Cana: the moment of glory, the symbolic submission of humanity; then the beginning of the (adult) dark journey, the descent into the waters, the brooding Dove, the Voice declaring, promulgating, the sonship of Christ; and so, finally, the marriage of heaven and earth, the water of fallen humanity turned by the divine creative power (elicited by the Mother) into the wine of humanity redeemed and made glorious. So the dark journey will end with the new dawn, the ascension to heaven, and thence the pentecostal light and fire; so the rosary, which begins with joy but goes on to sorrow, to the way of the Cross, ends with ' the crowning of the Mother and the glory of all the saints '.

But before the glory there must be the sorrow; before the light, the darkness; before the gladness of the wedding-feast, the anguish of separation.

That idea of separation would seem to be the key to the mysterious story of how when he was twelve Jesus went with his parents to Jerusalem and, when they began the return journey, stayed behind. (There is a legend that Moses was twelve when he left his father's house to become a teacher of mankind; Samuel too, according to tradition, was twelve when he received the divine call, and Solomon the same age when he gave his famous judgment concerning the child. Jewish girls were legally marriageable at this age. An old Jewish rule says: ' At ten the Mishnah, at thirteen the Commandments': twelve is the borderline, the threshold of manhood, the apotheosis of childhood.)

---

[1] In the east there is, at the beginning of the feast, a rite of blessing of waters in which the faithful then bathe or with which they are sprinkled; one of the old names for the feast is ' the day of lights ' because lights were carried (as they still are in our rite of baptism) to symbolize the baptismal rebirth. In the western office for the feast references to Christ's baptism are frequent, and Cana also is mentioned in the hymns at Vespers and Lauds, the former containing the line (which perhaps was the source of a more famous though less felicitous line of Crashaw, *Aquae rubescunt hydriæ:* ' The water pots are ruddy grown ' (as the Marquess of Bute's translation puts it).

'And they, thinking that he was among their travelling companions, had gone a whole day's journey before they made enquiry for him among their kinsfolk and acquaintances. When they could not find him, they made their way back to Jerusalem in search of him, and it was only after three days that they found him. He was sitting in the temple, in the midst of those who taught there, listening to them and asking them questions.'[1]

A boy of twelve is often to be met with in myth and story: he is the *puer æternus*, the eternal boy who is the symbol of immortal youth or of youth regained; like the blessed in St Thomas's picture of heaven,[2] he is usually naked, as in the representations of Eros or the young Dionysus, of the Renaissance cherubs and *putti*, the nude youths of the Sistine ceiling, the *Sacrifice of Isaac* of Ghiberti or Bazzi, the *St John in the Desert* of Domenico Veneziano, for he is also the symbol of freedom; at the same time he is often associated with the paradise-garden symbol because he expresses humanity's longing for the lost paradise or, in christian terms, for the joy and beauty and freedom of heaven, and often he is to be found on an island, i.e. in close connection with the sea. In mythology we meet for instance Eros, the young Dionysus, Tammuz, Attis, Adonis, the Eleusinian Iacchus and the Etruscan Tages. In Islamic legend there is the 'eternally youthful Chidher' or 'Khidr', the 'Verdant One', born as a 'son of the watery deep', who imparts his wisdom to Moses. Dr Jung notes that the 'rapid growth of the hero [to wisdom], a recurrent motif, seems to indicate that the birth and apparent childhood of the hero are extraordinary because his birth is really a rebirth, for which reason he is able to adapt so quickly to his heroic role'; so Tages, also, the 'boy who sprang from the freshly-ploughed furrow', is a teacher of wisdom. The *puer* is of course often to be met with in poetry—'of course' because the poet expresses those unconscious themes which to his more prosaic contemporaries are a closed book—as also in fiction and imaginative literature generally. He is usually twelve years old; usually naked. For Meleager, Eros

[1] *Luke*, ii, 44–7 (Knox). [2] *Compend. Theol.* clvi.

34

was the 'most beautiful of gods , Hölderlin cries, 'all hope lies in youth renewed', and in his symbolism of that youth brings together the images of sea, earth, wine and sun:

> *There on the loveliest of the islands . . . there lay beneath*
> *The vines, O mother Earth, thy loveliest child—*
> *And the boy raises familiar eyes*
> *To Father Helios.*[1]

But the *puer* is also the symbol of separation: the apotheosis of childhood, after which adolescence begins and with it the gradual process of separation from the mother: he must begin gradually to make his own life, to follow his own vocation, to embark on his own dark journey. As Dr Buber puts it, 'all living is meeting'; but if there is to be meeting there must first be separation. The child is, so to speak, part of its mother; if they are to 'meet', the boy must cease to be that, he must go away, he must become a personality in his own right; only then, when he has done that, can he return and *meet* his mother. It is significant that El Greco, in his painting of Christ meeting his mother, does in fact depict them precisely face to face; not one bending down to the other but on the same level: the lack of understanding is all over now, there is perfect understanding; and with deep insight Miss Dorothy Sayers in her dramatization of the life of Christ, when she depicts the scene of the meeting of mother and Son on the way to Calvary, makes Mary say, in answer to another woman who urges her to speak to Jesus, 'We have no need of words, my Son and I'.

But the separation is a sort of death; and, as Dr Jung has pointed out, the losing-finding theme is simply a variant of the pattern of death and rebirth. 'The forward-striving libido which rules the conscious mind of the son demands separation from the mother, but his childish longing for her prevents this by setting up a psychic resistance that manifests itself in all kinds of neurotic fears—that is to say, in a general fear of life. The more a person shrinks

[1] For all this, cf. Jung: *Symbols of Transformation*, and *Psychological Types*; also, for some of the references, W. P. Witcutt: *The Child in Paradise* (Guild of Pastoral Psychology, Lecture No. 29).

from adapting himself to reality, the greater becomes the fear which increasingly besets his path at every point.' But ' life calls us forth to independence, and anyone who does not heed this call because of childish laziness or timidity is threatened with neurosis ' [1].

The application of all this to the christian pattern of living is clear. Christians are to be children of that ' Jerusalem which is above '[2], following now not the ' ways of flesh and blood ' but the ' ways of the spirit ' [3], and this new birth is expressed symbolically in terms of the heavenly city, of the well (cf. the words of Christ to the Samaritan woman), the cave, the tree, the river (the baptism in the Jordan) or sea (so Mary is the Star of the Sea), or again the Ark, the Ship of Peter which is the Church, and also the Rock which is Peter which is the Church.[4]

The rebirth or finding means life; the separation or losing is none the less harsh and painful; the lesson, then, that there can be no meeting without a previous separation, is a harsh one, and perhaps can only be taught in what seems a harsh way. For that is what makes this story so mysterious; the apparent inconsiderateness of the boy. ' Think,' his mother says, ' what anguish of mind thy father and I have endured, searching for thee.' He might have told them beforehand that he was staying behind; he did not. He might at least have said he was sorry; he did not. It is curious that biblical scholars never seem to notice this mystery; the only reference to it one has come across is in a letter from Bernard Shaw to his friend Dame Laurentia, abbess of Stanbrook, written from Damascus on St Patrick's Day, 1931: ' He was a most inconsiderate boy where his family was concerned, as you would realize if you travelled over the distance (at least a day's journey without a Rolls Royce) his mother had to go back to look for him when he gave her the slip to stay and argue with the doctors of

---

[1] Jung, *op. cit.* pp. 297, 304.   [2] *Gal.* iv, 26 (Douai).   [3] *Rom.* viii, 4 (Knox).
[4] Cf. *Isaiah*, li, 1: ' Think of the rock you were quarried from, of the hidden depths whence you came '; and I *Cor.* x, 4: ' All drank the same prophetic drink, watered by the same prophetic rock which bore them company, the rock that was Christ ' (Knox). Cf. also Jung, *op. cit.* p. 213.

divinity'.[1] Why did he do it? 'The Word was made flesh, and came to dwell among us; and we had sight of his glory . . . full of grace and truth.' May it not be that St John had in mind, at least in part, the *youthful* qualities which the Word (and his mother) never lost as we do: the gracefulness and graciousness, the honesty, directness, candour, the inability to compromise, of childhood? A child will often say things which are hurting, not because he wants to hurt, but because he has not learnt the adult wiles of tergiversation. And, to return to the harsh lesson: if it has to be learnt gradually, with much pondering in the heart, may it not have to be given in that direct and hurtful way that it may really sink in? The keynote to this story is obviously the word ' father ': ' Think, what anguish of mind thy father and I have endured'; and he replies, ' Could you not tell that I must needs be in the place which belongs to my Father ? ' He must leave his father and go alone on his dark journey to his Father: the mystics tell us with one voice that we must do the same.

All living is meeting. We can never live fully if our relationship with persons and things is an I–It relationship, greedy, possessive, utilitarian; we have to learn to treat everything as a Thou, an end in itself which we can meet. We have to go forth from the security of home to meet reality, as Columbus left the land that he knew and set his sails and ' went west '.

The phrase ' to go west ' has already in late Middle English the sense of disappearing, dying, perishing; in the death-life theme of symbolic language there is a similar idea of darkness, danger, death, which have to be faced if life is to be found. As the sun goes down into the darkness of the western ocean, so Christ goes down into the baptismal water and then into the dark kingdom of the dead, the ' sombre caverns of the underworld ' as a Syrian baptismal liturgy puts it; so in the christian rite of baptism the neophyte goes down into the dark waters and there renounces Satan, the ' black one ', who dwells in the dark west, and he turns instead towards ' Christ the king of light, who comes from the

[1] Cf. *In a Great Tradition*, by the Benedictines of Stanbrook, p. 250.

37

east like the sun and brings him the illumination (*photismos*) of baptism '.[1]

' The Gabilan Mountains to the east of the valley were light gay mountains full of sun and loveliness and a kind of invitation, so that you wanted to climb into their warm foothills almost as you want to climb into the lap of a beloved mother. They were beckoning mountains with a brown grass love. The Santa Lucias stood up against the sky to the west and kept the valley from the open sea, and they were dark and brooding—unfriendly and dangerous. I always found in myself a dread of west and love of east. Where I ever got such an idea I cannot say, unless it could be that the morning came over the peaks of the Gabilans and the night drifted back from the ridges of the Santa Lucias. It may be that the birth and death of the day had some part in my feeling about the two ranges of mountains.' [2]

To look back is always to court disaster: the penalty of refusing the life-challenge is always immobilization. So it was with Lot's wife who, like the people of Pompeii, was overtaken and killed by the sulphurous flow, or with Daphne in Greek legend who, refusing the advances of Apollo the life-bringer, was turned into a tree. Columbus goes on despite the mutterings and cowardice of his men; he will not look back; and so he comes in the end to the new world, with its Sea Pacific—and as life goes on one realizes more and more that if there is one thing more important and rewarding than joy it is peace.

In human relationships true discovery and meeting so often depend on discarding a false idol-projection: this is not a goddess on a pedestal but a real woman with a woman's faults, shortcomings, incomprehensibility: now that I have discovered that, we can begin to make a life together, to be real, to go west hand in hand. So it is in religion: it is easy to make a fantasy-figure god to suit one's own needs; to live at an infantile level; to hide behind the skirts of Mother Church and seek refuge from thought

[1] Cf. Rahner, *op. cit.* pp. 395, 399.   [2] John Steinbeck: *East of Eden*, Viking edition, p. 7.

in what William Law called the ' outward forms and modes of religion '[1]. For here too the theme of losing and finding, of death and rebirth, has its application: we may have to lose God in order to find him, as the mystics have discovered who for long periods have known nothing but aridity and darkness.

There are many forms in which darkness can come to us: it may be the loss of health, of money, of those we love, or of faith in ourselves, in humanity, in God, or again it may be some moral collapse: all these can be creative in so far as they teach us to live at a deeper level. Even sin, and the consequent estrangement from God, can lead to a deeper meeting with God when there is real sorrow and repentance.

They found the Boy in the temple, listening to those who taught there and asking them questions. Often it is tempting not to ask questions of life, to let sleeping dogs lie, but that too is a refusal of life. To live fully we have to go on exploring, trying to find God, trying to learn wisdom, trying to find our real selves, trying to understand the pattern. And often that will mean a temporary losing of life, it will mean a series of deaths and rebirths, till the dark journey is accomplished and life is found in its fullness.

When the time came for Jesus to leave his home he went to be baptized by John in the Jordan. Later on he was to say: ' There is a baptism I must needs be baptized with, and how impatient am I for its accomplishment! '[2] He was referring there to his death-agony as a birth-agony. Here it is the other way round: the baptism of water is a sort of going down into death to be reborn. (The darkness is also illumination; Paracelsus speaks of Jonah seeing ' mighty mysteries ' in the belly of the whale; John the Baptist had urged his hearers to a *metanoia*, a renewal of mind and heart.) Thus a new stage of his dark journey begins. But our Lord himself was baptized, as Ambrose says, *non mundari volens,*

[1] Is there not an urgent need that Superiors in charge of theological colleges and seminaries, or of novitiates in monasteries and convents, should see to it that those under their care not only progress in an intellectual apprehension of their faith but also grow to an emotional maturity which will save them from the disasters and torments of religious infantilism?

[2] *Luke*, xii. 50 (Knox).

39

sed mundare aquas,[1] wanting not to be himself cleansed but to cleanse the waters, and so to make effective what had before been merely significative.

There is in the Church's liturgy a profound appreciation of the way in which evil has affected not merely man but Nature as well, so that things need to be cleansed and blessed if they are to be life-bringing. The hero must go down into the dark waters, into the sea: but the sea can be either pacific, tranquil, welcoming, or it can be angry, destructive, devouring. So the baptismal water, and the salt which is put into it (for this water is the christian's ' sea ') must be exorcized and blessed so as to become the instrument of rebirth. That motif of rebirth is very clear in the liturgy for the blessing of the baptismal font (the word font itself coming from *fons*, a source) where the priest prays that God may ' send forth the spirit of adoption to beget new life in them that are born unto thee in this font of baptism ', and that he may ' render this water fruitful for giving rebirth to mankind, that whosoever is sanctified in the stainless womb of this font may be born again as a new creature, and come forth as an offspring of heaven ', and that the water may become ' a living fountain, a water that regenerates, a stream that purifies '.

The baptistery should be below the level of the rest of the church: the neophyte goes down into the waters—and the rite for the baptism of adults speaks of him as *qui in hujus sæculi nocte vagatur incertus ac dubius*, wandering in doubt and uncertainty through the night of this world—and then, clothed in white and with lighted candle, symbols of life, he comes up into the church and faces the altar, the east, the rising Sun, the Life-bringer: the new life has begun.

But baptism is not to be thought of as just a rite to be once performed and then forgotten: it is the initiation of the pattern, and the pattern must be repeated again and again, for the christian life is a series of deaths and rebirths. ' In this earthly life, he who has received the initiation of baptism is indeed possessed of life

[1] Cf. St Thomas: *Sum. Theol.* III, xxxix, 1.

everlasting . . . but his possession of it is not secure. The mystery of baptism is a lifelong decision between light and darkness, between Christ and Belial, life and death. Or else, to use another early christian image, the mystes has already reached the harbour of the transcendent world, and yet his perilous voyage continues; he bears in his soul the seal that opens all gates on his heavenward journey, but his ascent is still threatened by demons and spirits. This is the paradox of the mystery. . . . In the primeval ship, the ark built of the wood of the Cross, the mystes traverses the black bitter sea of the world; he is in deadly peril, yet he has already reached the haven, and his ship is safe from harm, as long as the mast that is the Cross remains in its place. . . . Christ on the Cross has gained the final victory, he has achieved peace; and so the mystes, who like Odysseus in his mystical voyage has himself tied to the mast—in this case, the Cross—is already certain of his home-coming.'[1]

Again, every time the penitent goes into the darkness of the confessional the pattern is repeated; but also, as we have seen, every entry into any form of darkness can be a repetition of the same theme, a baptism-journey leading to a renewal or an en-riching of life, a strengthening for the *agon*, the struggle with the adversary.

So, immediately after his baptism, Christ is led by the Spirit into the desert to be tempted. (So, too, the newly baptized christian is now a 'hero', equipped to start on his own *agon*-journey.) In the myths the struggle is an external one: the hero battles with dragon or serpent or sorcerer; here the struggle is internal, with Satan as merely the *agent provocateur*: our Lord was really torn between the path mapped out for him by his Father with all its pain and agony and that suggested to him by the adversary with its promise of easy and resounding success. So it must be with the christian; the struggle cannot just be stated, externalized, in myth or rite, it must be lived out: we have to choose between what we should like, what Satan suggests to us, and what God wills for us.

[1] Rahner, *op. cit.* pp. 398–9.

The tempting of Christ is preceded by the forty days of solitude and fasting in the desert.[1] In psychological terms, ' solitude and fasting have from time immemorial been the best-known means of strengthening any meditation whose purpose is to open the door to the unconscious '; and we may recall how Hiawatha ' builds himself a hut in the forest in order to fast and have dreams and visions ': in thus hiding himself again ' in the lap of nature, what he is doing is to reawaken the relationship to the mother, and to something older than the mother, and it is therefore to be expected that he will emerge reborn in some other form '[2]. In religious terms we can similarly say that from time immemorial solitude and fasting have been the preliminary either to moments of great illumination or to the initiation or renewal of great activity. A simple and common form of this spiritual ' introversion ' or *recueillement* is to be found in the practice of making a ' spiritual retreat '; a period of silence and thought and prayer, of ' being alone with God ', in order that the personality may be renewed and strengthened and deepened.

With us as with our Lord who went before us to show us the way there is indeed the external adversary to face, but he will try to destroy us by playing on our own evil propensities. Thus, while it is true that we have to battle against ' princedoms and powers . . . with malign influences in an order higher than ours '[3], it is also true that we have to battle against ourselves. Here again we can draw instruction from Dr Jung's analysis of the story of Hiawatha, who ' wrestles with himself in order to create himself ', for while it is with Mondamin the corn-god that he struggles in the ' purple twilight '—the setting sun, the west—Mondamin is in fact a god sprung from Hiawatha's own unconscious, the ' prototype of Hiawatha's heroic destiny ', since ' Hiawatha has in himself the possibility, indeed the necessity, of confronting his dæmon '. So the battle is engaged, and goes on for three days; from it Hiawatha derives new strength; in the end he conquers; his adversary

---

[1] For an analysis of the tempting and of the symbol ' 40 ', cf. *Stones or Bread?* by Gerald Vann and P. K. Meagher, O.P.   [2] Cf. Jung, *op. cit.* p. 334.   [3] *Ephes.* vi, 12 (Knox).

dies and is buried by Hiawatha in the earth his mother, and soon afterwards, ' young and fresh ', the corn ' sprouts from his grave for the nourishment of mankind '. Had the struggle gone the opposite way, Mondamin would have ' killed ' Hiawatha and usurped his place, so that Hiawatha would have become ' possessed ' by a demon.[1]

The application to ourselves is obvious. Christ was tempted to abuse his messianic power: to employ it in ways and for purposes which would have run counter to the will of his Father.[2] We in our turn have our own puny powers to use or to abuse, to employ in God's service or in the service of our own vanity, pride, lust for power or, in a word, our egoism. To be possessed by these is indeed to be possessed by a demon. So Dr Jung comments: ' Christ successfully resisted the temptations of the power-devil in the wilderness. Whoever prefers power is therefore, in the christian view, possessed by the devil. The psychologist can only agree '[3].

The struggle of Hiawatha with Mondamin inevitably recalls that of Jacob with the angel.[4] In the former case it is not, as one might expect, the man who is vanquished and dies and is reborn. but the god; the same is true with Jacob, to whom at the end the angel says: ' Jacob is no name for thee, thou shalt be called Israel, one that prevails with God. If thou hast held thy own with God, how wilt thou prevail over men! '[5] Some of the Fathers took Jacob's adversary to be the Son of God himself, the more common view is that he was an angel, taking human form and representing the Son and acting in his power and authority; he has also been identified with Jacob's guardian angel, inciting him to a struggle, and a victory, which will give him the courage he lacks to meet human struggles and dangers (his meeting with Esau).[6] Jacob is able to be the conqueror, so some of the exegetes tell us, because God restrained the might of the angel; on the other hand the angel is able, at a touch, to wither the sinew of Jacob's thigh, to show him that, if in spite of this exhibition of power he is able to conquer,

---

[1] Jung, *op. cit.* pp. 336-7.   [2] Cf. *Stones or Bread?* ch. vii.   [3] Jung, *op. cit.* p. 337, n.52.
[4] *Gen.* xxxii, 24-30.   [5] *Gen.* xxxii, 28-9 (Knox).   [6] Cf. infra, p. 102.

it must be owing not to his own power but to the power given him by God.

Jacob's wrestling goes on through the night. As in the myth the corn-god is vanquished and dies as adversary and is born again as nourishment for the people, so here, with the coming of the dawn the angel ceases to be an adversary and becomes the giver of blessing and of the promise of greatness. We must not think of the assaults of Satan as being independent of God's providence and love. God allows us to be tempted; he proves the just, as the Bible shows us: ' Moses told his people, " The Lord your God trieth you, that it may appear whether you love him with all your heart, and with all your soul, or not ".[1] And this appears to be the lot of all the just, for we read of them that God has tried them and found them worthy of himself. Now the purpose of the trial is certainly not to show God the true disposition of the soul: that he already knows. It must then be for the enlightenment of the man tempted, and perhaps of others also. Man is largely a mystery to himself . . . " What doth he know, who hath not been tried? "[2] asks Ecclesiasticus; it is only when temptation comes to search him that he discovers himself.'[3] Further, God allows us to be tempted, both to remind us of our weakness and preserve us from pride and presumption, and also to harden and strengthen us, to be ready for whatever struggles the future may hold. As we are led to think of Christ's human nature as coming exalted, ' filled with the Spirit ', from his baptism; so we may think of him coming with human soul more poised, more calmly assured of its own strength, perhaps even with human mind (in its ' experimental ' workings) more vividly and clearly aware of the way which lay before him, from his encounter with the dark angel. And as though to underline the victorious issue to the struggle which had gone on within him, we are told of darkness succeeded by dawn, of how the dark angel withdrew from him and angels of light came and ministered to him.

At the end of the three temptations the devil left our Lord ' for

[1] *Deut.* xiii, 3 (Douai).   [2] *Eccl.* xxxiv, 9 (Douai).   [3] Cf. *Stones or Bread?* pp. 47-9.

a time '—for we are to suppose that the essential temptation went on through the three years of his ministry—and ' angels came and ministered to him '. It is foolish to forget or to minimize the power and malice of Satan; it is also foolish to neglect the power and benevolence of the good angels. The hero has his adversary but also his ' helpers ': so it is with the christian; the psalm which the devil quotes in the pinnacle-temptation applies, as the Church makes clear, to us, singing it as we so often do at Compline: ' He has given charge to his angels concerning thee, to watch over thee where-soever thou goest; they will hold thee up with their hands lest thou shouldst chance to trip on a stone '[1]. We wander in doubt and uncertainty through the night of this world, but we have mighty helpers and we should call upon them; above all we should call upon him who is infinitely mightier than they: for in that ' he himself hath suffered and been tempted he is able to succour them also that are tempted '[2].

Through the three years' ministry the agony continues: the darkness, the loneliness, the homelessness; and it reaches its climax in the garden of Gethsemane.

But as the onset of childhood-sorrows were preceded by the moment of glory we call the Epiphany, so the final gathering of storm and cloud and darkness is preceded by that other moment of glory, that other epiphany, we call the Transfiguration. And it is as though to underline for us some deep connection between the two events, the transfiguring and the agony, that we are told how in each case Jesus took with him Peter, James and John. Why are these three taken? If we view the events purely as historical events we may suppose it was because Peter was to be head of the Church; James and John were asked " Can you drink the chalice that I shall drink? '; and John of course was ' the disciple whom Jesus loved '. But perhaps we may also see the three as types, as symbols, of im-mediate relevance to our own experience.

When we look back at our own lives, whether our years are few or many, we too find that certain events stand out from the

---

[1] *Ps.* xc, 11-12 (Knox). [2] *Hebrews*, ii, 18 (Douai).

rest, high lights of joy or of sorrow, of glory or agony, of ecstasy or of something like despair. But when we say, ' I did this ', ' I suffered that ', what do we mean by ' I '? Certainly ' I ' means this individual human personality, means John or Mary; but, as we know from bitter experience, we are inconsistent creatures, untidy, unpredictable in our behaviour, so that in a true sense it can be said that within the ontological unity of the personality there is a psychological multiplicity, there are several, perhaps many, personalities; and perhaps we are not always capable of predicting which of these personalities, in any given situation, will take charge, or whether it will be in fact the right one. Sometimes we find ourselves diffident and inhibited when we should be energetically active; sometimes we are officious when we ought to be quiet and retiring; we are now too quick, now too slow, to speak or to do. If we see these three disciples as symbols (though to do so necessarily involves doing violence to them as real, historical human beings) we shall see Peter as impulsive, headstrong, impelled in any great event or crisis to take action of some sort, to be, like Martha, busy about many things: it is Peter who exclaims how fortunate it is that they are there, since they can build three leafy arbours, for our Lord, for Moses, for Elias, but there is in fact no need for arbours since in a moment a cloud will shelter them. James, overshadowed by his brother, has been further obscured by historical accident: almost nothing is known of his later life; (the other James, moreover, seems to have been made bishop of Jerusalem, less for any qualifications of his own than because he was the ' brother of Jesus '): we may take the name here, then, as a symbol for those who are shy of the limelight, who feel inadequate, in face of responsibility, and are slow to act. John was still a boy when he was called to follow Christ; but if he has about him the aura, the unspoilt quality, of childhood he is also already the eagle, the seer, whom history would know as John the Divine, the theologian who did not learn about God from books but learned God from God, ' leaning his head back upon Jesus' breast '[1].

[1] *John,* xiii, 25 (Knox).

In many of us there is a Peter, liable to burst into activity at moments when action is pointless and may be disastrous; there is a James, liable to be found sleeping when action is required. The three disciples fell asleep both here on the mountain and later in the garden; but here they awoke to the sight of Christ's glory, in the garden they slept on till the end. And perhaps this too is true of human experience as a whole: first, that we are more likely to fail our friends—not through any lack of love necessarily, but through lack of understanding—in their moments of dereliction than in their moments of glory; secondly, that the same is true of the selves within ourselves: we may not even suspect our lack of inner resources until in the moment of crisis we discover we have none. Or rather, perhaps, our real—and, in a moment of crisis, our only—resources are so deeply buried that we cannot draw upon them, we remain unaware of them though they are there: for somewhere deep down in all of us John does exist; and though all three disciples sleep through the agony, John goes with Jesus to his trial and his Passion and his Cross, and if we are given moments of dereliction, of near-despair, perhaps it is in order to awaken, to evoke, this John-figure in us, the God-seer, the contemplative, who but for the crisis might have gone on placidly sleeping.

In fact there are times when we need to be active and times when we need to refrain from activity, but whether we are doing or not doing we need to be seers. Psychologically speaking we need to integrate our various ' personalities' into a unity, a completeness; theologically speaking we need to make sure that, whether active or inactive, we are under the governance of the wisdom and will of God. For transfiguration is not something we can achieve; it is something which only he who is mighty can bring about in us. Our Lord's transfiguration here on the mountain led on through agony and death to the final transfiguration, the glory of the risen life, and of that life St Peter was to say later, in his sermon to the men of Judæa, that it was God who ' raised up this man, Jesus, from the dead ': how much more obviously in our own case is it the power of God alone that can raise us up and

release us from the ' pangs of death ' [1]! We say truly of our Lord
that he went forth into the wilderness to meet the tempter; but
the deepest truth is in the words of the Gospel: he was ' led by the
Spirit' into the desert, and, when the devil had gone from him
' angels came and ministered to him '. The same truth is conveyed
to us in the contrast between Martha and Mary: there are times
when action is irrelevant, impertinent, a nuisance; but deeper than
that, the activity which is in fact essential, the daily tasks and
struggles, the taking up of the daily cross, all this is of value only in
so far as we are led to it and in it by the Spirit, that Spirit on whom
we are dependent for the kindling within us of the divine fire, the
transfiguring love.

But here the question arises whether, in thinking of *alternations*,
in our Lord's life, of moments of joy or glory and moments of
sorrow and dereliction, we are not distorting the facts of that life.
It seems that we must be, unless by such alternations we mean
merely to say that there were moments in which joy *predominated*
over sorrow or sorrow over joy. For could Christ ever, in his
human feelings, be wholly happy or wholly sad? When he stayed
at Bethany with the friends he loved so much could he (as we should
say) ' forget' the Passion which lay before him? Even when, as
a very small child, he was happy in his mother's arms, could he
be unaware of the Cross? The story of Palm Sunday seems to
give us an answer.

He had in fact been at Bethany; the news of the raising of
Lazarus had become well-known; and as he approached Jerusalem
a multitude came out to meet him and escort him into the city, and
they spread garments and palm-branches for him and cried ' Blessed
is he that cometh in the name of the Lord '. It was a modest
triumph; as Lagrange remarks, if a Roman officer had chanced to
pass by, in his helmet and armour and astride a good horse, he would
no doubt have smiled mockingly at this untidy procession, so
unlike the glory of a Roman triumph. [2] But the shouting, the
homage, were sincere, heartfelt; it would have been inhuman not

[1] *Acts*, ii, 32, 24 (Knox). [2] *The Gospel of Jesus Christ*, vol. II, p. 123.

to be touched by it; and our Lord was never inhuman. And he seems to voice his own triumph when, to the Pharisees who would have had him rebuke his disciples, he replies: 'I tell you, if they should keep silence, the stones will cry out instead '[1].

And yet the story, in St Luke's account, goes on immediately: ' And as he drew near, and caught sight of the city, he wept '.

He wept because he knew, he saw, the future, the tragedy of his city and his race. We for our part often cheat fate in our moments of happiness because we do *not* see the coming collapse of happiness; equally our anguished moments may be blacker than they need because we do not discern the joy or consolation that lies beyond them. But is our lack of fore-sight sometimes wilful rather than fateful? It is characteristic of childhood experience to be thus wholly white or black: as A. N. Whitehead pointed out somewhere, when we are young ' despair is overwhelming ' because ' there is then no tomorrow, no memory of disaster survived '; for the child, the pleasure or pain of the moment—objectively so insignificant perhaps that an adult would hardly notice it as being the one or the other—can be immeasurable ecstasy or heartbreak simply because it fills the whole horizon of awareness, there is no room for anything else. Do we sometimes deliberately continue this childhood concentration of consciousness into adult life, refusing to allow our moments of happiness to be spoilt by the intrusion of gloomy ideas, truths, realities; or in moments of misery being so determined to wallow in self-pity that we exclude any thought that might bring us comfort? And if we do, and if the second thing, the wallowing, is clearly odious, what of the first? Are the mixed experiences, the fusions of joy and sorrow, more valuable to us, deeper and richer, than ' pure ' joy or sorrow could ever be? (We are not concerned here with the pure joy of heaven, the pure misery of hell: we are *in via*, and the question is to discover which kind of experience is most likely to be helpful to us on our journey. Even *in via* there are doubtless in some lives moments of glory—of natural or mystical ecstasy—so dazzling, or of misery

[1] *Luke*, xix, 40 (Knox).

so abysmal, that they cannot be other than 'pure', but our concern here is rather with what happens, or can happen, day by day in the ordinary course of life.)

Inevitably we come back to the basic *fact* of our existence: the pervasiveness in it of paradox, of that ambivalence in reality which symbol can capture and convey so much more easily than can discursive reasoning. There is paradox (for our human modes of thought) even in God: he is just and merciful; but that means that his justice *is* his mercy: how can it be? There is paradox in our approach to God: he is the infinitely perfect, the *mysterium tremendum*, whom we approach with awe, in fear and trembling, yet he is also our Father whom we are to approach with the gay and loving confidence of a little child. We are urged to receive the Bread which is God as often as may be: we are to be eager therefore, yet our sense of unworthiness is no less than that of our forbears whom it caused to approach the sacrament only very rarely. It is the same with our experience of earthly things: *odi et amo*, the Roman poet cries: and sometimes we mean 'I love this in him but I hate that' but sometimes perhaps it is the same 'this' that we both love and hate, and we are torn in two.

Let us return to the question. You find yourself living some moment of great joy: you can, if you will, enclose yourself in the joy as in a fortress, shutting out everything that might throw a shadow over your joy; or, if you will, you can leave yourself open to these other things: if you are lost in music you can let it tell you of the *lacrimæ rerum* even while it lifts you up to heaven; if you are lost in love you can know how fragile and fugitive it is even while you know its reality and eternity. There is a joy that is close to tears; and is it not that joy precisely that is the deepest joy we know?

There is one moment in religious experience to which these thoughts seem especially to apply: the moment when the penitent sinner knows himself to be restored to life, to God; the moment of sacramental absolution. The load is lifted, and with it the sense of being lost, the loneliness; but the joy does not annul the sorrow;

rather, the joy and sorrow become fused into a single thing, for which we have no name unless perhaps it be love. (Inevitably we are reminded of how Christ gently and subtly made plain to Peter the fact that he was forgiven for having thrice denied him by asking him thrice the same question, ' Simon, son of John, lovest thou me?' and of how Peter, no longer 'protesting too much' as he had done before the denial, replied simply, 'Lord, thou knowest that I love thee '[1].)

But if we are to know this moment of joy-and-sorrow we must first have two other things: a sense of what it means to be close to God (which in turn involves being in love with God) and therefore what it means to have lost that closeness; and a sense of sin. It is necessary nowadays to add that a real sense of sin means a sense of real sin. It is difficult not to suspect a complete lack of any sense of sin if a penitent says that since his last confession a year ago he may perhaps have told a few small lies and that is all :[2] if his story were true it would mean, surely, that he was the greatest of all saints except the mother of God—but the confessions of saints, or those who are close to sanctity, are very different, filled with a deep shame for their inadequacy, their faithlessness, their lack of generosity. But the lack of a real sense of *real* sin is revealed in two ways: first, by inventing sins, as those penitents do who say they have missed Mass on Sundays and then, when questioned, admit that they were in hospital: this is not religion but superstition, a sense not of sin but of pseudo-sin; secondly, by evincing a false scale of values, as those penitents do who, after a long list of peccadilloes, will say as an afterthought that perhaps they should mention that they have not been to Mass, or have not been on speaking terms with their families, for the past year: they have thought of the offering of Mass as just one among many ecclesiastical laws; it has never occurred to them that to reject it indefinitely is to starve the soul to death, that we need the grace of the sacraments and above all of the sacrifice-communion not merely in order to keep the commandments, the natural law, but in order to *live*—that it is

---

[1] *John*, xxi, 15-17 (Douai).   [2] Cf. *infra.*, p. 63.

literally a matter of supernatural life or death; similarly it has not occurred to them that if sins of weakness can be grave, and sometimes very grave as was the case with St Peter, still the greater sins are those which are hateful because full of hate, and hurtful, full of the will to destroy what should be dear and precious, and a black, deliberate revolt against God and the order of things.

Now real sorrow for sin, contrition, is essentially a question not of feelings but of will: a real awareness of one's own sinfulness and then a determination to repent, to change what needs changing.[1] The goodness of a confession is not measured by the extent to which we feel sorrow: we cannot turn on appropriate emotions at any given moment as one turns on a tap. But emotions are important because they can so strongly help or hinder the will: it is much easier to be sorry if one feels sorry. And if we think often and deeply about the two things, closeness to God and separation from God, love and sin, if we gradually steep mind and heart in these realities, they are likely to become for us, at least at times, a deeply felt as well as a deeply known and deeply lived experience.

Let us then reformulate the question to fit this immediate context. Will these two things, the joy of love, the sadness of sin, grow in us most deeply if they grow together? The sequel to Palm Sunday, the story of Holy Week, seems to suggest that they will, as does also the christian liturgy. In the moment of triumph, on the Sunday, Christ spoke of how he would draw al' hings to himself if he were ' lifted up from the earth '[2]—but his hearers knew that by that phrase he meant his crucifixion; on the other hand, at the end of the Last Supper discourse, just before crossing over the brook Cedron to his agony, he prayed to his Father to glorify him[3] and he spoke of his joy.[4] At his trial he proclaimed his kingship, yet he allowed the cruel mockery of the crowning with thorns ;[5] and on the cross, though earlier he had spoken of the legions of angels at his command, he made no reply to the taunts of those who called on him to save himself ;[6] the moment

[1] For a fuller discussion of confession and sorrow cf. *infra*, pp.116 *sqq*.   [2] *John*, xii, 32 (Douai).   [3] *John*, xvii, 1, 5 (Douai).   [4] *John*, xvii, 13 (Douai).   [5] *Matt.* xxvii, 11, 29. [6] *Matt.* xxvi, 53 ; xxvii, 40.

of darkness over the earth is also that of the rending in two of the veil of the temple which, if it presages the destruction of the temple itself and the end of the old Dispensation, can also be taken as symbolizing the glory of the new Dispensation, the fact of God's accessibility to man; and the cry of dereliction, ' My God, my God, why hast thou forsaken me?' neither contradicts nor is contradicted by the cry of triumph, *Consummatum est*.[1]

In the Palm Sunday liturgy the two strands, of triumph and of pain, are interwoven; and the same is true of the week as a whole. On the Thursday the dominant theme is the Last Supper and therefore the holy communion; and the maundy, the washing of the feet of the poor, underlines for us that idea of God's prodigal self-giving to man; on Good Friday we concentrate on the Passion, the Sacrifice; but Communion and Sacrifice are one and the same thing, the Mass. Even the Lenten purple (of vestments and hangings) has this ambivalence: coming relatively late into liturgical use, it is now associated in our minds with penitential days and seasons, yet it also suggests imperial pomp and majesty: so Fortunatus, in his great hymn, *Vexilla Regis prodeunt*, apostrophizes the Tree:

> *Arbor decora et fulgida,*
> *Ornata Regis purpura—*

' Tree of beauty and splendour, adorned with kingly purple '. Finally, in the Easter Vigil service night and day, darkness and light, come together, for this is the ' blessed night ' (as the deacon sings in the *Exultet*, the blessing of the paschal candle) ' of which it is written, *nox sicut dies illuminabitur*, the night shall shine as the day '. It was on the day of his triumphal entry into Jerusalem that Christ spoke of how the grain of wheat must die if it is to bear fruit ;[2] and later, perhaps as the sun was setting,[3] he told his hearers: ' The light is among you still, but only for a short time. Finish your journey while you still have the light, for fear darkness

---

[1] Cf. *infra*, p. 187, n.5.   [2] Cf. *John*, xii, 24.   [3] Cf. Lagrange, *The Gospel of Jesus Christ*, vol. ii, p. 127.

should overtake you.... While you still have the light, have faith in the light, that so you may become children of the light'[1].

The fulfilment we hope for is the eternal light which is also eternal rest; but even here on earth, *in via*, where there is both light and darkness, where sometimes it is darkness that seems to predominate, but where in any case we perhaps learn best how to live when we welcome and absorb reality in its *chiaroscuro*, even here it is light that must predominate in our minds since it is light that is ultimate, not darkness, and since he who is the Light told us: 'I am come a light into the world, that whosoever believeth in me may not remain in darkness'[2].

But we have been anticipating; and must return to the moment in which, for our Lord himself, it was certainly darkness that predominated: the moment of his agony.

It is John, concerned more with symbol than with biography, who, in describing Christ's agony, uses the word 'garden'; the synoptists say simply 'a plot of land'; there is in the Passion story an echo, in a sense terribly ironical, of the theme of the *puer æternus*: the paradise-garden is now the garden of agony, and the naked laughing Eros is replaced by the Man of Sorrows stripped of his garments in ultimate indignity; for, once again, the pattern has now to be lived out, and the living of it is often crude and cruel and sometimes terrible; it is John too who will tell us that when Christ cries 'I thirst' they give him vinegar to drink not, as in the synoptists, simply on a sponge, but on a sprig of hyssop, reminding us again that this was the 'baptism wherewith I am to be baptized', for to catholics the word 'hyssop' inevitably suggests the ceremony of sprinkling the faithful with holy water at the beginning of Sunday High Mass while the words of the psalm are sung: 'Thou wilt sprinkle me with hyssop, Lord, and I shall be cleansed: thou wilt wash me and I shall be made whiter than snow'.

To reach the garden he must first cross the brook Cedron. (Again it is St John alone who mentions this.) In symbol-language crossing the river means overcoming the longing to retrogress, to

[1] *John*, xii, 35-6 (Knox).   [2] *John*, xii, 46 (Douai).

sleep, to turn away from life and its struggles; in mythology the dragon lives in or near a spring or other waters of which perhaps it is the guardian: it is beside the water that the struggle takes place, and the hero, having killed the magic animal, can clothe himself in its skin and so acquire giant strength for the struggles that lie ahead.[1] Perhaps it is with this sort of setting in mind that we should read what William Law, for instance, has to tell us of Cedron: all life is fire, he writes, but the soul is a dark fire-breath, an anger-fire, until it is reborn by repentance into the real image of the divine fire; but there can be no repentance until we see this deformity and are terrified at it; we must with Christ ' cross the brook Cedron and sweat drops of sorrows '—the temptation is to turn back to sleep, to ' keep all things quiet in us by outward forms and modes of religion '[2].

Sacrifice, as universal as the monomyth, follows essentially the same pattern as the monomyth: whether you think of the simple animal sacrifices of some nomadic tribe or the terrible human sacrifices of Aztecs or Moabites, it is always the same theme: the victim is offered to the god—death—in the hope that thereby the gift, the boon, the elixir, will come from the god—life; and once again the myth which expressed humanity's longings is made fact and reality in the life of Christ. We are not to think of the Passion as ending with the death and burial of Christ, or indeed with resurrection and ascension, but only with the coming of the Spirit upon the apostles at Pentecost.

But first, before and leading up to the climax of crucifixion, there is the *transitus,* the carrying of the cross. Here too the pattern must be lived out, not only by Christ himself, but by all his followers: each man is to ' take up his cross daily and follow ' his Lord; as St Paul puts it, each of us will ' have his own load to carry '[3]. And it is indeed ' his own load ', in the narrowest, strictest, sense, i.e. himself. If, like Hiawatha, we are to wrestle with ourselves in order to create ourselves, it can only be by shouldering

[1] Cf. Jung: *Symbols of Transformation,* pp. 326–7.   [2] W. Law: *Selected Mystical Writings,* ed. Hobhouse, pp. 11 *sqq.,* 39, 50 *sqq.*   [3] *Gal.* vi, 5 (Knox).

our whole burden, our whole being, and carrying it to the place of sacrifice, the sepulchre, the cave. What is to be achieved is an integration of the personality: let us take in their broad sense St Paul's words about the flesh lusting against the spirit: there is at issue within us light and darkness, good and evil, life and death, being and non-being. But nothing is wholly evil, not even the Prince of Darkness: what is dark and deathly and evil in us has to be first recognized and then loved, accepted (for we are to love ourselves, not part of ourselves) and so in the end, through God's grace, be converted and live—in the totality of the self made at one with God. So, when we pray to the holy Spirit on the feast of the pentecostal fire we do not pray that the ignoble in us be destroyed but that it be cured and ennobled:

> *Lava quod est sordidum,*
> *riga quod est aridum,*
> *sana quod est saucium.*
> *Flecte quod est rigidum,*
> *fove quod est frigidum,*
> *rege quod est devium.*
> *Da tuis fidelibus, in te confidentibus, sacrum septenarium.*[1]

Our Lord then, does not command us to take up *his* cross: he commands us to take up our own. Each man has to do the best he can to fulfil his own individual vocation, using what gifts, of nature and grace, God has given him to fulfil the task and surmount its difficulties. And in this context too we can say, adapting St Paul, ' to each his own gift ': as one man is more gifted in mind or body than another, so one man is more gifted in soul, more engraced, than another. Nothing is more foolish or dangerous than to confuse trying to be perfect, as Christ bade us, with perfectionism, which is a refusal to accept one's limitations and therefore

---

[1] ' Cleanse what is foul in us; water the arid soil in us; heal what is hurt in us. Bend our rigid wills, warm our stone-cold hearts, discipline our deviousness: give to thy faithful, who trust in thee, thy holy sevenfold gift.' (By the sevenfold gift is meant the seven ' Gifts of the holy Spirit '—effects of the indwelling Spirit upon the soul—wisdom, understanding, knowledge, counsel, fortitude, dutifulness and the fear of the Lord.)

in the last resort is a form of egoism. For John Smith, being perfect does not mean becoming a John of the Cross because (in all probability at least) he has not been given the graces given to John of the Cross.[1]

Each his own load: but he does not have to carry it unaided. The hero in the myth has his ' helpers ': here there is first of all Simon of Cyrene :[2] he was an unwilling helper to be sure, but a helper none the less; and if his help began in reluctance, who is to say how it ended, and what riches of faith and love flowed into him on the way to Calvary from the wood? Secondly, there is the mysterious figure whom we call Veronica,[3] who wiped our Lord's face with a towel which, tradition has it, thereafter bore upon it the imprint of his features.

We know nothing of this woman, not even, it may be argued, her name (since Veronica, True Image, would seem to have been given her *post factum* because of this event): her whole life and personality are sunk in her function *as* a helper, in this one event; and if Simon is the symbol of the fact that we can rely on help (from our Lord, the angels, the saints, those we love and who love us), Veronica is the symbol of the way in which we in our turn are to give help, selflessly, humbly, on our knees because not so much giving as receiving a boon, whether it is Christ we are called upon to help in his redeeming work, or our fellow men in their trials and sorrows.

The crucifixion follows. Some of the martyrs have suffered similar physical tortures, though they could not experience anything remotely resembling Christ's agony of spirit; most of us are not required to endure pain or sorrow in any such dramatic form. But even for us, for all our weakness and pettiness, pain and sorrow there must be; and as at Calvary ' from the sixth hour there was darkness over the whole earth, until the ninth hour '[4] so it must sometimes be with us. But the end, for us too, is to be not darkness but glory, the fire of the Spirit, kindling within us

---

[1] Cf. Vann and Meagher, *op. cit.* p. 41. [2] Cf. *infra*, p. 224. [3] Cf. *infra*, p. 225.
[4] *Matt.* xxvii, 45 (Douai).

the flame of love. For 'behold the veil of the temple was rent in two from the top even to the bottom':[1] hitherto the divine presence had been veiled, there was no access save once a year when the High Priest, and he alone, entered the holy of holies; now the veil is torn down, the Light is accessible, God is with us; and our journey is meant to end in the life and light and energy of the mighty wind and fire, in flame giving out flame, in the radiance and transfiguring power and charity of the saints.

[1] *Matt.* xxvii, 51 (Douai).

3

The Pattern in the Commandments

As a desiccated and jargon-ridden treatment of dogma can make the whole *corpus* of christian doctrine seem remote and unreal, so too with the ten commandments: taken out of their context and made indeed (psychologically speaking) into tables of stone, they may easily cease to have much relevance to everyday living, or at least may easily lose the greater part of their meaning. The first commandment will come to mean no more than 'having difficulties' about the faith, probably with the quite mistaken implication that having difficulties is sinful; the second commandment all too commonly means no more than saying 'O my God!' in moments of stress; while the third, interpreted simply in terms of avoiding something called 'servile work', is likely to be made nonsense of by modern working conditions.

We need then to revivify our understanding of the commandments, to get back again to their real meaning; and the first step is to see them in their context, and their context is poetry, is the poem we call the Old and New Testaments. The trouble with so much catechetical work, so many sermons and instructions, seems to be that they attempt to 'paraphrase' the poem: obviously, no matter what examiners in 'English Literature' may say, you just cannot paraphrase a poem, and if you try you will merely kill it, for a poem is not a scientific formula to be apprehended by reason but a mystery into which one enters; and this is above all true of the *mysterion tou theou*, the mystery of God. 'The christian mystery', writes Fr Rahner, 'is the "drama of truth": the plan of salvation hidden in God is revealed in Christ crucified, and beneath the cloak of his human life is concealed the unfathomable "mystery of godliness".[1] Everything that happens in the historical unfolding of his plan of salvation—that is to say, in the Church—partakes of this character of mystery: everything is both revealed and hidden, and beneath the simple visible cloak is hidden the unfathomable wisdom of God that will be manifest only at the end of days, the "wisdom . . . in a mystery".[2] Thus the Church itself is a "great sacrament",[3] because its now manifest presence is the revelation of the secret intimated to Adam and Eve,[4] but for this very reason the Church itself in its historically tangible form is also a cloak for a secret to be revealed only eschatologically, namely the secret of its innermost bond with Christ,[5] from which one day the *doxa*, which now works in secret, will burst forth.'[6]

A vast abyss seems to separate the ordinary modern approach to the mystery from that of the early christian. Of the latter, the pseudo-Chrysostom is typical: 'O crucified one, thou leader of the mystical dance! O Spiritual marriage feast! O divine Pascha, passing from the heavens to the earth and rising again to the heavens! O new feast of all things, O cosmic festive gathering, O joy of the universe, O honour, O joy, O delight. . . . The people which was in the depths arises from the dead and proclaims to the hosts above: the chorus of the earth returns!'[7]

This sort of ecstatic attitude of mind has to be contrasted, not only with the fire-and-brimstone formula for sermon and admonition (which in any case is now, we may hope, outmoded) but with the characteristically modern tendency to concentrate on the *minutiæ* of little 'pious practices' which can often lead away from, instead of to, the central mystery. The keynote of that mystery is joy: as we have seen, it is comedy rather than tragedy which reveals man's destiny to him; it is with Wisdom at play that creation begins, and with dance and music that the drama reaches its fulfil-

---

[1] *Tim.* iii, 16 (Douai). [2] I *Cor.* ii, 7 (Douai). [3] *Ephes.* v, 32 (Douai). [4] *Gen.* ii, 24. [5] *Col.* i, 27. [6] *op. cit.* p. 370. [7] Cf. Rahner, *op. cit.* pp. 386-7.

ment: for 'this is the mountain beloved of God, no longer the scene for tragedies, like Cithaeron, but devoted to the dramas of truth. . . . O truly sacred mysteries! O pure light! . . . The Lord reveals the sacred signs, for he himself is the hierophant. . . . And thou shalt dance with angels around the unbegotten and imperishable and only true God, and God's *Logos* shall join with us in hymns of praise'.[1]

We shall see too how in a sense we must think of deity as androgynous:[2] seeing Wisdom and *Logos* as one, seeing Spirit and Mother as one; and this is particularly important with regard to the commandments, for we shall distort their meaning and purpose if we see them simply in terms of Jovian thunderbolts; equally we shall distort them if, wrenching them from their poetic context, we see them simply in terms of prosaic actions to be done or to be avoided.

St Paul's rebuke to some of his fellow Jewish-christians, his opposition to the judaizers (an opposition which led him to withstand even Peter to his face), and the sharp contrast he draws between faith and the 'works of the law': all this is very relevant here. 'Now you, my reader, who bear the name of Jew, take your stand upon the law, and are, so to speak, proud of your God. You know his Plan, and are able through your knowledge of the law truly to appreciate moral values. You can, therefore, confidently look upon yourself as a guide to those who do not know the way, and as a light to those who are groping in the dark. You can instruct those who have no spiritual wisdom: you can teach those who, spiritually speaking, are only just out of the cradle. You have a certain grasp of the basis of true knowledge. You have without doubt very great advantages. But, prepared as you are to instruct others, do you ever teach yourself anything? You preach against stealing, for example, but are you sure of your own honesty? You denounce the practice of adultery, but are you sure of your own purity? You loathe idolatry, but how honest are you

[1] Clement of Alexandria, *Protrepticus*, quoted Rahner, *op. cit.* p. 355.   [2] but cf. *infra*, p. 270.

towards the property of heathen temples? Everyone knows how proud you are of the law, but that means a proportionate dishonour to God when men know that you break it! Don't you know that the very name of God is cursed among the Gentiles because of the behaviour of Jews? . . . I have come to the conclusion that a true Jew is not the man who is merely a Jew outwardly, and real circumcision is not just a matter of the body. The true Jew is one who belongs to God in heart, a man whose circumcision is not just an outward physical affair but is a God-made sign upon the heart and soul, and results in a life lived not for the approval of man, but for the approval of God.'[1]

St Paul's point is that the law, apart from the grace of God,[2] is indeed a way of life but not a way to life: the latter is to be found only in faith in him who is the way, the truth, the life—and faith in the Pauline sense: not just an intellectual assent to propositions about God but a personal commitment to and communication with God, and a communication which begins with the humble admission that we can do nothing of ourselves. The trouble with the Jews, St Paul says, was that ' their minds were fixed on what they achieved instead of on what they believed ' :[3] so, in our Lord's parable, it is not the Pharisee, for all his achievements, but the sinful Publican, who goes down from the temple justified. St Paul is of course at pains to point out that we are not to sin because now ' it is grace, not the law, we serve '; on the contrary we are to think of ourselves as dead to sin, as living and moving in a new kind of existence.[4] It remains true, however, that we do sin; but if we rely not on achievement but on belief, not on the works of the law but on Christ, that fact will not lead us into despair. Paul himself, who swept through the world like a forest fire, setting men's hearts aflame, spoke of his own experience of the warfare between flesh and spirit, of willing one thing and doing another, of becoming himself a castaway; but he declared roundly his con-

---

[1] *Romans*, ii, 17 *sqq.* Cf. J. B. Phillips: *Letters to Young Churches*, pp. 22–3. It is useful to read this passage to oneself substituting ' christian ' for ' Jew ' and making other corresponding adjustments, which is one reason why it is quoted here in this modern English version.   [2] Cp. *John*, i. 17.   [3] *Rom.* ix, 32 (Phillips).   [4] *Rom.* vi, 15.

viction that nothing could separate him from the love of God. A penitent once came to confession and, having confessed that he had done this, that and the other, went on to say that, because of these things, he had felt unable to come to church and so had missed Mass for some considerable time. What a sad, and misguided, argument! The more we do this, that and the other wrong thing, the more we need to pray and to go to Mass; and if we find our-selves in such a muddle that we have to admit to ourselves not merely that we have done these things but that we intend to go on doing them, then most of all we need prayer and the Mass: we need to pray unendingly that pre-communion prayer: Never—in spite of myself, in spite of my sin, in spite of my will-to-sin—never let me be separated from you; for if the will-to-sin is offset by the will-to-sorrow, if we go on and on, hoping, praying, trying, then we can and must recall—if only, as it were, from afar off—St Paul's words: 'Who will pass sentence against us, when Jesus Christ . . . is pleading for us? . . . Of this I am fully persuaded; neither death nor life, no angels or principalities or powers, neither what is present nor what is to come, no force whatever, neither the height above us nor the depth beneath us, nor any other creature, will be able to separate us from the love of God, which comes to us in Christ Jesus our Lord '[1].

St Paul's conviction of his own sinfulness is of course charac-teristic of the saints; but deep, vivid, anguished as it is, it never quenches their hope or their joy. The confession story quoted above is a sad one; but it is infinitely less sad than that of a woman who, having found nothing to mention in confession except some-thing which proved to be no sin at all, was then asked, as is custom-ary, to mention some sin in her past life, that there might be some definite 'material' for absolution; whereupon she announced that she could not: there were no such sins. But had she never been to confession before? Oh yes, regularly. Then surely she must have found something to confess: must sometimes have been unkind or told lies or something of the sort? Oh no, she had always been

---

[1] *Rom.* viii, 34–9 (Knox).

a good-living woman. . . . What could one do? What one *wanted* to do was to shout very loudly: ' Good grief, woman, then quite literally for heaven's sake go out and peer at yourself through a spiritual microscope; go to your best friend and beseech her to tell you, without any dilutions or reservations whatsoever, just what she thinks of you: no doubt it will mean the end of a beautiful friendship, but it may conceivably mean the beginning of salvation for you. . . .'[1]

In our approach then to the ten commandments the primary emphasis must be not on works to be achieved but on a *theoria*, a perception of the God whom we thus approach, and on the attitude of heart and soul which that *theoria* is to awaken in us, in other words, on faith in the Pauline sense. And the *theoria* demands its setting: the story of God's love and mercy as revealed in Old and New Testaments.

The story begins with the Spirit-Mother brooding over the dark chaos and bringing forth from it form, beauty, light, distinction. We are shown the ' garden of delight '—and according to one reading it is ' in the east ', whence the Sun of righteousness comes—and in it is the tree of life and about it flow the four rivers: for this paradise-garden is the beginning, not the end; we can see it as the abode of the *puer æternus* but not as the heaven of the saints, for between the two there lies the whole of history, the whole of the process of re-integration whereby, in and through Christ, harmony is restored between man and God, between matter and spirit, between the four elements of the human psyche, between man and Nature. For the first garden is in fact lost to humanity through the wiles of the serpent-dragon; and the angel with the flaming two-edged sword bars the way to the tree of life, that tree which is in the middle of the garden and which is also in the middle of history, for the tree is Christ, the life-giving *Logos*: the *alpha* of Eden, the *omega* of Heaven, and, in the middle, in ' the whole world's midpoint ', the redeeming Tree, rising from Adam's grave, the water of life flowing beside it.

[1] Cf. *supra*, p. 51 and *infra*, pp. 116 *sqq.*

We cannot get back to the paradise-garden; nor on the other hand can we forget it. The *nostalgie du paradis* seems to be part of our humanity: we find it expressed among primitive peoples and archaic cultures in myth and ritual, and in our own world in romantic literature. But there is another, contrary urge, revealed both in literature and in human behaviour, the *nostalgie de la boue*, the longing for self-degradation; and there would seem to be a close connection between the two. Is the latter perhaps especially characteristic of the frustrated perfectionist? Certainly evil as such seems to have its fascination for fallen human nature, and the pursuit of it involves self-degradation; but when it is precisely the degradation that is the object of pursuit it seems plausible to argue that the motive, whether conscious or not, is either a desperate urge to be outstanding and so to win acclaim; or an expression of rage, like a child destroying the work or toy it cannot finish; or finally an attempt to escape despair by numbing the sensibilities and retreating from life. Milton gives us a picture of these three types of reaction to failure in his description of the conclave of the devils: Mammon would make hell a substitute-heaven: if we have lost the sun there is always electric light, if we have lost love there is always a brothel round the corner; for Moloch the best way of escape from intolerable sensations and situations is blind rage, to behave like a rat in a trap; Belial is in favour of being very quiet and learning to adjust to the new situation, to live at a lower level and to forget.

If I cannot be a great saint I can make sure of being a great sinner; if I cannot win love and admiration for my goodness I can at least achieve notoriety by my wickedness, or I can use my degradation to win me attention, sympathy, pity. On the other hand if I destroy myself it may be that I am simply venting my spleen against God, for not making me one of his favourites, by destroying his handiwork. Or, finally, if awareness of my situation is too painful I may escape from it by escaping from consciousness.

We are supposed to keep before us the ideal of perfection, but not to be perfectionists. The ideal is not the original paradise, now irrevocably lost to us, but the new Jerusalem to which we must hope one day to come through God's mercy but which is in essence that 'kingdom of God' which is meant even now to be 'within us'. We are, then, to be humble realists: not wasting our lives in futile yearnings nor destroying them out of rage or pique but accepting them, and ourselves, according to God's designs for us and so giving them back to him in sacrifice, quietly confident that if we do so he will 'make us whole'.

As a sun-symbol the sword means life, but it is life achieved through struggle. In medieval alchemy the sword separates the elements and so produces chaos, but it is in order that from the chaos a new and more perfect body may be fashioned. So the body of Christ is pierced with a lance on the cross, but from the darkness the glorious body bursts forth; so too in the Mass the mystical separation is followed by the mystical resurrection in the 'commingling' of body and blood. The essence of the Bible story is that the Fall, the disintegration, is permitted in order that a greater good may come; and so the sword is an essential part of the pattern. There is a hint of this in the creation-narrative itself: in the beginning all is 'waste and void': there is no form, shape, pattern, direction; one thinks of the words of *Job*, xii, 24: 'He . . . causeth them to wander in a wilderness where there is no way'; but light and form are made, and the Hebrew verb used to describe the making suggests fashioning by cutting; moreover the narrative retains the imagery of the Babylonian myth, in which creation is described in terms of a struggle between Marduk and Tiamat, Marduk splitting Tiamat 'into two parts like an oyster' and so making the heavens and the earth; and again when we read in *Genesis* that the Spirit 'moved' over the waters we may recall that the verb used in the Septuagint version has the meaning of bearing down on, assailing—a wind therefore driving over the face of the waters, as in the Babylonian myth Marduk conquers Tiamat by hurling the four winds at her. But the idea of cutting occurs again in the account of the Fall: the original harmony is disrupted, the tree of life is lost and the way to it barred by the fiery sword, though there is the promise of a new creation to follow. [1]

The Tree, which is Christ, is lost to mankind through the folly of mankind's pride; for it is life-giving only in so far as it is worshipped. The first sin was in fact the refusal of worship, of obedience: the attempt to be as God, to achieve mastery through the experiential knowledge of good and evil. The point of the special creation of Adam is that the Lord God ' breathed into his nostrils the breath of life, and made man a living soul ' :[2] he was given a certain autonomy, he was able to rebel, and he did so: he refused life, refused the Tree, refused the Way. The first commandment forbids the making of graven images to be worshipped; we may admit if we will that a superstitious veneration of images, amounting in fact to something like idolatry, is to be met with among the peasant population of certain countries; but what goes deeper than this, and is far more insidious, is the worship—to be met with, one may suppose, in all countries—not of a graven image but of oneself: the sword has not been used to separate the self from the devouring mother, from satiety and rest and sleep; there is no journey therefore in search of God; there is only the complacency of self-worship where there should be the faith, hope and charity which, according to the catechism of the Council of Trent, are the essence of the first commandment.

If the first mode of life-refusal is the refusal of worship, the second is the attempt to turn religion into magic. We may think of the second commandment—indeed we must—as concerned with the use of the name of God or of Christ as an oath; but again there is something deeper in it than that. The idea that to know a person's name is to have power over him is as old as history; it crops up in various forms of sorcery, in the conjuring of spirits, in the abracadabra of black magic. Magic is religion turned upside down: it means attempting to *use* God, to summon and employ divine power for one's own purposes instead of submitting oneself

---

[1] Cf. *Gen.* iii, 15; *Apoc.* xii, 1-17.   [2] *Gen.* ii, 7 (Knox).

and one's will to the will of God. (The most horrible and terrifying example of the exercise of magic is the renegade priest's use of his power of consecration for some satanic purpose.) It is tempting to see certain current superstitions, such as touching wood, throwing salt over the shoulder, not sitting thirteen to table or passing under ladders and so forth, as degradations or vestiges of christian beliefs and practices; however that may be, there is no denying the importance attached by some christians to what are in effect simply talismans; the wearing of this or that medal or scapular, the performance of this or that pious practice, regarded as of magic rather than of religious efficacy. No doubt these things are of no great importance in themselves; and certainly it would be the greatest folly to dismiss all popular forms of devotion as so much superstition—to light a candle before an image of the Mother of God, for instance, is as reasonable, and as symbolically meaningful, as it is beautiful; but it has to be quite clear that we are not pinning our faith to outward observances regardless of our inner dispositions, we are not gambling on the efficacy of a tin medallion or a scrap of wool: it may be possible to make a pact with Satan, it is never possible to make a pact with God. ' Not every one that saith to me, Lord, Lord, shall enter into the kingdom of heaven: but he that doth the will of my Father who is in heaven, he shall enter into the kingdom of heaven.' [1]

When we come to the third commandment we find ourselves faced with the direst confusion. On the one hand there is the sort of sabbatarianism which attempts to turn Sundays into days of unadulterated boredom and gloom; on the other hand the traditional textbook formulas concerning the avoidance of servile work have either become entirely meaningless, as is the case with those for whom Sunday work is an economic necessity, or else have become irrelevant simply because the old distinction between servile and liberal pursuits has ceased to have any significance. True, attempts to impose the (very confused) letter of the law linger on; but they merely serve to remind us of St Paul's disquietude:

[1] *Matt.* vii, 21 (Douai).

68

'You have begun to observe special days and months, special seasons and years. I am anxious over you; has all the labour I have spent on you been useless?'[1]. *Non oportet christianos iudaizare,* the Council of Laodicea roundly declares: christians are not to imitate the Jewish law by abstaining from servile work on Sundays: they are to abstain every day from the servility of sin. True, the Sunday was to be kept holy; but the identification between the christian day of worship and the Jewish day of abstention from labour seems to have come about partly through a confusion of thought and partly through secular legislation from Constantine onwards.[2]

'The Sunday,' writes Fr Jungmann, 'is not the continuation of the sabbath in the sense that, following the example of Old Testament practice, the men of those days wanted to set apart one specially holy day each week but desired to choose for this purpose a different day. The idea of a " day of rest ", which underlay the Jewish practice, was completely absent from the christian celebration. In fact they even used to poke fun at the Jews for spending a whole day in idleness each week. Many centuries were to pass before it occurred to anyone to connect up the christian Sunday with the third commandment. This commandment was interpreted allegorically in terms of the sabbath rest of the spirit which christians were observing all the while, or else of the sabbath rest of eternal life towards which they were ever striving.'[3]

In the early Church then ' servile work ' was interpreted ' spiritually ' as meaning sin; but gradually, in the Middle Ages, the idea of Sunday rest came to be taken as deriving from the Old Testament law concerning the sabbath, and to be interpreted with great severity.[4] Confusion was increased by an uncertainty as to whether the ' servility ' of the prohibited work was to be seen simply in terms of the nature of the work in itself (i.e. as proper to a servant

---

[1] *Gal.* iv, 10 (Knox).   [2] Cf. L. L. McReavy: *Servile Work* (*Clergy Review*, April, June, 1935).   [3] J. A. Jungmann, S.J.: *The Sacrifice of the Church*, pp. 24-5.   [4] The ' Cain Domnaig, an Irish document, which Priebsch dates from the ninth century ' forbids, among many other things, shaving, washing, bathing, aimless running, baking, house-cleaning (cf. McReavy, *op. cit.* p. 277).

or slave) or whether the idea of working for gain was essential. It seems no more than common sense to suggest that our present-day definitions of servile work should in fact take cognizance of present-day conditions, so as to exclude (from the prohibition) any labours which in fact are to be regarded as recreations or hobbies; the one essential thing, however, is to do what St Thomas did in his attempt to rescue first principles from the morass of piecemeal legislation, and to make it clear that the primary purpose of the law is to keep the Sunday *holy*.[1] We may note, moreover, as Dr Erich Fromm has pointed out, that the idea of 'sabbath' means much more than a relaxation from labour: it means a cessation from 'work' in the sense of any interference by man, whether constructive or destructive, with the physical world; it means, in other words, a state of peace between man and Nature, an adumbration of that messianic kingdom where lion and lamb lie down together and swords are turned into ploughshares.[2] We may recall again that seven is the sacred number signifying completeness, but a completeness crowning effort or indeed struggle: so on the seventh day God ' rested' after the work of creation; so Christ's *consummatum est* comes at the end of the seven words on the cross and Mary's apotheosis is the crowning of that com-passion we think of in terms of the seven swords; seven times Naaman the Syrian was to wash in the waters; for seven days Laban pursued Jacob; when Eliseus raised to life the son of the Sunamite woman he breathed into his mouth and the boy yawned seven times and opened his eyes; so also the supernatural power given the christian to complete his journey is summed up in the seven sacraments and the seven gifts of the Spirit. The word sabbath (the Babylonian *sappatu*) itself means completeness, and so denotes not so much a day of rest as a day on which sacrificial ceremonies bring peace to the worshipper; so St Thomas teaches that the purpose of the third commandment is to ensure the 'mind's rest in God ', *quies cordis in Deum*, a tranquillity which is a foretaste of the peace of eternity.[3]

---

[1] *Sum. Theol.* II, II. cxxii, 4.   [2] Fromm: *The Forgotten Language*, pp. 206 sqq.   [3] *Sum. Theol.* I, II, c, 5; II. II. cxxii, 4 ad 1.

All this we can certainly apply to our concept of the christian Sunday, but with another essential element added. If 'seven' is still significant here, so also is the number eight. 'A basic idea which underlay the christian weekly Sunday was the same as that of the yearly Easter—namely, to keep vivid the consciousness that we have been redeemed by Christ. According to the outlook prevalent amongst us today we might have expected that for this purpose choice would have fallen on Friday as being the day on which Christ died upon the cross. But early christians did not analyze into constituents the various phases of the work of our redemption; they regarded the redemption as one dramatic occurrence, as one great battle which Christ had fought for the salvation of mankind. . . . Hence Sunday is the day of triumph, of exultation and of certain hope for all christians. It is the day of new creation. That is why, as early as the second century, it was frequently called the "Eighth Day". For in six days God had accomplished the first creation; on the seventh day, the sabbath, he had rested from his work; but on the eighth day, Sunday, he had resumed his work and brought it most wondrously to completion in the resurrection of Christ by which there has been opened to us the way to the everlasting kingdom of God.'[1] The idea of the number eight as a symbol of perfection and completion is, as we shall see,[2] very ancient; and so the idea now finds a new richness in christian symbolism: '*octava summa virtutum est*, "eight is the sum-total, the essence of all virtues", we read in the lesson by St Ambrose in the breviary'.[3]

But, as Fr Jungmann goes on to point out, 'the name which was most characteristically attached to this day . . . was *Kyriake, Dominica*, "The Lord's Day" ',[4] not in the Old Testament sense of 'the day of the Lord' but as the day of resurrection, of triumph, in other words 'Christ's Day'; but the eighth day was the day of Helios; the early christians were accustomed to think of 'the sun

[1] Jungmann, *op. cit.* pp. 25-6. [2] Cf. *infra*, p. 112. [3] Jungmann, *ibid.* [4] Jungmann, *op. cit.* p. 27.

as a symbol of Christ, and of sunrise as a symbol of resurrection ' ; [1] and so we arrive at the name Sunday, *Sonntag*.

Sunday then is the day especially devoted to the joyful remembrance of the work of redemption; but remembrance, not in the sense of a simple calling to mind of past events, but as a re-enactment, symbolic and effective, of those events. ' For the christian of early times the renewal every Sunday of the *memoria passionis* must have been the fulfilment of a self-evident need.' (It was only gradually that the Mass came to be celebrated on other days also.) In those primitive times ' we find no trace of any commandment to go to Mass on Sunday, only plentiful evidence that in point of fact all who dwelt in the town or country did actually assemble for Mass. In the Diocletian persecution the martyrs of Abitene asserted: " Without the *dominicum* we cannot live " '.[2] But quite apart from persecutions, it was difficult to fit the assemblies for Mass into the existing economic framework of society, so that they had to be held, as Pliny says, *stato die ante lucem*, before dawn [3]; but under Constantine the time of Mass was fixed at the third hour of the morning—the normal hour for transacting business—and the prohibition under later emperors ' of all business in the law courts and of noisy functions such as public circuses and the like; also of noisy forms of trading ' seems to have been concerned simply to keep the day holy. It was not until the sixth century that all work on Sundays was prohibited in the west; and this ' was brought about partly through suggestion from the now christianized German races, and partly from the adoption of pertinent regulations taken over from the Old Testament. But the emphasis remained for a very long time on the requirement of one communal service. The Church became on Sunday visible and tangible as a Church '. [4]

Not abstention from work for abstention's sake, not the pharisaic sabbath, not sabbatarianism, but simply a measure of external quietude in order to make possible the *quies cordis in Deum*, keep-

[1] *ibid.*   [2] *ibid*, p. 29.   [3] *ibid.*   [4] Jungmann, *op. cit.* p. 31.

ing the day holy by the recalling and offering of the sacrifice of redemption: this is the essential meaning for the christian of the third commandment, and it is in this idea that the meanings of sabbath and Sunday, of the seven and the eight, are seen to coalesce.

There is a significant contrast between the quietude of the Lord's sabbath and the frenzy of the witches' sabbat: between the sacred dance and the *Walpurgisnacht*. The aim of the latter is destruction, disintegration, hatred, discord, non-being, achieved through defiance of God and the worship of the mystery of iniquity; the aim of the former is unity, peace, love and life, and the way is through the mystery of the wood, the *sacramentum ligni vitæ*. So, once again, the Tree, which is Christ, is the focal point of all three commandments: for the first enjoins on us faith, in the Pauline sense, in the Tree; the second bids us call upon the name of the Lord in humble worship and dependence and trust; and the third commands us to do what we may to re-establish the original harmony which was disrupted by sin, the harmony between man and Nature, the harmony within man himself, the harmony between man and God.

Now it was suggested above that we may arrive at a deeper idea of the commandments if we see them in the context of the Bible as a divine poem. But the Bible can rightly be seen in terms not only of poetry but of music: as in a symphony, you find the same theme occurring again and again, now simply stated, now elaborated, now altered by the addition of fresh material or a new colour in the orchestration; as in the Elgar *Enigma Variations*, you will find the theme sometimes hidden by some other theme which has been superimposed upon it; or you will find dramatic changes of mood, as in the overwhelming change from minor to major in the second movement of the Sibelius second symphony. In the Bible, ' in the beginning ', the main themes are quickly and simply stated, and thereafter they are never far distant: water, wood, dragon, life, sword, the darkness of chaos, the form and definition and beauty to which the light gives birth.

The Mystery

We are not told explicitly in *Genesis* that God created all things out of nothingness: on the contrary, the imagery used suggests a picture of the dark chaos as being in some sense the pre-existent material out of which the cosmos was fashioned. This picture is useful when we apply the history of the macrocosm to our own individual microcosm: God sets about his creative work, but it is through *bara*, through cutting and cleaving, that form emerges from chaos; then the form is disrupted through the wiles of the dragon, the harmony of the first sabbath becomes a discordant jangle, order and beauty are destroyed; but the Fall is not ultimate: we are to see the disorder, the evil, thus permitted by God as permitted in order that an even greater good may come about than could otherwise be the case: a deeper, richer revelation of the meaning of love. So there must be more destruction, more cutting away: but that a new creation may come to be, greater than the old. Professor Mircéa Eliade points out that ' whatever the religious context in which they occur, the function of the waters always remains the same: they disintegrate, they abolish forms (wash away sin)—at the same time both purifying and regenerating ';[1] and Fr Beirnaert, quoting this, points out the ' identity of structure ' in ' the deluge which reabsorbs the world and humanity into water (instituting a new epoch)[2], the periodic lustrations which remove the tarnish of time and use, the immersion of sacred statues which restores the spent forces of divinity, etc.', since ' in each case the passage through water signifies the return to a principle[3] anterior to all forms, a sort of chaotic totality of energies in which qualified existence is dissolved into indifferency in order to rise again according to a new mode. The alchemical formula recalled by Jung,[4] *Aqua est quae occidit et vivificat*, expresses in lapidary terms the

---

[1] *Traité d'Histoire des Religions*, p. 187.   [2] That the flood was not a world-wide but merely a local one seems to be proven not only by the findings of science but by the plan and style of the biblical author: the plan was one of gradual elimination: first the Cainites are dismissed in order to concentrate on the Sethites; then the descendants of Cham and Japheth are disposed of in favour of the Semites; and so on; but it is characteristic of the author's style to apply universal expressions—' all flesh ', ' all men ', etc.—to the particular group with which he is dealing.   [3] *In principio,* ' in the beginning ': not a temporal concept so much as a question of source, derivation; cf. *infra.*, p. 151.   [4] *Psychologie der Übertragung*, p. 130.

universal function of water: water is that which slays and which gives life. A fragment of Heraclitus asserts, " It is death for souls to become water ".[1] It is death also for humanity and for the cosmos. But at the same time it is life. So an Indian text states: " Water, you are the source of everything and of all existence ".[2] Hence this strange ambivalence of waters, at once the object of a sacred terror because one fears to drown there and of a passionate attraction because in the bosom of the waters lie concealed youth and immortality. On the one hand the waters are the sea of death, the abyss with its devouring jaws, the retreat of monsters and dragons which in the Indo-European tradition represents a permanent danger for all formal existence. On the other hand it is in the depth of the ocean that Gilgamesh will find the marvellous plant, it is in the depths of lakes and seas that lie the majority of magic cauldrons which in Celtic legends confer youth and transform men into heroes.[3] The water is the water of Life '[4].

If then we are ever to find God, to walk with him again ' in the cool of the evening '; if we are to rise to the realities of religion and not sink back into magic; if we are to arrive at the *quies* and harmony of the sabbath, it can only be through undergoing the cutting and cleaving of the sword, through entering the death-dealing and life-bringing waters. The same is true of the moral realities with which the rest of the commandments are concerned. The first table of the law, as St Thomas points out, deals with our love of God; the second, with our love of our neighbour and with the main types of behaviour which militate against that love. We shall find plenty of examples of such behaviour in the Old Testament; and perhaps we can discern a common pattern or theme in all of them. The myths and mysteries express man's yearnings: they can be seen as remote adumbrations of the true pattern; the

---

[1] Fragment 68. [2] *Bhavicyottarapurana*, 31, 14. [3] Eliade, *op. cit.* p. 182. [4] Louis Beirnaert, S.J.: *The Mythic Dimension in Christian Sacramentalism* (Eranos-Jahrbuch, 1949) tr. by Erwin W. Geissman, *Cross Currents*, Fall, 1951, pp. 68-9. Cf. *Selection I*, ed. Cecily Hastings & Donald Nichol (Sheed & Ward, 1953), pp. 43 *sqq.* Cf. also *infra*, pp. 110 *sqq.*, 144 *sqq.*

sins described in the Bible, on the other hand, are not adumbrations of the pattern (though they recall its themes) but a turning upside-down of the pattern: not a fumbling attempt to find life through expressing a harmony, but a defiant attempt to seize on life through disharmony. It is that attempt to seize, to grab, to dominate, which is characteristic of all the main forms of human wickedness, reflecting as it does the attempt of the first human beings to seize life and to be gods by snatching the fruit from the tree; and the idea is of particular relevance to the modern western world, in which to live (or to succeed) and to grab are so often synonymous. We might recall here some trenchant words of Ananda Coomaraswamy: ' Cain, who killed his brother Abel, the herdsman, and built himself a city, prefigures modern civilization, one that has been described from within as " a murderous machine, with no conscience and no ideals ". . . . The modern traveller—" thy name is legion "—proposing to visit some " lost paradise " such as Bali, often asks whether or not it has yet been " spoiled ". It makes a naïve, and even tragic, confession. For this man does not reflect that he is condemning himself; that what his question asks is whether or not the sources of equilibrium and grace in the other civilizations have yet been poisoned by contact with men like himself and the culture of which he is a product. . . . The bases of modern civilization are to such a degree rotten to the core that it has been forgotten even by the learned that man ever attempted to live otherwise than by bread alone. . . . Mrs Handy's record of the Marquesas Islanders, that " the external aspects of their culture have been almost wiped out by the white man's devastating activities ", is typical of what could be cited from a hundred other sources '[1].

Let us agree that this is a one-sided picture of our civilization as a whole; it remains true that the side is there for all to see; that our civilization must in fact appear to many who have suffered at its hands as a smash-and-grab raid—and there is nothing very uplifting to the spirit in the reflection that if in the past the accent has been on the grabbing it is likely in the future to be on the smash.

[1] *Am I My Brother's Keeper?* (Asia Press, N.Y.), pp. 1-7.

Yet it must be admitted also that we are only doing, in our own particularly vulgar fashion, what has always been done *ab initio*, from the first fatal disruption. The discovery of life must involve a killing and a hating; and the mystics tell us of these things in no uncertain terms; but humanity, after the first rebellion, was quick to fall into a fundamental confusion and to suppose that the killing and the hating must be external. There is a sense in which the father (that is, the ' father-figure ') must be slain that the son may himself grow up and reach maturity; there is a sense in which the son (that is, the *puer æternus*, the boy in us) must be slain lest the man end up not as a mature human being but as an aged, and therefore repulsive, Peter Pan; what in fact you find in human history, from the earliest times, is the real, objective killing or dishonouring of father by son, son by father, brother by brother, as though brute force at its most brutish, the masculine element in us isolated and exaggerated and degraded *ad absurdum*, could seize upon the boon of life. So we are told that it was the sight of the world filled with corruption and oppression and violence that led God to destroy it with the deluge. [1] It is not by killing other things that we shall find life ourselves; it is not the ' blood of bulls and goats ' that will take away our sins; [2] the only life-bringing sacrifice is self-sacrifice: but that is a lesson it took mankind a long time to learn.

In one of the prayers of the Canon of the Mass we recall the sacrifices of Abel, Abraham and Melchizedech; [3] and Dr Jung has pointed out how in this sequence there is a sort of crescendo. ' Abel is essentially the son, and sacrifices an animal; Abraham is essentially the father—indeed, the " tribal father "—and therefore on a higher level. He does not offer a choice possession merely, but is ready to sacrifice the best and dearest thing he has—his only son. [4] Melchizedech (" teacher of righteousness "), is, according to *Hebrews*, vii, 1, king of Salem and " priest of the most high God ", El 'Elyon. . . . By virtue of his priesthood, Melchizedech stands

[1] *Gen.* vi, 11–12. [2] *Hebrews*, x, 4. [3] Cf. *infra*, p. 215. [4] Cf. *infra*, p. 86.

above the patriarch, and his feasting of Abraham has the significance of a priestly act. We must therefore attach a symbolical meaning to it, as is in fact suggested by the bread and wine. Consequently the symbolical offering ranks even higher than the sacrifice of a son, which is still the sacrifice of somebody else. Melchizedech's offering is thus a prefiguration of Christ's sacrifice of himself.'[1]

The seven commandments show us how man, instead of sacrificing his own egoism, tries to achieve life by doing violence, by being aggressive, to other things and people. And the first and worst form of such violence is that done to one's own parents and thence to one's home, one's brethren, one's *patria*. For St Thomas, the fourth commandment is a sort of bridge between the first three and the rest, having, as he says, a ' certain affinity ' to the precepts of the first table inasmuch as our parents are the ' particular principle of our being, just as God is the universal principle ';[2] the story of our disruption begins with man's repudiation of the universal principle, and soon there follows a dishonouring of the particular principle, in the story of Noah and his sons. In the ninth chapter of *Genesis* we read of how Noah tilled the earth and grew a vine and made wine and then, ' drunk with it, lay all naked in his tent '[3]; the details of what followed are not clear: Cornelius à Lapide thinks that the boy Chanaan first discovered Noah in this condition and mocked at his nakedness and then joked about it to his father, Cham, *qui pueri petulantiam non repressit sed probavit*, who approved instead of repressing the wantonness of the boy;[4] Sem and Japheth on the other hand, with averted gaze, cover their father; and the story ends with the cursing of Chanaan.

In its imagery the biblical account of Noah thus includes a number of the themes with which we are concerned. The name Noah itself means rest or repose, and recalls the sabbath-theme; on the other hand the word ' Chanaanite ' is used to signify a trader

[1] *Transformation Symbolism in the Mass*, in ' The Mysteries ', Eranos Yearbook, pp. 286–7. [2] *Sum. Theol.* II. II. cxxii, 5. [3] *Gen.* ix, 21 (Knox). [4] *Comment. in Genesim, in cap. ix*, v. 22.

or trafficker, and one thinks of the destruction of the ' quietude of the heart in God ' by rapacity, and of the traffickers whom our Lord expelled from the temple. In Noah's story we have the wood of the ark and the water of the flood, and then, in this incident, the wine, the *puer*, the laughter (in this case mocking, irreverent and therefore sinful), and the nakedness which provokes the laughter.

Let us be clear about this last: these early human beings were in the happy position of never having heard of puritanism, and they regarded the organs of generation not as shameful but as what indeed the Romans called them, *verenda*, objects of veneration. So when, at the approach of death, they would exact a most solemn oath, Abraham and Jacob both use the same formula: ' Put thy hand under my thigh '—where ' thigh ' is a euphemism for the generative power. [1] On the other hand, Adam and Eve were ashamed of their nakedness after their sin because, we are to suppose, having striven for divine mastery they found that they had lost their human mastery, had lost their dominion over their own bodies as they had lost their dominion over the beasts. The story of man might have been a song of innocence; but because of sin it became a song of (bitter) experience; Eden is lost and there is no returning to it; the *puer* is lost (Chanaan is cursed); the carefree nakedness cannot be recaptured. But the solution is not to be found in any form of puritanism, in regarding sexual experience or the genital organs as shameful in themselves or nakedness in itself as indecent: the only solution is to embark on the *agon*, the dark journey through the waters, to the nakedness of heaven.

The *puer* is usually depicted naked, as we have seen, because nakedness is primarily a symbol of freedom; but it is also a symbol of candour, honesty, openness—and therefore, as between man and God or man and man, of understanding. There is bound to be some connection between figleaves and fraud or at least dissimulation, and

[1] *Gen.* xxiv, 2; xlvii, 29; cp. the reference in *Gen.* xlvi, 26 to the sixty-six souls who went with Jacob into Egypt and who had come ' out of his thigh '; cf. Fr. E. F. Sutcliffe, S. J., *Genesis*, in *A Catholic Commentary on Holy Scripture*, p. 197.

therefore lack of oneness (or, after dissimulation, of at-one-ment) with God or with man; so it is that after his sin Adam hides from God and can no longer walk with him in the garden in the cool of the evening. We must suppose too that Adam could no longer walk with Eve in perfect understanding; there is a picture of the loss of understanding between man and man in the story of Babel, the ziggurat which would enable them to mount up to the very heavens but which in fact showed them that they could not live together in understanding and amity because, not in the technical but in the colloquial sense, they ' did not speak the same language '; (so St. Paul tells us: ' Use, all of you, the same language. There must be no divisions among you '[1]); and that discord within humanity finds a more forceful, an ultimate, expression in the murder of Abel by his brother. ' And the Lord said to Cain: Where is thy brother Abel? And he answered, I know not: am I my brother's keeper? '[2] The divine answer to that terrible question is in the story of the good Samaritan; and that story has been restated again and again in different ways by men of vision, as in Dostoievsky's ' We are each responsible for all '. But Cain becomes thenceforward a ' fugitive and a vagabond ' upon the earth: homeless, rootless for all that he built a city: not homeless in the creative sense, not homeless like the hero who ' puts away the things of a child ', of a *puer*, and leaves his home and sets out on his journey; not ' without father or mother or genealogy ' like Melchizedech who for that very reason represents a priesthood higher than that of the sons of Aaron, the eternal priesthood of Christ; but homeless because he has, by killing his brother, killed in himself not what ought to have been killed, his pride and egoism, but what ought to have been preserved through no matter what wanderings, his power to rest in God in the end, his power to hallow and to enjoy the sabbath of heaven.

The fourth commandment is concerned primarily with the duty of children to show *pietas*, dutifulness, to their parents; but it is also concerned with the duty of all members of a family to

---

[1] I *Cor.* i, 10 (Knox). [2] *Gen.* iv, 9 (Douai).

show *pietas* to their family. Children must respect and honour their parents by being obedient to them; but parents must respect their children in wielding authority over them. Both obedience and authority have limits: a parent may not be a tyrant any more than a child may be a rebel: when the father is acting within the limits of his God-given authority the child has no right to rebel; when the father goes beyond those limits he has no right to command. Too often in fact the two generations find that, like the builders of the tower of Babel, they speak a different language, and so the family unity is wholly or partially destroyed and the members of it become, metaphorically if not literally, fugitives and vagabonds.

All this is a return to chaos; but it is the wrong sort of return, sterile instead of creative. A return there must be, through the waters that ' kill and quicken ', to the chaos out of which a new creation can be fashioned: man must go back to the beginning for, once again, this beginning is a question not of time but of principle, of source, of a return to receptivity, malleability, a return to the ' original mother-waters from which all qualified existences have risen, every form of life, in a procession which takes its rise at once from struggle and from childbirth. The rite of the waters repeats and re-actualizes for concrete existence its *archè*, and if it realizes death it is so that the return to the origin can be made without the destruction of the forms and figures which precisely suppose a rising out of the waters '. So, ' from the first centuries of the christian era ', the Church recognized in the waters of baptism ' a death-dealing and maternal function '; Cyril of Jerusalem speaks of it as ' both a tomb and a mother '; for the pseudo-Denys the immersion symbolizes ' death and the burial in which all form disappears ', while on the other hand Ephrem the Syrian speaks of the font as a ' second womb ' for the ' sons of the kingdom of heaven ', making young men out of old as the river Jordan once restored Naaman to his youth.[1]

A death there must be, a killing; quite obviously we distort the

[1] Cf. Beirnaert, *op. cit.* pp. 69-70.

whole meaning of the Bible if we try to tone down its stark realities, to sentimentalize it; but the killing is not of something other than ourselves, nor is it in any ontological sense a killing of ourselves or any sort of self-mutilation; it is indeed a killing of something *within* ourselves, but in the last resort that something is the effect of a lack or privation, is the egoism which comes of the lack of theocentricity. There must be a killing, a denuding, but—and this is the elementary lesson which some spiritual men seem never to learn—if it is to be life-bringing it must be done not with hate but with love. Cain kills his brother because he hates him and so the end is nothingness, rootlessness; but if we see these brothers as symbols of a duality within ourselves—let us say the light and the dark sides of our personalities—then we must change the story radically: there must be love, not hate, of the dark shadow, amity not enmity, so that the end may be not a destruction, and therefore a residual half-personality, but an integration.

As we shall see, another of the prayers in the Canon of the Mass links together the two ideas of accepting and blessing: there must be the acceptance of the fact of disintegration before there can be the blessing of integration. The psalmist's ' they have numbered all my bones ' must go side by side with Christ's ' the very hairs of your head are all numbered ': for creative Love is both fierce and tender: the sword cleaves the waters; the mighty wind and fire fill the house; laboriously Eliseus breathes life back into the nostrils of the boy; Mary is troubled at the angel's news; Christ is troubled in spirit and weeps at the raising of Lazarus his friend; always the condition of life is tension, polarity, for integration means the reconciliation of opposites, of Cain and Abel, and that in its turn means the at-one-ment of man with God, and, yet further, that means being naked to God, naked to the thrust of the sword as Sebastian was naked to the arrows and Christ himself to the lance. It is in this sense that we may read the words of Job: ' Naked came I out of my mother's womb, and naked shall I return thither '[1].

---

[1] *Job*, i, 21 (Douai).

'In nearly all the mystery cults, the mystes undergoing initiation had to perform innumerable purifications and ablutions, in preparation for which he removed his clothing'; so Plotinus speaks of the ascent to the Good and the Godly in terms of the Orphic version of the Eleusinian mysteries, that is to say, of 'appointed purifications' and 'the entry in nakedness'[1].

What then, in a word, is the fourth commandment telling us? It is telling us that we must give honour to, and be humbly receptive of, influences greater than ourselves, influences both divine and human. There are the waters above the firmament and the waters below; and the latter remain for us dark and chaotic: we cannot of ourselves grasp the boon, find life, reach maturity: first the fierce and gentle rain must fall from heaven and only then can there arise in us the fountains springing up into life everlasting. The soul is feminine to God: Cain was cursed for his arrogance and hatred and brutality, but our Lord told us, Blessed are the meek, for they shall possess the land.

It is good to be naked; to fling off one's clothes and bask in the sunshine or bathe in the sea, to know with one's body the feel of earth and wind and sun. It is psychologically useful inasmuch as it can help us to face and see ourselves, to throw off the 'conventional husk' and enter into that 'stark encounter with reality, with no false veils or adornments of any kind' in which a man 'stands forth as he really is and shows what was hidden under the mask of conventional adaptation: the shadow. This is now raised to consciousness and integrated with the ego, which means a move in the direction of wholeness. Wholeness is not so much perfection as completeness. Assimilation of the shadow gives a man body, so to speak; the animal sphere of instinct, as well as the primitive or archaic psyche, emerge into the zone of consciousness and can no longer be repressed by fictions and illusions. In this way man becomes for himself the difficult problem he really is. He must always remain conscious of the fact that he is such a problem if he wants to develop at all. Repression leads to a one-sided develop-

[1] Cf. Hans Leisegang: *The Mystery of the Serpent*, in 'The Mysteries', pp. 236–7.

ment if not to stagnation, and eventually to neurotic dissociation. Today it is no longer a question of " How can I get rid of my shadow "—for we have seen enough of the curse of one-sidedness. Rather we must ask ourselves: " How can man live with his shadow without its precipitating a succession of disasters? " Recognition of the shadow is a reason for humility, for genuine fear of the abysmal depths in man. This caution is most expedient, since the man without a shadow thinks himself harmless precisely because he is ignorant of his shadow. The man who recognizes his shadow knows very well that he is not harmless. . . . [But] the advantage of the situation, despite all its dangers, is that once the naked truth has been revealed the discussion can get down to essentials; ego and shadow are no longer divided but are brought together in an —admittedly precarious—unity ' [1].

The relevance of humility is yet more obvious when we transfer these ideas to the religious sphere, when we think of confronting not only ourselves but God in nakedness. For our nakedness to God can no longer be the carefree nakedness of Eden, of the *puer*. True, St Cyril of Jerusalem reminds his catechumens that at baptism they will be ' publicly naked and yet unashamed ' as Adam was in the earthly paradise [2]: the baptismal rebirth is in a true sense a rebirth of innocence; but the past cannot be undone, the way to glory must lie now through darkness, and as for St Paul baptism is a sharing in Christ's death so for St Cyril the neophyte is ' stripped and naked, thereby imitating Christ's nakedness on the Cross ' [3]: we cannot approach God save in humble consciousness of our own sin and of the fact that the regenerative waters are waters of sorrow, though because of our identification with Christ it is to glory that they lead so that they are also the waters of joy, and when we bathe in the waters we immerse ourselves in the bridal bath of Christ and his Church, so that, as the same St Cyril tells us, ' the soul must not put on again the garment it has previously taken off. As the Bride of Christ says: I have put off my garment, how shall I put

---

[1] C. G. Jung: *Psychology of the Transference* (in ' Practice of Psychotherapy ', Collected Works, vol. XVI, pp. 238-9). [2] *Catechesis Mystagogica, lect.* III, c.2. [3] *ibid.*

it on?'[1]: the nakedness is indeed a recovery of youth and joy and freedom which we must not lose.

These themes are restated, these truths underlined, by the story of Abraham and Isaac. Abraham dwells among the oaks of Mambre and sets up an altar there (turning to the west when he parts from Lot, as Lot had chosen to go eastward); his posterity is to be as number-less as the sands of the sea (though Sara his wife is barren); his sword defeats Chodorlahomor and the kings who were with him, and divides the sacrificial animals that God may make a covenant with him;[2] at sunset he falls into a deep sleep and a great dread assails him; but in the darkness of night he sees in vision a torch of fire that passes between the pieces of flesh; henceforward every male child is to be circumcised when he is eight days old, a ritual whereby 'the source of life, the natural means whereby the race was propagated, was consecrated to God'[3]; he is promised a child, but Sara, listening behind the tent door, laughs mockingly—again the wrong sort of laughter, as in the case of Chanaan—and then, ' overcome with terror ', denies the charge of laughing but is told by the Lord (or the angel speaking in his name), ' Ah, he said, but thou didst laugh '[4]; later the boy is born and Abraham gives him the name Isaac, Laughter, and Sara cries out, ' God has made me laugh for joy '; but at the feast that Abraham made for the day of the child's weaning Sara finds Ishmael mocking her son—another echo of Chanaan's behaviour—and the slave woman is sent away.[5] Abraham is greatly distressed at this but is consoled by God's promise for Ishmael's future. The rest of Agar's story continues the familiar imagery: she goes away with her child and wanders in the desert of Bersabee; when at last all the water in the bottle with which Abraham had provided her is exhausted she leaves her son under a tree and goes to sit down at a bowshot's distance: ' I cannot bear

---

[1] *ibid.* (cf. *Song of Songs*, v. 3). [2] *Gen.* xv, 10; ' An ancient mode of making a covenant was for the parties to pass between the parts of a divided animal, the original symbolism being apparently that they called down on themselves a similar fate should they violate the treaty '; in this story God adopts the ritual usual among men. Cf. E. F. Sutcliffe, S.J.: *Genesis*, in *A Catholic Commentary on Holy Scripture*, p. 194. [3] *ibid.* p. 195. [4] *Gen.* xviii, 15 (Knox). [5] *Gen.* xxi, 8-10.

to see my child die'; but then God gives clear sight to her eyes and she sees a well with water in it, so that she gives the boy to drink; and thereafter God is with him, he grows up and becomes a great archer.[1]

The command to sacrifice Isaac follows[2]: a command which affirms God's absolute dominion over human life while its revocation implies both a condemnation of the human sacrifices then common among the Chanaanites and an affirmation of the principle we have been considering, that, in the last resort, the only acceptable sacrifice is self-sacrifice. Abraham is told to sacrifice his ' only-begotten ', his beloved son; to give up his hope in the promises; to go to the land of vision and there give back to God his Laughter —his story is indeed a song of experience—and so he rises in the dark hours before the dawn and saddles his ass and sets out to face his agony, as Another would one day set out for his last journey seated upon an ass; and on the third day he sees in the distance the place to which he is to go; so he leaves his servants and the ass and goes on alone with. the boy, who asks him, Where is the victim ? and he replies, God will provide; then having set up the altar and bound his son he takes up the knife to slay him, but his hand is stayed and he offers instead a ram caught by its horns in a thicket; so his Laughter is restored to him, and he returns to Bersabee, where he had planted a grove of trees[3]—and the name of the place means the seventh well or the well of satiety—and there he dwells.

His laughter was given back to him: he had not attempted to cling to it against God's will, to possess it by force. And it was given back to him, we must presume, a hundredfold, since we always prize more what we have nearly lost. Thus he anticipated those other words of our Lord, Blessed are they that mourn for they shall be comforted. Just as the fourth commandment covers all that refers to *pietas*, to our dutifulness to parents, family, home, fatherland; so the fifth commandment covers all injuries inflicted

---

[1] *Gen.* xxi, 11-12 (Knox). [2] *Gen.* xxii. Cf. *supra*, p. 77 and *infra*, p. 216. [3] *Gen.* xxi, 33.

on the person of our neighbour (as the precept forbidding theft covers all damage done to property);[1] and we might do well to think of laughter sometimes in this context, for perhaps we seldom think to accuse ourselves of ' black ' laughter, even though we know the deep damage and hurt it can do to others; on the other hand, how many spiritual directors or religious superiors think to remind those under their guidance that ' white ' laughter is a good and perhaps a holy thing, that it can be an important duty, an important part of charity, and that it is a sin to go about with a mouth like a coat-hanger? Mockery and dourness alike can injure and even kill.

We need not abandon these trains of thought, these themes, if we turn now to another commandment, the prohibition of stealing. Melchizedech is king of Salem, which means peace; for peace is the fruit of poverty of spirit as solicitude and anxiety are the fruit of avarice and covetousness and the attempt to satisfy these cravings by the use of violence, literal or metaphorical. Melchizedech, as we have seen, stands in sharp contrast to Cain; for the latter was rootless, a vagabond, because through his violence he had torn up his roots; Melchizedech is without father or mother or genealogy because he is the symbol of that freedom from care which comes of total self-dedication, of being absorbed in a God-given office or function; he is a king, but our Lord will say: Blessed are the poor in spirit for theirs is the kingdom of heaven. Mysterious figure that he is, he seems to come upon the scene as though, like creation, *ex nihilo:* without background, he is the symbol of all those who stand ' poor and stripped and naked ' before God and so, instead of trying to enrich themselves forcibly at the expense of others, are able to receive all the riches which God's prodigality offers to his human creatures.

There are many figures in the Bible who symbolize this process of being stripped of everything before God, being reduced to nothingness or rather to the awareness of one's nothingness. And it is significant that these figures are often if not always figures of

---

[1] Cf. *Sum. Theol.* II. II. cxxii, 6, *ad* 2.

the *puer* or son; for, once again, it is only through the process thus symbolized that, with Eden lost to us, the child can come to maturity in God. Isaac is one example, in the story we have just been considering; Joseph the son of Jacob is another. His brothers mockingly call him ' the dreamer': he is the seer, the visionary, associated therefore like Isaac with a ' mount of vision '; as a boy of sixteen he is stripped of his coat of many colours; he is thrown into a waterless well, and his father is told that a wild beast has devoured him; then he is sold into slavery, and as a slave meets with further trouble and is cast into the darkness of a dungeon; but thereafter he prospers and becomes the deliverer of his family from famine. The blessing given him by the dying Jacob is not without its obscurities, but we may notice the reference to the arrows of his enemies (his brothers?) harassing him—again the Sebastian figure—but his own bow ' rests in the strength that does not fail him '; and, most important, there is the promise that God will bless him *benedictionibus coeli desuper, benedictionibus abyssi jacentis deorsum*, with the blessings of dew and rain from heaven, of wells and fountains from the depths of the earth: thus here again there is life because here again the two waters meet. Man must be born of water from below and Spirit from above; so at Christ's baptism the brooding Dove descends upon him as the waters of Jordan envelop him. These blessings will rest upon Joseph's brow: he is to be clothed with glory as with a crown. We are not to be solicitous about wherewith we shall be clothed: as Abraham said, *Deus providebit*, God will provide: our concern must be to be naked, to be stripped as Christ was stripped on the cross; there are to be no figleaves, none of the falsehood of prudery, the shallowness of formalism, the arrogance of man-made attempts to make order out of chaos, attempts which can end only in a meaningless babel.

The waters above and below are joined; heaven and earth remain distinct but there is marriage between them; as when the Church in God's power first exorcizes and then fills with blessing the material things of earth, there is an ' interinanimation ', the fountains spring up, the earthly can be taken up into the seventh heaven. Blessed are the poor in spirit for theirs is the kingdom: stealing means first of all taking for one's own what belongs to others; but it also means taking for one's own what belongs, through God's gift, to oneself. We are only stewards of the things that are ours; and that applies not only to material possessions and blessings, but to all our gifts and qualities, all that makes up our psycho-physical 'estate': all these are God's gifts and presents to us, as a prayer in the Canon of the Mass expresses it, and they are to be offered back to him that our self-sacrifice may be unrestricted, a holocaust, and our self-dedication complete.[1] Another prayer begs God to 'accept and bless' our offerings[2] and the two ideas have their application here. If there is to be blessing there must first be acceptance: acceptance of the facts (in this case, about ourselves) as they are, that we are neither angels nor brute animals, and are not meant to be; that if on the one hand we can think of ourselves as only a little less than the angels,[3] on the other hand we cannot be blind to the disruption into which we have fallen and which makes us subhuman: to cry with the psalmist, I am a worm and no man,[4] is not maudlin self-pity but plain statement of fact, for in so far as the image of God is destroyed in us we become subhuman—and we can rise again to our proper stature only by acknowledging our brutishness and looking to the waters that are above, the Spirit, to give us rebirth; so Nabuchodonosor, in his dream, was a tree in the midst of the earth, a tree great and strong and reaching up to heaven, but the Watcher came down from heaven and cried out that the tree must be felled, though the stump must be left and bound with iron and brass: the king must be driven out and dwell among brute beasts and eat grass, ox-fashion, and be drenched with the dew of heaven for seven seasons; then, when he has learnt his lesson, that all power is from above, his throne and glory are restored to him. Christ takes upon himself our brutishness: as a baby in the crib he is traditionally portrayed with the ox and the ass; in the wilderness he is 'with beasts'; it is

---

[1] Cf. *infra*, p. 201.   [2] Cf. *infra*, p. 167.   [3] *Ps.* viii, 6.   [4] *Ps.* xxi, 7 (Douai).

when flogging and torture have robbed him of human dignity, and there is now 'no beauty in him, nor comeliness '[1], that Pilate announces, Behold the Man, for out of that divine degradation man can be born again—provided always that he accepts his death, his own degradation.

'Before plunging into the [baptismal] piscina with the victorious assurance of faith, the candidate has known the agony of the approach to faith. The security which he enjoys in the course of his descent into the piscina has been preceded by the ordeal of a typal situation symbolized by the archetypal image of the night and of the tomb. In the face of the transcendent power which presents itself to him, he has had to admit to himself a deep-seated insufficiency, even more a radical impurity whose existence makes him intolerable to himself. It is a humiliation which touches him at an unfathomable depth, at the gateway to the shadow and the night which are beyond every immanent archetype, for the experience of such a situation rises only before the Other—the Love which falls upon one beyond all else . . . It is the situation of " he who is not " before " He Who Is ", of the sinner before the All-Holy. . . . It is a question of recognizing oneself as nothing and as sinner before him who alone creates and purifies, and of renouncing self-sufficiency and sin in accepting salvation, beloved by the Love-agape made known in the dying Christ. . . . The victorious assurance of the baptismal descent crowns and fulfils the certitude conceived in grief. The piscina is not only a sepulchre, it is also a maternal womb. Water is feminine.'[2]

In mythology the hero is often pictured riding on a horse or ass or other animal: the animal can be the symbol of the animal nature within us with which we have to come to terms, which we have to try to domesticate. Adam, in the beginning, was given dominion over the beasts, they were all ' domesticated ', but through striving to grasp at a greater dominion he lost what he had: he lost his dominion over the animal creation, and over the animal in himself. We were thinking just now of the ass which

---

[1] *Isaiah*, liii, 2 (Douai).　　[2] Beirnaert, *op. cit.* p. 82.

comes into the stories of Abraham and of Christ: in each case there is a triumphant conquering of 'nature', of the revulsion of senses and feelings and instincts against what is to come. The animal has been mastered, domesticated, (not, of course, destroyed): there are times when it has to be 'left behind'; so Abraham left the ass with his servants, so Christ rode into the city indeed but not to Golgotha; there are times when instincts and senses and feelings have to be set aside lest they overwhelm and subjugate the will; but we cannot do without them (even dedicated men, even prophets, sometimes need a little 'horse sense', as Balaam did who was rebuked for his blindness by the beast he was riding); we are restored to our true stature only through their restoration, but that restoration means a re-domestication, and that in turn means a surrendering of possession, a poverty of spirit with regard to them.

To be poor in spirit means to be stripped of everything before God; but it also implies—as an ideal which is not indeed demanded of us by Christ but is held up to us as a 'counsel of perfection'—a readiness to strip oneself of everything for the sake of men: 'Go, sell *all* that thou hast, and give to the poor'. But the fundamental idea of 'having nothing yet possessing all things' is of universal application. Every temptation echoes the original temptation: why not be like God? why not snatch this fruit—you want it, why not have it? But no: 'let this mind be in you, which was also in Christ Jesus: who being in the form of God thought it not robbery to be equal with God, but emptied himself, taking the form of a servant'[1]. It is not only to Christ that the idea of *kenosis* refers, but to every other-christ as well. Blessed are the poor. The rhythm of creation is also the rhythm of re-creation: the six days of labour but then the quiet of the sabbath; there must be activity but it must be rounded with a little sleep; life is to be a series of deaths and rebirths; we return to the dark chaos in order to be refashioned, the sabbath comes round and in its quiet moment we offer God what has been done, and draw in life and energy for what

---

[1] *Phil.* ii, 5–8 (Douai).

is next to do. 'Come to me . . . and I will give you rest': our Lord condemned the pharisaic idea of the sabbath because it turned what was meant to be a rest into another burden. The sabbath must be re-creational, and to be that it must be recreational. We need the rhythm of work-and-play; sometimes we must lie fallow, like the fields in the Hebrew sabbatical year. Woe to the rich—to the greedy and grasping and avaricious—because they put themselves outside the rhythm: they cannot stop, relax, rest, always there must be the tension, the relentless grind, because if for a moment they relax their attempt to lay hold on the fruit—whether the fruit be material riches or human love or divine life—the fruit, they think, may escape their grasp; in reality it is the other way round: what immense theological reverberations are sounded off by the nursery injunction, Don't snatch! It is when you snatch at the fruit that it eludes you, because it disintegrates in your hand. The rich in spirit cry 'Wherefore this waste?' when they see a lovely useless gesture like the pouring out of the spikenard over Christ's feet; they cry 'Wherefore this waste of time?' when they see the prophet sleeping under the tree, the saint resting in the Lord, the child which is man being cradled in God's arms. It is no good being active unless you can be contemplative; it is no good labouring unless you can rest. Of themselves the works of the law bring nothing to perfection; the sea does not conquer the shore in one movement, it ebbs and flows; and every day goes gently down into darkness, and every week into the sabbath pause, and the end-feast of the Jewish liturgical year is Tabernacles—tents to remind us that we are sojourners, that here is no abiding city, but that our journey to the eternal city must be like the incoming of the tide, flowing and ebbing, working and resting, active and passive, making and being made.

The feast of Tabernacles was a joyous occasion, coinciding with the vintage season; the 'tents' were in fact huts of leafy branches; the festivities included the waving of branches of palm and willow and other trees, the sounding of trumpets, illuminations in the court of the women and libations of water from Siloe mixed with wine.

It was associated with the deliverance of the Hebrews from their Egyptian bondage: ' From the fifteenth day of the seventh month, when you shall have gathered in all the fruits of your land, you shall celebrate the feast of the Lord seven days: on the first day and the eighth shall be a sabbath, that is a day of rest. And you shall take to you on the first day the fruits of the fairest tree, and branches of palm trees, and boughs of thick trees, and willows of the brook, and you shall rejoice before the Lord your God. And you shall keep the solemnity thereof seven days in the year. It shall be an everlasting ordinance in your generations. In the seventh month shall you celebrate this feast. And you shall dwell in bowers seven days: everyone that is of the race of Israel shall dwell in tabernacles, that your posterity may know that I made the children of Israel to dwell in tabernacles when I brought them out of the land of Egypt ' [1].

It was, then, at the time of this feast that Jesus set out for his last journey: a final incoming of the tide leading to the final over-whelming by the dark waters. It was of living waters that our Lord was to speak. The feast was held at a time of year (September–October) when the soil was sun-dried: the water of Siloe poured out on the altar symbolized no doubt the rain for which the soil thirsted. But ' on the last and great day of the festivity, Jesus stood and cried, saying: If any man thirst, let him come to me, and drink. He that believeth in me, as the scripture saith, Out of his belly shall flow rivers of living water. Now this he said of the Spirit which they should receive who believed in him ' [2]. But the ' dissension among the people because of him ' [3] was growing more and more marked; the warring of darkness against the Light more and more fierce; and so Jesus took the man born blind, and cried out ' I am the light of the world ' and then spat on the ground and made clay of the spittle and spread the clay on his eyes and told him, Go, wash in the pool of Siloe; and ' he went therefore, and washed, and came seeing '. [4] And this was on the sabbath day.

[1] *Levit.* xxiii, 39–43 (Douai).   [2] *John*, vii, 37–9 (Douai).   [3] *John*, vii, 43 (Douai).
[4] *John*, ix, 1–7 (Douai).

I must work the works of him that sent me, whilst it is day: the night cometh when no man can work.'[1] Night and day, dark and light, the clay—the slime of the earth—out of which man is made: there must be a constant renewal, but it can come only from the Spirit, the rain must come down from heaven if the waters are to spring up from the belly of mankind, of earth: it means that there can only be renewal if you can stop and be still and receptive, so finding, like Jacob, wherever you are, that ' God is in this place ', and so, refreshed, you can start off again, on to the next place; the ultimate end is still afar off and yet in a sense you already have it, the kingdom within you, and so the cyclic rhythm goes on, and ' in my end is my beginning '. The first Eve was greedy (of knowledge and power) and snatched at the fruit and it turned to dust in her hand; the second Eve knew her lowliness and could wait on the Lord and so the Fruit grew slowly within her, and thenceforth all generations, like the angel, have called It blessed. ' What is said universally of that virgin mother which is the Church is also said particularly of Mary; and what is said of Mary the virgin mother is rightly understood in a general sense of the virgin mother the Church: in such a way that when one undertakes to speak of one or the other, what one says is applied indifferently to one or the other and in an intermingled fashion. Every faithful soul also is the spouse of the Word of God—mother, daughter and sister of Christ. Every faithful soul ought to be called both virgin and fruitful.'[2]

Adam was meant to tend the paradise-garden, but to be a gardener you need patience and he was impatient: he wanted the fruit straight away. But the second Adam was not impatient; he could adapt himself to the sluggish tempo of human stupidity, he could suffer patiently the hideous effects of human greed; in his garden he knew agony, but he tended his garden. In Gethsemane the tending was the agony; even in the garden of resurrection there was still question of work yet to be done, as the Magdalen

[1] *John*, ix, 4 (Douai).   [2] Isaac de l'Etoile: *Sermo li, In Assumptione*, quoted Beirnaert, *op. cit.* p. 3.

discovered: she was not to clutch at or cling to the fruit even of this divine and glorified Tree in the midst of the garden. The tilling and watering and tending were still not yet quite over. In the dim light of the early morning she thought the one she saw before her was the gardener,[1] and it was not until she heard the voice of the Word calling her by her name that she knew her error. And yet, in the light of this context of thought, we can see that she saw better than she (afterwards) knew; for it was indeed the Gardener.

The commandments tell us that we too have to tend the garden, not with a contemptuous voltairean detachment from the affairs of other men, but with a complete self-dedication to God and other men: trying not to disrupt the family or destroy its *pietas* but to keep and tend it in and for God; not to destroy or disparage life but to honour and enrich it for God; not to arrogate to ourselves the ownership of anything but again to be good and responsible gardeners, helping to tend and keep the garden for God and for men.

Let us turn now to the remaining commandments, which deal with bearing false witness (and with all the other ways of being untruthful), with adultery (and all sexual and sensual sins) and with covetousness (and envy and jealousy). We may remind ourselves again that for St Thomas all the mandates of the second Table are concerned with a man's relationship to his neighbour—in other words, with sin as anti-social behaviour; at the same time we can recall the importance of seeing the social implications of sins which at first sight might be thought to be purely private. To steal means primarily to take for one's own what belongs to another; but it also means to take for one's own what belongs to oneself—to sin against poverty of spirit by being a grabber: and to be a grabber is itself anti-social. The same is true with regard to lying. The commandment expressly forbids the bearing of false witness, because this is the gravest form of lying: it is a sin at once against both general and particular justice (against a man's duty to his society and to his

[1] *John*, xx, 15.

individual neighbour) and against the virtue of religion (since the swearing of an oath is usually involved); by implication all other forms of wronging one's neighbour by lying and deceit are also forbidden; but more than that, to be false to oneself must be forbidden too, for this too is anti-social: to be false to oneself is in the end to become disintegrated, and that in its turn means in the end to be a disintegrating influence on society. If you are living a lie you cannot expect to be honest in your dealings with your neighbour, just as if you are ' full of grace and truth ' yourself you cannot but be honest with others.

Learning to live fully means in fact learning to understand and accept and live the truth about oneself. Let us consider the story of Jacob in the Old Testament. His elder brother Esau sold him his birthright for ' a mess of pottage '; later, when their father Isaac was near to death, Jacob presented himself before the blind old man and, declaring himself to be Esau, begged for the blessing due to the first-born. The older writers were at pains to find ways of exonerating Jacob from the sin of lying to his father; later, Cornelius à Lapide for instance admits that Jacob sins, but considers the sin only venial; modern biblical scholars are more inclined to see Jacob's behaviour as without question a lie—and indeed we need not suppose that even the greatest and holiest of the patriarchs were sinless, while it would be foolish to suppose that their moral standards were as clear-cut as the codifications of a modern theological textbook. But the important thing, for our present purposes at least, is to see such events as these *figuraliter*, as symbols; St Thomas remarks that Jacob spoke in mystery—he ' mystically declared that he was Esau, the first-born of Isaac, since the rights of primogeniture were now *de iure* his ' [1]: we have already noticed how for the Hebrews a name involves the essence of a personality, a function, an office (so our Lord speaks of the Baptist as Elias): throughout this episode Jacob is acting at the instigation of his mother and is in effect embarking on a process of integration— trying to find life and therefore trying first of all to find truth,

[1] *Sum. Theol.* II. II. cx, 3, *ad* 3.

integrity, wholeness. Psychologists tell us that this means coming to terms with one's *anima*, and this presupposes returning to the womb and integrating the dark shadow; ethnologists and spiritual writers describe the same process in their own different idioms. Prof. Eliade, in a valuable discussion of initiation rites among primitive peoples, points out how a ritual death-and-resurrection is always a constitutive element in such rites, for the initiate is to become really and completely man, and indeed a new man (and often he will bear a new name, as Jacob here becomes Esau and later on will become Israel), while at the same time there may be surgical operations such as circumcision or subincision, symbolizing the giving of feminine attributes to boys or masculine attributes to girls, for the whole point of these rites is that they are ' *un essai d'androgynisation symbolique des candidats*': ' one cannot become really man or woman without first becoming, at least symbolically and in a transient manner, perfect man, " total ", androgynous man '[1]. But first there must be the ritual death: the candidate must in some way symbolically re-enter the womb and there face his dark shadow. Centuries ago Walter Hilton described this dark journey in terms which are closely paralleled by those of Jungian psychology. The christian, he says, must turn away for a time from all outward and bodily things and look into his own heart; and what then will he find? Nothing but a dark and ugly image of his own soul, all inwrapped with ' black stinking clothes of sin '; this dark shadow he bears about with him wherever he goes; and if he would know just what it is, the answer is that it is ' nought else but darkness of conscience, a lacking of love and of light, as sin is nought but a wanting of God '. Yet in this dark conscience the christian must ' swink and sweat ' and ' abide awhile therein ', for within this nought is Jesus hid in his joy ' whom thou mayest not find by thy seeking but if thou pass through the murkness of thy conscience '[2].

[1] Mircéa Eliade: *Chasteté, Sexualité et Vie Mystique chez les Primitifs*, in *Mystique et Continence*, (*Etudes Carmélitaines*, 1952), p. 33.   [2] Walter Hilton: *The Scale of Perfection*, ed. E. Underhill, chs. lii–liv.

The shadow thus appears black, sinister, gloomy; but it is not wholly evil; psychologists will tell us that it comprises three components; first, the ' qualities rejected from the *persona* after mature reflection '; secondly, ' the far more numerous qualities rejected with no personal reflection at all '—because of the disapproval of some mother-figure for instance—and thirdly, ' the qualities never evoked by life and consequently lying as primitive, undeveloped potentialities ' [1].

But if the shadow is not wholly evil, it is certainly unattractive; and the temptation is to refuse to accept it, to keep it well out of sight. ' " If I have an ashpit or cesspool behind that screen, is that any reason for stirring it up and making a stink for myself and my neighbours? How much happier and better we should be without all this psychological investigation." Thus the man who fears his shadow. The answer is threefold. First of all, there are all the seeds mixed up with the shadow, all the undeveloped potentialities crying to heaven for their *Lebensraum*. Secondly, there is the awkward fact that one's neighbours are often more aware of one's cesspool than one is oneself until one turns it out; it is no service to them to try and ignore it, because they then get all its underground seepage. Thirdly, there is the curious tendency of these matters to force themselves on the attention in adult life. If they cannot get their business attended to by presenting their credentials honestly they fall to all kinds of subterfuges, and disguise themselves as tiresome character-traits, runs of " bad luck ", neurotic symptoms, physical illnesses and all manner of unpleasant things which interfere with the sensible, rational programme of the practical man.' [2]

The shadow, then, must be faced: we must do our swinking and sweating. ' Hilton will not let us off lightly,' writes Fr Victor White. ' The shadow indeed is nought, a symbol, an image merely; but it is the symbol and image of a reality which must be faced, in which we must " swink and sweat ", which must be examined and analyzed in detail . . . if we are to realize and be, and

---

[1] K. Forsaith Lander: *A Map of the Psyche* (Guild of Pastoral Psychology Lecture No. 24), pp. 18–19. [2] Lander, *op. cit.* pp. 30–1.

so see, the image of Jesus, the re-formed integrated Self within. And indeed, in this life it will not be fully accomplished; the shadow is always with us and in us. But he tells us that what, with divine grace, we *can* achieve is this—that we shall be enabled to bear the shadow and not be borne about *by* the shadow.'[1] Hence the necessity, first, of acknowledging and recognizing our own sinfulness, and secondly of forgiving others: ' Hilton does not use Jung's language; but he knows all about the human propensity to project the shadow on to others, and thereby to try to evade it in ourselves. " Thou art busy upon thy might for to stop the rivers without, but perhaps the spring within thou leavest whole." Jung, in his turn, will tell us that " the other is always guilty " is the master-principle of the paranoiac, of the thoroughly divided man. But there is something of that within us all. Mutual forgiveness is no arbitrary command; it is from the very nature of the case the necessary condition of the integration of the personality, and so of reconciliation with the Father '[2]. Hilton's theme is the ' re-formation of the divine image which is man, and this means the harmonious life of the *whole* man. . . . Hilton is a catholic, in every sense of the word, and as against all theories of the total depravity of human nature, he holds that the original image of God in man is not annihilated, but disintegrated, rent asunder, by sin. There is, indeed, no way back to the original innocence of Eden; we cannot again become Adam and Eve. The way forward is shown to us in Christ, the acceptance to the full of the consequences of sin and the full consciousness and acknowledgement of the disintegration which sin brings about. It means the death of the ego, the autonomous disintegrated part, and the acceptance of the whole, and the living of the whole. It means living from the centre, and not in the periphery; where no part of the periphery and no one corner of it masters, but all is mastered. That centre, he holds, (whether we know it or not), is to be realized only in filial relationship in Christ to God as our Father, through the unifying life and love of

---

[1] Walter Hilton: *An English Spiritual Guide* (Guild of Pastoral Psychology, Guild Lecture no. 31), p. 16. [2] *ibid.*

the Spirit. Conformed to the pattern of Christ the incarnate Son, and by his grace, we realize the Christ within, and in so doing we are caught up into the life of the blessed Trinity. Hilton knows that this can never be fully realized in this life; the guidance he offers is only that we may *begin* to form the pattern, and have ourselves formed according to that pattern'[1].

Let us return then to the story of Jacob and his struggle with Esau. The struggle begins in the womb: Jacob seizes his brother by the foot, the *planta pedis*, for he is to be the 'supplanter'[2]: he is to take to himself the Esau-qualities that he may be made whole. Esau, we read, was red and hairy, and became a hunter, loving the open plains; Jacob was smooth and gentle, and became a tent-dweller and a man of peace. Esau is his father's favourite; Jacob is his mother's darling, and to be whole he will need to acquire something of the earthy quality, the toughness, of his brother. And he does in fact begin to display these qualities as his story proceeds: he drives a hard bargain with Esau over the right of primogeniture; he roundly asserts, to his father, that he is Esau the first-born; and the blessing he receives is a prayer that he may receive an earthy abundance: ' dew from heaven and fruitful soil, corn and wine in plenty '—so that in fact the blessing ' brings the unworldly Jacob into the world of reality and into the sphere of practical circumstance. He is torn out of the one-sidedness of his unworldly security in the tents, and forced to realize his humanity in the everyday world. He, so remote from the world, receives as supreme blessing the promise of deepest roots in the earth '[3]. So he leaves the protecting home where Rebecca had 'mothered' him and sets out on his own journey; he comes to a place called Luz, which means separation or departure, and it is there that he has the dream of the ladder ' standing on the earth, with its top reaching up into heaven; a stairway for the angels of God to go up and come down '. Fr D'Arcy has pointed out how the gnostic, ' who

---

[1] White, *op. cit.* pp. 4–5.   [2] This is the meaning of his name, Jacob.   [3] H. Westmann: *The Old Testament and Analytical Psychology* (Guild of Pastoral Psychology, Guild Lecture no. 3), p. 17.

considers the soul as imprisoned in the body, who reckons all that is visible and finite to be illusion ', ' makes himself a ladder out of this world and longs to be able to kick the ladder away '[1]. But life, for us, is to be found only in the marriage of heaven and earth, the meeting of the waters above and the waters beneath— the coming of the dew from heaven and then the springing up of the fountains from the earth. So Luz, separation, is renamed by Jacob, Bethel, the house of God; and he takes the stone which had been his pillow and sets it up as a monument and pours oil over it, and goes on his way renewed and strengthened. His new strength is underlined in the incident of the well-stone, which follows: having met the shepherds from Haran, and seeing Rachel approaching, he himself removes the great stone from the mouth of the well, though normally it was a job done by several men together. And his physical strength is paralleled by a moral strength: he is willing and able to work and wait for seven years to win Rachel, ' and they seemed to him only a few days, because of the greatness of his love '.

Rachel is the *anima*-figure; and she is beautiful in Jacob's eyes because he has met and faced his shadow. The Jungian plan of the psyche shows us the shadow ' as blocking the way to the *anima*, the feminine " other side " of the male psyche. Hilton's language is different, but we need not be surprised to find the same idea. We remember that when Hilton's contemplative first looked into his home he found both " stinking smoke " *and* a " chiding wife ". No wonder she was chiding, poor woman, suffocated and obscured in the stinking smoke of the unassimilated shadow. When the shadow is made conscious and so rendered powerless and clearly seen, the smoke dissipates, the " other side " appears in all her beauty, and the way is ready for tranquil and happy union with her '[2].

But Jacob's struggles are of course not at an end once he has married Rachel. The story goes on to tell us of his eventual escape from his uncle Laban (who, incidentally, pursues him for seven

---

[1] *The Mind and Heart of Love*, p. 51. [2] White. *op. cit.* p. 18.

days) and of his mysterious struggle with an angel before he is finally reunited with Esau. First he crosses the ford Jabbok: ' the crossing of a river represents psychologically an attempt to overcome an obstacle in order to arrive at a different attitude to life on the opposite side. It is a gulf, an abyss, which must be crossed despite all terrors, in which all dangers must be met face to face without assistance, in which the individual can rely only upon himself. He only is the hero who successfully accomplishes the dread journey through the darkness in himself ' [1].

The night-long struggle follows. As we have seen, there are different views as to the identity of the being with whom Jacob wrestled through the night: was it an angel assuming human shape? was it God himself—for ' it is a terrible thing to fall into the hands of the living God '? was it Esau? For our present purposes we can see the adversary *figuraliter* simply as once again Jacob's own shadow: this is the climax of his struggle with himself, with his own demon; and it ends in victory—and Jacob henceforth is to be called Israel, one that prevails with God, and ' as soon as he had passed beyond Phanuel, the sun rose '.

The application of all this is clear enough: as long as we remain wilfully blind to our own shadow we bear false witness to ourselves: it is only when we have faced it, accepted it, and come to terms with it, that we can be said to be on the way to integration and to becoming useful members of society. And what is true of this ontological truth or falsehood is true in degree of all forms of veracity and deception. The question of the morality of lying is a complex one; and perhaps it is best approached precisely against this ontological background. According to the thomist view, every *locutio voluntaria contra mentem*—every deliberate and serious [2] affirmation that something is the case when we know it is not so—is a sin; and it is easy to argue that such a view is both heartless and unrealistic. But the answer to Pilate's question is that truth is God; and therefore to

---

[1] Westmann, *op. cit.* pp. 21–2.   [2] ' Serious ' because it is not a lie to say jokingly something which is obviously untrue, or to use expressions which are manifestly ironical, hyperbolical or not to be taken literally. (Cf. e.g. Prümmer: *Manuale Theologiae Moralis*, t. II, p. 151.)

do violence to the truth is ultimately to do violence, as it were, against God, to do violence to the nature of things. *Omnes viæ tuæ veritas*, the psalmist says; *All thy ways are truth*; and as all laws lead back ultimately to the eternal law which is God himself, so all falsehoods mean in the last resort a going outside the true order of things, a destruction therefore of a cosmic order. Satan is the Father of Lies not only in the sense of being the great deceiver but also because he is the supreme embodiment of the lust for disorder, disintegration, non-being. Certainly we can argue that this or that small lie will not rock the universe to its foundations; but we have to consider in fact not this or that individual lie but the whole ' tangled web ': social disintegration must as surely follow upon the practice of deceit, of lying to one's neighbour, as personal disintegration must follow upon lying to oneself. In both cases we are concerned, not just with verbal mis-statements, [1] but with a disruption of the order and nature of things.

All this is equally relevant when we come to the question of sexual morality. It is adultery which is expressly forbidden, because adultery especially disrupts the order of things: destroying the integrity of the husband-wife relationship it also destroys the integrity of the home, the family, and in so doing attacks also the order of society. In the development of western moral theology one can discern a trend of thought which deals with questions of sexual morality rather in isolation from the idea of the total order of things, the *ordo universi*; and this certainly does not seem to reflect the mind of the Old Testament. The first biblical allusion to sexual sin is the mysterious reference in *Genesis*, vi, to the ' sons of God ' and the ' daughters of men '; the Fathers usually understand these as being Sethite men and Cainite women; some scholars argue that as the Cainites have now been dismissed from the story (in accordance with the author's general principle of gradual elimination) we must understand both men and women as belonging to the tribe of Seth and explain the appellation ' daughters of men '

---

[1] A mis-statement is not necessarily a lie, nor a lie necessarily a mis-statement. If I say ' X is Y ', I am lying if I think X is Z, even though in fact X *is* Y; I am not lying if I really think that what I say is true, even though in fact it is not.

as given to the women, 'not because they do not figure in the genealogy but because the Sethites in their licentious polygamy took to wife whosoever pleased their fancy'[1]; in either case we are clearly concerned with a disruption of social order; but it is interesting that the passage was taken by some early writers to refer to a commerce between spirits and women, and the idea of such commerce is to be found, not only in apocryphal Hebrew literature but also as a commonplace of medieval thought: the activity of demons as *succubi* or *incubi* is mentioned in many medieval trials and confessions and is dealt with as a matter of course by moralists in their treatises on sexual vices. It has been debated whether such intercourse was 'real' or 'phantasmal': the important point for our present purposes is that the idea in itself emphasizes dramatically the idea of sexual sin as a going outside of the true order of things, since it implies a diabolic travesty of the Incarnation, a mingling of alien natures for the defilement, degradation and disintegration of humanity. (We might compare with this the biblical use of the word 'fornication' to mean the following by Israel of false gods.)

A similar change of emphasis seems to have taken place in connection with the sins of Sodom and Gomorrah. It is at least arguable that in the account given us in *Genesis* the sins referred to were not sexual sins at all, or at least not primarily; eventually the 'sin of Sodom' did come to be identified with 'sodomy', but there is an interesting intermediate stage in this evolution of thought, in which the emphasis is put on the fact that the sin concerned (again) another order of beings, the angels who were Lot's guests, and that its heinousness lay precisely in this *deordinatio*.[2]

Parallel with the emphasis on what may be called the purely private aspects of sexual sin, to which allusion has been made, may be noted an emphasis on its purely biological aspects, and this too can lead to a forgetfulness of the essential complexity of human nature and human behaviour. The degree of guilt involved in a particular action cannot be adequately measured without any re-

[1] Cf. E. F. Sutcliffe, S. J.: *Genesis*, in *A Catholic Commentary on Holy Scripture*, p. 189.
[2] Cf. D. S. Bailey: *Homosexuality and the Western Christian Tradition*, for a detailed discussion of the development of thought and shift of emphasis in this matter.

ference to its social effects, any more than it can be measured without any reference to the psychological conditions of the agent. Thus, for example, homosexual sin is traditionally referred to as ' unnatural vice ' and this is correct inasmuch as biologically speaking it is further removed from the natural purpose of sex than is, for instance, fornication; but we ought not in practice to separate the biological from the psychological and the sociological: and so the homosexual is using the word in a permissible psychological sense when he says that for *him* heterosexual intercourse would be ' unnatural '; similarly it is questionable whether the nature and order of human society are not damaged less by private homosexual acts between consenting adults than they are by adultery.

Another example of this biological emphasis is to be found in the fact that the term onanism has come to mean solitary sexual sin whereas in the Bible-story of Onan it is clearly the anti-social character of his action in failing to complete the act of intercourse and so ' beget children in his brother's name '[1] that is reprobated. Nature shows herself very little concerned with physiological redundance or wastage; and the moralist in his turn must be concerned not just with the physiological aspect of a situation but with the situation as a whole, not with the purely biological or purely animal but with the *human*.

All this is not to say that what might be called purely private sexual behaviour, which has no immediate effect on other individuals or on society, is therefore to be brushed aside as of no moral consequence. On the contrary; the traditional catholic teaching treats any and every sexual sin as being of its nature grave—so that here, as in the case of lying, it is easy to make that teaching look cruel, heartless, unrealistic and, in its condemnation of certain modern eugenic techniques, obscurantist. As with lying, therefore, it is well to put the whole matter firmly into its wider context, as the Bible does. To say that every sexual sin is a grave sin is of course to speak of objective standards, not of subjective guilt: there are all sorts of factors which can make a sexual sin, like any other

[1] *Gen.* xxxviii, 8 (Knox).

sin, either no sin at all or only a venial one. But even so, is it not altogether too rigorist to say that even objectively speaking every sexual sin is a grave one? No, precisely because the judgement is based not just on biological considerations but on an appraisal of total human situations. Human sexual activity is specifically different from that of animals precisely because it is always, inevitably, not just a physiological but a psycho-physical—and, in the last resort, a socially significant—affair; and if the traditional catholic teaching on the matter seems rigorous it is not because it despises or disapproves of sex but because of the very great importance, dignity and beauty it sees in it. You do not treat lightly a mystery in which you see, *in figura*, the union of Christ with his Church. And while some forms of sexual sin are more serious than others because more anti-social, more disintegrating to individuals and society alike, it remains true that all sexual sin is in the last resort anti-social because in the last resort it does tend to bring about the disintegration of the individual, and a society of disintegrated individuals is a disintegrated society.

Going outside the true order of things, the *ordo universi*, always means a rejection of life, a lust for disintegration and death. In the present context the perfect example of this is to be found in that manicheism which, under various names and forms, has beset christianity through the ages. Dualism is indeed a perversion of the true order of things since it begins from the assumption that matter is evil; if matter is evil, clearly marriage and procreation must be evil too; desire is exalted to infinity but it must be the desire for complete fusion which is to be found only in death. 'I have two luxuries to brood over in my walks,' wrote Keats to Fanny Brawne, ' your loveliness and the hour of my death. O that I could take possession of them both in the same moment [1].' Keats's choice of verb, taking possession, is interesting: the rejection of marriage as evil, if it meant the cult of virginity among the *perfecti*, soon came to mean for the majority the cult of adultery and other sexual deviations, and in romantic literature the Tristram-Iseult theme is

[1] Cf. D'Arcy, *op. cit.* p. 27.

to be found with all the trappings of pursuit and possession, of the falling of the citadel, of surrender—a predatoriness at one level which can cohabit comfortably with idealizations, with what Mr Thurber has aptly described as pedestalism, at another. To take possession of another human being can only mean to destroy him, and therefore to destroy the possibility of any relationship with him; to take possession of death is either a meaningless expression or else must signify the cult of deliberate disintegration, of self-destruction, of nihilism.

In manicheism the death-wish is dominant; but in all of us it exists somewhere, lurking in the shadow, an urge to destroy oneself in one way or another, to seek death rather than life. And the Bible reminds us forcefully that we can destroy not only by deeds but by thoughts. We sometimes use the expression, ' If thoughts could kill . . .' The tragic truth is that in the long run they can. So the commandments forbid not only adultery but the coveting of another's wife, and our Lord will speak of committing adultery in one's heart, and of the thoughts which defile a man—and, through him, the society of which he is a member.

We have a dramatic example of the lusting after another's wife, and the terrible consequences of it, in the story of David. Here once again the familiar themes confront us: he is, in the early stages of the story, another *puer* figure: a shepherd boy in Bethlehem, the youngest of eight brothers, ' red-cheeked, fair of face, pleasant of mien '; he is anointed with oil by Samuel; he enters the camp of Saul riding upon an ass; and there his struggle begins. But it begins with an external enemy. Saul for his part allowed himself to be destroyed by his own darkness till ' the Lord's spirit passed away from him ' and instead ' an evil mood came upon him that gave him no rest ' and he sank into madness and death. David was to learn how to find life; but he did not learn quickly. His victory over Goliath, the external enemy, was not enough, nor were his struggles with Saul. When he danced naked before the ark of the Lord he was mocked by Michol, of whom we are previously told that he had fallen in love with her and that she for her part had become his 'loving wife': in this incident with its mixture of gaiety and mockery he thus stands halfway between the Eros-figure of the paradise garden and the naked Man of Sorrows; and if we see Michol here as the *anima* we may suppose that the love between them was imperfect because he still had not fully come to terms with his own shadow, he had not yet gone down fully into the depths of his own soul. But then he sees Bethsabee and commits adultery with her; and to conceal his guilt causes her husband to be killed in battle so that he himself can take her to wife; whereupon the prophet Nathan is sent to him by the Lord, and tells him the story of the rich man who, having to entertain a foreign guest, would take no toll of his own abundant flocks and herds but stole from a poor man a ewe-lamb which was his sole possession and which ' he had bought and reared, letting it grow up in his house like his own children, share his food and drink, sleep in his bosom; it was like a daughter to him '; and David, ' burning with indignation at the wrong, said to Nathan, As the Lord is a living God, death is the due of such a man as this '; and Nathan said to David, ' Thou art the man ' [1]. It is after this incident that David's personality and reign are changed, his family life darkened by sins and sorrows, his own adultery finding an echo in the rape of Thamar by his son Amnon, his murder repeated in the fratricidal act of Absalom. So it is that he goes down into the depths at last, and out of the depths cries unto the Lord to hear his voice, for with the Lord there is mercy and with him there is plentiful redemption. . . .

David entered into his own sin, went down into his own darkness; we all have to do likewise in order to rise into life. Black thoughts, like black laughter, can destroy; but when sin leads to sorrow and thence to self-understanding and an understanding of God and his mercies, darkness turns into light. When power and pride and complacency and triumph have been taken away and we are left naked, then it is possible to sing the psalms of sorrow and repentance, to pray our *de profundis* and learn to be poor in spirit, putting all things into the hands of God and making our own those

[1] Cf. II *Kings*, xii (Knox).

words of the psalmist which were to find an echo later on in the words of Mary to the angel: *Sicut oculi ancillæ,* ' See how the eyes of servants are fixed on the hands of their masters, the eyes of a maid on the hand of her mistress! Our eyes, too, are fixed on the Lord our God, waiting for him to shew his mercy '[1]. So, at last, it is possible, in integration, to be one with God and man: not a fugitive from life, like Cain; not a self-destroyer, like Saul; not dancing a death-dance in a sabbat of destruction, deceit, disorder; but given wholly to God, like Isaac, in holocaust and therefore, in the divine power thus acquired, able like Jacob to prevail with God, to join in the sacred life-giving dance of the One in the Twelve,[2] of Christ in his Church.

[1] *Ps.* cii, 2 (Knox).　　[2] ' Thus Jacob becomes the central figure of the twelve tribes, which, projected into the zodiac as an image of a perfect mandala, corresponds to the symbol of the Self. Through these twelve tribes, like the symbolical radii of a circle—the image of rounded completeness and perfection of man—the life of the individual radiates into the reality of the world.' (Westmann, *op. cit.* pp. 20-1.)

4

The Pattern in the Sacraments

THE CHURCH tries to teach us through symbol as well as through dogma; and so we shall not be surprised to find the pattern repeated or recalled again and again in the sacraments and sacramentals, in the words and gestures and actions of the Church's worship, in the material things it makes use of, in the way a church is built and furnished.[1] This is above all true of the Mass; but before we turn to it it may be useful to look briefly at the other sacraments.

As we have seen, Christ was baptized that thereby the waters might be made holy and fruitful for us, that through our own baptism we might be brought to the new, the everlasting life. So the baptism rite begins with two questions and answers: What dost thou ask of the Church of God? Faith. What doth faith bring thee? Life everlasting. And the priest breathes three times gently into the face of the child: breath and wind are synonymous, in Hebrew, with spirit, the life-giving principle; so, when Eliseus breathed life into the son of the woman of Sunam, ' rising from his prayer, he laid himself down on the dead body, mouth to mouth, eyes to eyes, hands to hands, bending down close, till the boy's flesh grew warm. Then he went away, and walked to the end of the house and back, and now when he mounted the bed and lay down, the boy yawned seven times, and opened his eyes '[2]. At the same time he commands: ' Go forth from him (or her), unclean

---

[1] Cf. *The Water and the Fire*, ch. vi: The Church's Daily Life.   [2] IV *Kings*, iv. 34–6 (Knox).

spirit, and give place to the holy Spirit, the Paraclete ': Satan, who would lure us into death, destruction, non-being, is commanded to give place to the ' brooding Dove ', the giver of life. Then, if the salt is not already blessed, there is the magnificent prayer of exorcism and blessing, that the salt may become a ' salutary sacrament for the putting to flight of the enemy '; and a little of it is placed on the baby's tongue: ' Receive the salt of wisdom: may it be to thee a propitiation to life everlasting '; then again the unclean spirit is commanded to go forth in the name of Father, Son and holy Spirit, for he commands it who ' walked upon the sea, and held out his right hand to Peter as he was sinking '; the sign of the cross is made on the child's forehead, and Satan, the accursed one, is warned never to dare to violate it. Then there comes a prayer to God the author of light and truth: that the child may be illumined with the light of God's mind; and this is followed by the invitation: Come into the temple of God, that thou mayst have part with Christ unto life everlasting. Later the priest, echoing but much more than echoing the Gospel story, puts his finger on his own tongue and then touches the child's ears, saying ' *Ephpheta*, which is to say, Be thou opened ', and then the nostrils, with the words ' To the odour of sweetness '. Later again he takes oil and with it makes the sign of the cross on the breast and then the back of the child, saying: ' I anoint thee with the oil of salvation in Christ Jesus our Lord, that thou mayst have everlasting life '; and then finally the baptism itself is given in the name of Father, Son and holy Spirit, the water being three times poured out in the form of a cross over the head of the child, or the child being three times immersed. Next the priest makes the sign of the cross with chrism on the child's head, and then places on it a white cloth and gives the godparent a lighted candle, saying: ' Receive this white garment and see thou carry it without stain before the judgment-seat of our Lord Jesus Christ, that thou mayst have eternal life; receive this burning light, and keep thy baptism so as to be without blame: keep the commandments of God, that when the Lord shall come to his nuptials thou mayst meet him in the company of all the saints in the heavenly court, and live for ever and ever'. And so, with a final 'Go in peace', the rite ends.

The end is peace: the peace of eternal life, gained for us by the Cross, for we are *per arborem vivificati*, quickened by the tree of life. 'The mystery of baptism', writes Fr Rahner, 'can only be understood in connection with the mystery of the Cross—the water of life springs up at the foot of the tree of life. For only through the redeeming power of God's death on the Cross has the water gained the power to give life. . . . Thus baptism is the fundamental mystery of christianity, the true initiation into participation in the divine life of the dead and resurrected Christ. . . . [It is] the " mystery of eternal life ".' Hence the ' basic distinction between the christian mystery and the ancient mysteries with their naturalistic yearnings for rebirth. . . . To express this gift of grace (so far exceeding any heathen yearning) " in familiar images " and to signify what he believed, in common with St Paul, about this approximation to the transfigured life of the resurrected Saviour, the ancient christian took from his religious environment a symbol that in its christian adaptation was to know a rich and varied history: the " mystery of the Ogdoad ", the symbol of the number eight. Christ arose from the dead on the eighth day, the day of Helios; this had been the first day of the creation and for the christians it became again the first day. . . . According to an ancient Pythagorean conception, the number eight was the symbol of perfection, of eternal, absolute repose. Eight is the number of the cube, the figure that presents the same area on all sides; eight is the number of the spheres moving around the earth. The ancient christian's belief in the efficacy of baptism, then, led him to find this mystical symbol everywhere and imbue it with a christian meaning. The Lord rose on the eighth day: on an Easter Sunday, the liturgical eighth day, the christian received baptism; and this is the day on which the " Spirit moved upon the face of the waters ". Eight persons rode the ark over the waters, and this wooden structure by which man was saved is a symbol of the Cross. Everything is full of secret signs and symbols. In the second *Epistle of Peter* (ii, 5) we read: " And [God] spared not the original world, but preserved Noah the eighth person, the preacher of justice ". This was a prefiguration of baptism, and the first *Epistle of Peter* (iii, 20–1) declares: ". . . wherein a few, that is, eight souls, were saved by water. Whereunto baptism, being of the like form, now saveth you also . . . by the resurrection of Jesus Christ ". . . . Thus baptism is rebirth to eternal life, to that eternal peace which is symbolized in the age-old image of the Ogdoad, the antithesis of earthly birth '[1].

Fr. Rahner goes on to point out how the early christians designed ' the earthly abode of the mystery, that " humble site full of all grace ", in accordance with the mystical symbolism of the number eight. They tended to build their baptisteries in octagonal form and surrounded the basin of life-giving water by an eight-cornered rail '. And he quotes an inscription written by St Ambrose for the baptistery of St Thecla at Milan:

> *The holy temple has eight niches,*
> *octagonal is the font, worthy of its sacred work.*
> *The house of our baptism must be built in the mystical eight,*
> *for in it eternal salvation is given to all peoples*
> *through the light of Christ resurrected who burst the bars of death*
> *and freed all the dead from their dungeon.*[2]

Baptism and the Cross, then, are but a single mystery; the ' mystery of wood and water ' which in baptism is but a ' partial aspect of the mystery as a whole '; together, ' baptism, cross, and descent into the darkness of the underworld constitute the mystery of the divine destruction from which new life surges, the night from which the new day dawns '; so the evening sun is immersed in the western ocean that tomorrow there may be a new dawn. In christian art a cross was placed in the middle of the river Jordan [3]; and ' the wooden cross as symbol of the humble, crucified

---

[1] Rahner, *op. cit.* pp. 387 *sqq.* Cf. also *infra*, p. 144.   [2] *op. cit.* p. 393.   [3] Cp. ' And they could not drink the waters of Mara, because they were bitter. . . . And the people murmured against Moses. . . . But he cried to the Lord, and he shewed him a tree, which when he had cast into the waters, they were turned into sweetness (*Exodus*, xv. 23–5, Douai).

Jesus gives light, it is alive with the fire that since the earliest period has been identified with the baptism of Jesus in Jordan '[1]; and so water, wood and fire come together in the mystery of eternal life and eternal peace.

The end then is peace; but before the peace there must be the struggle, the spiritual ascent of the christian, his ' gradual deification through the power of baptism '[2]. Origen speaks of our Lord going into the desert to be tempted as an athlete setting out to his trial of strength; in ancient Greece the boys and youths in the gymnasia rubbed their bodies with oil before their wrestling matches to make them strong and supple; so, as we have seen, the oil-symbol appears in the rite of baptism, but it will be emphasized in two other sacraments.

The first is precisely that sacrament of strengthening which we usually call confirmation. We return here for a moment to the *puer æternus* and the symbol of separation: as the child ceases to be a child and begins gradually to be capable of responsibility, to come to the ' age of reason ', so he needs strengthening to live his own life as God would have it lived, that he may come in the end to life eternal. So there is the anointing with oil, that he may be actively strong, full of the energy of the Spirit; and the symbolic blow on the cheek (but with Christ it was no merely symbolic blow when they ' fell to spitting upon his face and buffeting him and smiting him on the cheek ') that he may be strong to accept the pain, sorrow, insults, trials of every kind, which his service of God may bring him, without flinching.

All this brings to mind St Paul's athletic metaphors. ' When men run in a race, the race is for all, but the prize for one; run, then, for victory. Every athlete must keep all his appetites under control; and he does it to win a crown that fades; whereas ours is imperishable. I do not run my course, then, like a man in doubt of his goal; I do not fight my battle like a man who wastes his blows on the air. I buffet my own body, and make it my slave;

[1] *ibid.* p. 396.   [2] Rahner, *op. cit.* p. 393.

or I, who have preached to others, may myself be rejected as worthless.'[1]

The oil-symbol recurs in the sacrament of the last anointing, but here with a difference of emphasis: the purpose of the sacrament is first that the sick person may be restored to health; secondly, that if that be not God's will he may be given strength to go lovingly and manfully on his last dark journey and to arrive at the fullness of everlasting life; thirdly, that in either case he may be given peace of heart, to accept God's will whatever it may be.

The rite, then, begins with this keynote of peace: 'Peace be to this house, and to all who dwell therein '; then baptism is recalled by the 'sprinkling with hyssop' and by the lovely prayer to our Lord that 'all approach of demons be kept away from this place: that the angels of peace be present, and all malign discord flee from the house '; may there enter it, the priest prays, 'everlasting happiness, divine prosperity, serene joy, fruitful love, eternal health ', and may all who dwell in it be freed from 'every fear and perturbation '. Then, after praying, in the name of Father, Son and holy Spirit, that 'all power of the devil be extinguished in thee through the laying on thee of our hands ', the priest anoints the sick person's eyes, ears, nostrils, mouth, hands, feet and, formerly, in the case of men, the loins.[2] In each case, the priest prays that 'through this holy anointing, and through his loving mercy, our Lord may forgive thee whatever wrong thou hast done ' through eyes and ears and the rest.

Then there is the prayer that the sick person may be restored to health and may 'once more have his strength to take up his former duties '; and another asking God to 'raise him up by thy right hand, strengthen him by thy might, defend him by thy power,

---

[1] I *Cor.* ix, 24-7 (Knox); cp. *Heb.* xii, 1-14.   [2] This last was, for obvious reasons, always omitted in the anointing of women, and in the case of men was omitted too if, as the rubric says, the man's weakness made it difficult or dangerous to move him; nowadays the anointing of the feet is often, in practice, omitted also; but it may be noted that the complete rite brings the number of anointings up to seven, the symbol of plenitude and fulfilment (as in the 'septiform grace ', the seven Gifts of the Spirit, the seven sacraments, or the 'seventy times seven', of our Lord's infinite mercy).

and restore him to thy holy Church, with all desired prosperity, through Christ our Lord'.

So the sacramental rite ends, on this note of renewed strength; but if it be clear that death is imminent, the priest goes on to the ' commending of a departing soul', the prayers of which such magnificent use is made in the *Dream of Gerontius*. After the litany for the dying there follows the prayer ' Depart, christian soul', which ends: ' let peace come to thee this day, and let thy abode be in holy Sion'; and later the commending-prayer itself, in which the priest prays that Christ Jesus may ' place thee in his garden of paradise'.

So the ultimate dark journey is to be undertaken, not in fear—a special prayer begs the ' motherly intercession' of our Lady to prevent this—but in humble confidence and peace. But for most christians there will be many dark journeys before this last one is reached; and other sacraments are given us to help us with them.

As we have seen, sin-repented is itself a form of creative darkness; and we are given the sacrament of repentance and sorrow that this may be so. True, even without the sacrament, repentance and sorrow which are motivated by the love of God will achieve the same effect; but how difficult it is for some of us in our selfishness to be sure that our sorrow is of that sort! We must not indeed exaggerate the difficulty: for the ' profoundly christian soul', as has been wisely said, ' perfect contrition is easy, even very easy '— we have to remember that ' an act of perfect contrition' need not be ' a perfect act of contrition', and that whether one *feels* emotionally contrite is quite irrelevant. Contrition is ' psychologically the simple yielding to the attraction of God, the simple sorrow provoked by love, a beginning of a childlike self-surrender to the Father one has left or rejected, a reorientation of one's whole being towards God—Truth, Goodness, Beauty, Love '. The ' process of conversion' which contrition implies ' extends over an indefinite period of time, it may happen quickly or slowly, and is patient of a greater or lesser intensity, but in its very beginning it is perfect, in virtue of the end to which it tends—God who is all perfection '[1].

However, God's mercy has given us the sacrament; and the sacrament is itself a dark journey; if not physically, at least psychologically. It is not easy to unveil to another human being the murkiness and meanness and squalor of one's own soul. It is said that soon after Gilles de Rais had begun the confession of his enormities at his trial, the president ordered that a veil be put over the crucifix; and some of us may well be reminded of the story as we confess our own. His story is perhaps the most startling example of wickedness, repentance and divine mercy to be found in christian history: the condition of its completion in that mercy was the darkness of the confession; and so it may be with us.

Penitents can be divided into five main groups. There are those who have grave things to confess and who confess them simply, humbly, and with sincere sorrow. There are those who have grave things to confess but are in fact sublimely and blandly unconscious of the fact,[2] and spend most of their time (and it is usually a long time) in the confessional in describing their woes and the wickedness of their neighbours. There are the psychological exhibitionists who, with all the time in the world on their hands, will turn some trifling contretemps with a neighbour into an endless jeremiad. There are the truly good people who suffer —often agonizingly—from scruples. And there are finally the good people who have little to confess but who find a source of discouragement in that very fact: they long to love God deeply, perfectly, yet week after week or month after month they find themselves repeating the same little catalogue of sins, till finally the routine comes to assume an air of unreality, they wonder what use it all is since they seem to be making no progress, and they persuade themselves that they are not growing at all in the love of God. This is a difficulty common enough and serious enough to deserve careful consideration.

[1] Cf. *A Spiritual Cure for Scrupulosity*, *Blackfriars*, Nov. 1943, p. 416. [2] Cf. *supra*, p. 63.

First of all, many good people, especially those who become catholics in adult life or those 'cradle catholics' who (as does, alas, sometimes happen) had some harrowing and traumatic experience in a childhood confession, find confession difficult almost to the point of becoming a physical impossibility. What can be done to help them? We must presumably distinguish between a fear, which is based on something reasonable, and a phobia, which is not. Sometimes fear can be dealt with by a little frank and matter-of-fact discussion: some people will be helped if the confession is quite anonymous, i.e. if they go to a priest who cannot possibly know who they are or anything about them; others on the contrary may be frightened precisely by that atmosphere of impersonality, and in that case should go to someone who knows them well. Many penitents are helped to some extent by being reminded that the confessor is only a functionary and that they should try to think of themselves as talking not to him but through him to our Lord; and that in any case, if they cannot thus dissociate the man from the function, they can at least remember that the priest, unless he is a very wicked or a very stupid one, is far too conscious of his own sinfulness to be shocked by theirs.

A phobia is of course much more difficult to eradicate; but at least we can encourage penitents to take matter-of-fact advantage, with their doctors' advice and supervision, of the helps which modern medicine provides for this kind of ordeal. (It need hardly be said that it is not wrong but laudable and indeed a duty to take such natural means as are at hand to enable us to achieve some supernatural end; so the Church, in its recent legislation concerning the eucharistic fast, encourages the faithful to take tea, coffee and so on up to an hour before communion if that will make it possible or easier for them to get to Mass and communion.)

Secondly, there are those who become discouraged because, they say, as the years go by they make no progress: when they go to confession it is always the same story, and sometimes they are even tempted to give up in despair. To this there would seem to be two answers. First, the continuance of habitual failings is far from being incompatible with growth in the love of God, as the lives of some of the saints make plain to us, who seem to have retained their temperamental failings (as St Jerome, for instance, seems to have retained his irascibility and bellicosity) while becoming truly holy, love-filled and God-filled personalities; for such failings are often mere ripples on the surface of the soul, and leave untouched the depths, the ' fund of the spirit ', where God is sought and loved. The same thing is true even of habitual failings which objectively speaking are grave, if they have, for one reason or another, become a psychological rather than a moral problem. Again, because the little catalogue goes on and on unchanged through the years it does not mean that the sacrament is ineffective: its purpose is not only to cleanse from sin but also to strengthen and deepen the love of God, and whether this second purpose is in fact being achieved in us is something that we cannot know but must leave, humbly and hopefully, to God. Thirdly, it is indeed a boring routine to have to say again and again the same list of small sins; but we can view these small particular things as symbols or expressions of the general *sinfulness* which is in us still and of which we are only in part aware. ' Who knows his own frailties? ' asks the psalmist, and goes on, ' If I have sinned unwittingly, do thou absolve me '[1]. The reference is no doubt primarily to offences inadvertently committed against the Law and especially the ceremonial Law;[2] but we can well apply the phrase to all the things we do which are objectively speaking morally wrong but about which we have no anxiety of conscience because of our heedlessness or our imperfect sense of sin. (Perhaps one of the effects of regular confession—of the type we are now considering—is precisely a heightening or refining of the sense of sin, so that we become aware that episodes in our past life which at the time we regarded as in no way reprehensible, or at least brushed aside as of little importance, were in fact of considerable moral importance: and that realization is

[1] *Ps.* xviii, 13 (Knox).   [2] Cf. Boylan: *The Psalms*, vol. I, p. 69.

again no cause for discouragement but on the contrary for gratitude: it means that we are becoming clearer of vision and cleaner of heart. It is much easier to see our sins than our sinfulness; yet in the last resort it is the latter that we are telling God about. Confession may become a more or less unvarying routine, always the same ' wilful distraction at prayer, vanity, unkindness, laziness ' or whatever it may be; but these things can be seen as symbols of the deeper sinfulness we cannot apprehend or at least cannot fully appreciate while at the same time we know it is there and that it is that for which we have most to implore God's mercy and help.

Next there is the problem of scrupulosity. Here it is important to try to make the penitent see that this is simply an anxiety-neurosis: that as he for his part, emerging from one confessional, will become convinced that he has omitted something important and rush straight back to it or off to another, so other sufferers from the same essential malady will become convinced that they have, for instance, failed to put their foot on one particular crack between the cement blocks as they walk along the pavement and must go back and remedy the deficiency. The first essential seems to be to get them to remain faithful to one confessor, who knows their case and has shown himself sympathetic and understanding, and not to go rushing from one to another; secondly, to try to persuade them to put themselves trustingly in his hands, and to keep in their minds the thought that *he* is responsible for them, has care of them; and thirdly, to make them confine themselves in their confession to some all-embracing formula, such as ' I accuse myself of all sins committed since my last confession and in my past life, including any bad or imperfect confessions ' and to refuse to let them mention any particular sins, however heinous they may think them to have been. The point of this way of attempting to help the scrupulous is not of course to persuade them that they are not sinners (like everyone else) but that they are psychologically incapable of judging for themselves in what respect and to what extent they are sinners, and that therefore they must entrust themselves in this matter to the confessor, whose function as such includes precisely that of judge.

It must be emphasized too that the foregoing applies to bad cases of scrupulosity in which the sufferer is scrupulous about the moral life *as a whole*. It is quite possible to be scrupulous, in this sense of being neurotic, about one particular type of sin while being genially unscrupulous (in the ordinary sense) about everything else. In such cases the 'treatment' must obviously be adapted to the special circumstances. The refusal to listen to particularities where the neurosis is concerned may need to be balanced by arduous attempts to stir the conscience in other matters; in any case it has to be pointed out that the type of sin which occupies all such penitents' attention is not in fact the only one and perhaps not a very important one compared with many others: that this issue is not the whole of the moral struggle but only one element in it; and that if they could bring themselves to devote less attention to it they might have more time and energy to devote to more important things.

Finally, the confessor will have to go on reiterating again and again that God is not a hostile policeman, on the watch to catch them out in some misdemeanour, but a loving Father; and that the one essential gift he asks of them is love.

Go in peace, the priest says at the end; peace is the end of this dark journey too; and perhaps it may be that the deeper the darkness has been the deeper in the end will be the peace.

Two sacraments remain for us to consider, apart from the Mass: marriage and holy orders; and here too the same pattern emerges. These vocations are not the only vocations: there is no need for a man either to marry or to become a priest, any more than there is for a woman to marry or to become a nun; there are plenty of praiseworthy and important ways in which single people can serve God in the world. But they are the two vocations which carry with them special responsibilities and which therefore need special assistance.

Catholics sometimes romanticize the priesthood, and even restrict the word 'vocation' to it (and to the religious life) thinking of these as something quite arbitrary, a summons from God with no relation to the desires and aptitudes of the person concerned. In fact, all vocations have to be dealt with in the same matter-of-fact sort of way: does this life attract me, not just superficially but deeply? have I the necessary gifts and aptitudes to live it reasonably well? and finally, shall I be able to make of it, not an indulgence of pride or ambition or the lust for power or some other unworthy desire, but a real service of God? There are plenty of things in a priestly life to make a man happy if he is really fitted for it: the variety of interests, the joy of congenial work well done, the love of his people, above all, the joy of being the means whereby peace and divine life are brought or restored to sad and troubled souls. On the other hand there may be many hardships; there will be disappointments, frustrations, failures; there may be loneliness, or long periods of aridity; and always the sense of sin, the appalling sense of inadequacy, the memory of St Paul's words about preaching to others and becoming oneself a castaway. The youth, then, who is drawn to the priestly life must ask himself whether these happy things will really in a deep sense bring him happiness; whether he really has the gifts to enable him to do well the work he will have to do; and whether, with the grace of the sacrament, he will be strong enough to endure the darknesses and to turn them to good account. In the ordination service his hands will be anointed and then bound together with a linen cloth, palm to palm, in the attitude of prayer; it is to show that he must be strong, collected, single-minded; that he must be dedicated to the worship and service of God; that the sacrament empowers and dedicates him to bless and heal the souls and bodies of men and to bring them safely in the end to their eternal home.

When it is a question of marriage the same three questions have to be asked, but to be asked twice over: will married life as such bring me happiness in a deep sense, am I fitted for it, and will I be able to make it a service of God? but also, will married life with X make us both happy in a deep sense, and are we fitted for one another, and shall we help one another to love God? And here too there will be the same pattern; for marriage is not a perpetual honeymoon, there will be many hardships and difficulties to be overcome. The man and the woman will have to learn gradually and perhaps painfully to understand one another, to adjust to one another, till at long last they become of one mind and one heart; they will have to learn to be unselfish, first to one another and then in a common dedication to the good of their children; there will be darknesses—misunderstandings, quarrels, estrangements—between themselves, to be used creatively as means to a deeper understanding and love; there will be sorrows, losses, disappointments to be shared together and used together to strengthen their common love of and trust in God. The main symbol in the marriage service is the ring: the plighting of a troth, the mutual exchange of vows, the dedication to a life-work of love of one another and of their home and children, ' for better, for worse, for richer, for poorer, in sickness and in health ' till death parts them—though it can only part them for a time. So the priest begs God to bless the ring, that ' she who wears it may always keep perfect faith with her husband and remain always in thy peace and thy will, and that together they may always live in mutual charity '; while the man for his part, likely by nature to be the more aggressive, predatory, impatient, perhaps demanding, must declare his self-dedication: ' With this ring I thee wed; this gold and silver I thee give; with my body I thee worship; and with all my worldly goods I thee endow '; and the rite ends with the prayer that God, the author of the union of these two in one, may by his help preserve them, through Christ our Lord.

Any vocation must to some extent follow the ' pattern ', must have its moments of darkness, and these two vocations perhaps more than any others; but the end is meant to be light, and light eternal; marriage eternal, for we do not lose our loves in heaven, and the priesthood eternal, *sacerdos in æternum secundum ordinem Melchizedech.*

We were thinking earlier on of the way in which the water of baptism is made part of the one essential *mysterion*, the life-giving Cross. The same is true of these other sacraments. If Christ went 'as an athlete' to meet his adversary in the desert, still more is this true of his going to face his final struggle, to take up his cross and to endure torture and death; so too the christian must take up his daily cross like an athlete, and like an athlete therefore he is anointed with oil in the sacrament of strengthening; he must in the end face the final journey into darkness, and for this he needs the oil of the last anointing, that with the endurance of the athlete he may carry his burden faithfully to the end. The sacrament of repentance is a renewal of the life-giving function of the baptismal waters, and like them derives its power from the life-giving Cross. The whole purpose of the sacrament of Orders is to incorporate the *ordinandus* into the eternal priesthood in union with and as representing the priesthood of Christ: his essential function as a priest will be to mediate between Cross and people: bringing life from the Cross to the people through all the sacraments and above all through the Mass. Finally, in thinking of marriage we cannot forget how St Paul speaks of it as a 'high mystery' and gives to the (natural) union of man and wife 'in one flesh' a far deeper dimension within the christian mystery, likening their love to that of Christ and his Church. So St Augustine writes: *Dormit Adam ut fiat Eva, moritur Christus ut fiat Ecclesia:* Adam slept that Eve might be made; Christ died that the Church might be made; and the same saint speaks of the Cross as a nuptial bed whereon Christ was made one forever with the Church his bride.

So the sacramental system as a whole is linked with the Cross and integrated into the one essential mystery; and through all the sacraments alike the christian is reminded of, and empowered to live out in his own life, the one essential pattern which will lead him in the end to the everlasting light: for often, as life goes on, he will find himself, like the neophyte before baptism, wandering in doubt and uncertainty through the darkness of this world, but if he responds to the divine life and power that is offered him, if he tries to use the darkness creatively, then he can look forward with quiet confidence to the time when the darkness will be for ever dissipated and he will be led into that Light inaccessible which is the glory of God.

PART TWO

THE MYSTERY IN
THE MASS

5

The Mass of the Catechumens

THE MODERN PAGAN, wandering into a catholic church during Mass, might be expected to find it all very puzzling: the odd clothes, the strange actions and gestures, the mysterious Latin mumblings . . . Unfortunately, we catholics ourselves are not always very clear as to what the Mass in its detail is about: we know that it is ' one and the same sacrifice as that of the Cross ', the self-offering of the Word-made-flesh represented in a different mode but substantially the same offering; we know that at the central point of the Mass bread and wine are changed into God, and that at the communion God is brought to us; but if the pagan were of an inquiring turn of mind could we answer all his questions? If he supposed that this must be the strange rite of some esoteric sect could we sketch its history for him, down through the ages, and put it for him in the setting of the universal pattern of sacrifice? Could we in fact explain the odd clothes and actions and gestures and words? It is the purpose of the following pages to examine these things; but first of all, before going on to detail, we must try to see the Mass as a whole, not a haphazard series of prayers but a unity, a clearly defined pattern.

As we have already seen, the Mass is both remembrance and sacrifice: we both recall and offer Christ's redemptive sacrifice of himself to the Father. It is necessary to stress this dual aspect of the Mass because, since the Council of Trent, which had to fight against denials of the sacrificial character of the Mass, we have tended to concentrate on this aspect at the expense of the other. But, as Fr Jungmann points out, various elements in the Mass ' only really become intelligible when we try and understand them with the help of the idea of remembrance. Let us be clear about this: the remembrance of the facts of the redemption is essential and fundamental for christianity. This is what distinguishes christianity from all natural religions, be they pantheistic, polytheistic or mono-theistic. These religions as well as the Greek mystery-religions expressed their worship by representing the unchanging events of nature, embodied in a symbolical form. They were concerned only with the eternal return of spring and autumn, of flowering and withering, and they attempted to influence favourably these events of nature by magical powers and make them subservient to them. But these religions remained and still remain in the natural sphere. Christianity is entirely an historical religion. It builds upon this one historical fact which goes beyond nature, that Jesus Christ, the Son of God, came into this world and redeemed us. This he did at a definite point in time and space. The thinking back to this fact, the constant looking and referring back, is therefore essential. This referring back takes place in two ways: by means of sacred signs, sacramentally, so that the past act of redemption becomes effective for us; secondly through the psychological reflection and calling to mind by the christian people, because it should be an intelligent drawing on the source of salvation opened up for us; it should be a personal relationship with God. These statements are all the more important the more one relies on the ancient mystery-religions for throwing light on christian cere-monies. For in some of them we find redemptive acts; in others also the idea of participation in the fruits of redemption, and that by means of established rites. But then we come up against the fundamental difference: on the one hand are happenings on the mere plane of nature, while on the other is the fact that, in the fullness of time, God himself entered this world at a definite historical moment—the Word was made flesh and redeemed us by dying on the Cross' [1].

But this is not all. Fr Jungmann goes on to point out how within christianity we find this tendency to ' bring into religion what is purely natural ', how ' even within the Church there was the period of rationalism, when many people thought of christianity simply as a means of devotion, as a support for morality and virtue, when the only idea of Christ that remained was that of a great friend of mankind '; and he goes on: ' just think of most of the modern catechisms where the doctrine of grace and the sacraments follows immediately after the main chapter on the commandments, strictly orthodox and correct concerning individual points ' but tending to encourage us to think that ' we need grace only so that we may keep the commandments ': so that in the minds of those ' who do not understand the finer points of theology ' grace and christianity become simply means to ' help us do what is morally and naturally the right thing ' whereas the essential—that which essentially flows from the fact that christianity is a historical religion —is the living of the ' new life ', the ' putting on ' of Christ, the historical reality of ' Christ as the Son of God and the Son of man; the beginning of the new race; his work of redemption on the Cross, the source of salvation '; the fact that ' without him and therefore without the Church there is no possibility of salvation, but in him there is light and life and the aristocracy of the children of God ' [2].

Remembrance and offering; but there is a third essential element, included in the first and linking up first and second together: the element of thanksgiving. It is quite wrong to restrict the term *eucharistia*, thanksgiving, simply to the holy communion, to the sacrament as opposed to the sacrifice, as is now so often done. ' The liturgy of the Mass as we know it from early times (at least since the second century) has always been considered as a great prayer of thanksgiving. Even today we begin, after various preparations, the real *Actio* with the cry, *gratias agamus* ' [3], let us give

---

[1] *The Eucharistic Prayer*, pp. 2-3.　　[2] *op. cit.* pp. 3-4.　　[3] Jungmann, *op. cit.* p. 6.

thanks to our Lord God. This is included in the idea of remembrance, for indeed how can we recall all that Christ did and suffered for us and the immensity of the gifts we have in consequence received, without giving thanks? But we do not give thanks merely by words: we go on from words to deeds, to the offering of a gift, the offering of the sacrifice. This, as Fr Jungmann proceeds to show, is the force of the word *igitur*, 'therefore', at the beginning of the prayer (the *Te igitur*) which follows the *gratias agamus*, and in which we beg God to accept the offering about to be made. We express the fact that we are filled with gratitude to God and *therefore* we want to offer a gift, and we beg him to accept it.

But how can *we* offer *Christ's* sacrifice? Precisely because it is also *our* sacrifice: we pray, we bring gifts, we prepare them and offer them, Christ having enabled us to do so by making us one with him as vine and branches are one. Even so, how can we pray that God will accept the sacrifice? How could he do other than accept the sacrifice of his only-begotten Son? Because, again, the sacrifice is not only Christ's but ours, and must be so if we are to worship God ' in spirit and in truth'. Christ's own sacrifice has indeed 'already been accepted, and accepted definitively. But it is the sacrifice which *we* offer with him here and now that is concerned, and we offer this sacrifice in a worthy manner only when we possess that inner conviction of mind of which this sacrifice is the sign, and when we possess at least as perfect an obedience, and an attitude of mind as full of surrender, as the patriarchs'[1]—as Abel, Abraham, Melchizedech, whose sacrifices the Mass daily commemorates. ' Christ's attitude of mind must be our attitude of mind when we approach the altar of God, according to the exhortation of St Paul: " Let this mind be in you, which was also in Christ Jesus " (*Phil.* ii, 5), and then he goes on to write about the complete emptying of self and the sacrifice of the Man-God. At least this idea stands before us as a challenge, as a high ideal ';

[1] Jungmann, *op. cit.* p. 17 (cf. also pp. 14-15, 20).

for in fact we can make our offering in the way it should be made only 'when we do it with the consciousness that we are carrying out the work of Christ and that we are entering into his sacrifice and prayer' and when we 'enter into the world of the principles and convictions with which he went to his death'[1].

This question of how, and in what precise sense, we can offer Christ's sacrifice, demands closer attention; but first let us return for a moment—in order to emphasize it still further—to the essential difference between the Mass and all other sacrifices, which is indeed the same as that we considered earlier on between christianity and all anterior religions, between the christian *mysterion* and the cult-mysteries. Primitive and archaic religions are essentially 'anhistorical': they attempt as it were to escape from history, from the irreversibility of historical time; christianity is essentially an historical religion, not merely in the sense that it discerns the hand of God in the unfolding of historical events, but because it holds that at a given historical moment God became himself an historical event: the Word was made flesh, was born and lived and died, and his death was a sacrifice, the self-offering of God to God, to be continued and recalled indeed but never repeated. Time is thus irreversible; and the sacrifice is an unique event, which alone manifests the full nature and meaning of sacrifice. As Fr Victor White puts it: 'Calvary is not just one specimen (not even the best specimen) of the class "sacrifice"'; we 'may not judge whether or how what Jesus does is a sacrifice by comparing it with Old Testament or pagan standards, or with *a priori* definitions. Jesus on the Cross is himself the standard whereby other sacrifices, or definitions of sacrifice, are to be judged: it is illegitimate to make *them* the criterion of what *he* does'[2]. It is true that, as the same writer goes on to show, other sacrifices 'serve to illustrate, and help us to understand better, what it is that Jesus does': this is 'the underlying thought of the *Epistle to the Hebrews*', and though

---

[1] Jungmann, *op, cit.* p. 18. [2] V. White, O.P.: *The All-Sufficient Sacrifice, The Life of the Spirit*, June, 1957, p. 538.

St Paul is there concerned with Old Testament sacrifices, the same is true in degree of others, including the non-levitical sacrifices of Abel, Abraham, Melchizedech which are mentioned in the Mass; but what these other sacrifices enable us to understand better is ' what Jesus is and does " once for all ", subsuming and transcending them all and thereby rendering them obsolete '[1].

This is clear if we consider the four things which, as St Augustine pointed out, are part of every sacrifice, namely, what is offered, and to whom, by whom, for whom: in the Christ-sacrifice it is Christ himself who is all these four things, and ' it may be said that all other sacrifices, whether Old Testament or pagan, are so many attempts, and also so many inevitable failures, to achieve this identity of all these four elements '[2].

We can find in the phrase ' by whom ' a clue to the inevitable failure. Down to the time of the Hebrew prophets, it would seem, sacrifice was regarded as being an offering to God, of God (the ' sacred ' victim) and *by* God—not a human but a divine act.[3] It was so to speak an extra-temporal act in which the priest took part not as a human, temporal being but as an embodiment of the god. Yet it is *man* who ought to sacrifice; it is his duty as creature; and it is his duty to do so, not just at certain ' extra-temporal ' moments, but daily and in the world of ' profane ' events: ' as the psalmist says, *propter te mortificamur tota die*—on *thy* account *we* are immolated all day and every day. Already in the earliest reign, Samuel tells Saul that " obedience is better than sacrifices, and to hearken rather than to offer the fat of rams " (I *Kings*, xv, 22). The later prophets will stress more and more the need for the interior and ceaseless submission of a broken and humbled heart as against the external periodical ceremonials. . . . Did this mean that divine, ritual sacrifice is now to be *replaced* by human, interior acts of self-sacrifice . . .? But just this, we have seen, is humanly impossible. The claim to be able to sacrifice ourselves implies the claim to possess ourselves; and it is just this egoistic and illusory claim which

---

[1] White, *op. cit.* pp. 538-9.   [2] *ibid.* pp. 539-40.   [3] Cf. G. R. Levy: *The Gate of Horn*, p. 507, quoted White, *op. cit.* p. 540.

sacrifice surrenders. To *substitute* human, ethical self-sacrifice for divine sacrifice is not to recognize, but precisely to deny, the all-sovereignty of God. It is not to make sacred (*sacrificare*) the " profane ", but to profane the sacred; and atheistic or satanic moral autonomy is the logical outcome of such presumption. Only a God-man could resolve the dilemma. We may apply to sacrifice what St Anselm says of satisfaction: " Only God *can* make it, only man should make it; so it is required that a God-man makes it "[1].

Hence the Mass—the ' same sacrifice as that of the Cross '—is necessary not only as making the *gift* it brings available to us but also as making the *offering* available to us: it is Christ's *actio*, but it is also our *actio*: it is the sacrifice at once of Christ and of his Church. At the moment of consecration the priest speaks in the person of Christ—' This is *my* body '—but elsewhere he speaks for all the faithful around him and for the Church as a whole: ' Let *us* pray ' he says repeatedly, and most of the prayers in the Mass are in fact in the plural; but, as Fr Jungmann notes, ' to say these prayers in the name of all, and thus in the plural, was not considered sufficient. One also made sure of the express assent and joint action of the congregation. Here we have a very ancient christian tradition which can be traced back without hesitation to the apostles and also, partly, to the customs of the synagogue. The assent of the people was required in the *Amen* '[2]. Thus the collects are preceded by the greeting, The Lord be with you, and the *Oremus*, Let us pray; and end with the *Amen*, So be it, with which the faithful signify their endorsement of and participation in the prayer that has been offered. And the Mass as a whole is similarly *our* offering —*offerimus*, we offer—so that the Great Prayer itself, the Canon, concludes in the same way; and in ancient times, ' when the consecrated gifts lay upon the altar, when the offering to the divine majesty had been expressed and the mighty prayer brought to its conclusion with *Per ipsum et cum ipso et in ipso*, the entire com-

[1] White, *op. cit.* pp. 541-2. [2] *The Eucharistic Prayer*, pp. 31-2.

munity voiced its assent in the *Amen* '; and ' St Jerome recounts
how, in the Roman basilicas, this *Amen* used to resound like a
thunderclap ' [1]. It would be extremely helpful, as well as logical,
if the Great Doxology, the *Per ipsum*, could once again be said
aloud by the priest [2] and this great Amen restored to the people:
this doxology would then balance the earlier one, the Preface,
which is still said aloud or sung, and the beginning and end of the
Canon would thus be clearly marked. It would be useful too if our
missals were so printed as to show that the *Per omnia sæcula sæcu-
lorum, Amen* at this point does indeed mark the end of the
Canon and is not—as it seems to be in so many missals—a
sort of unexplained (and inexplicable) introduction to the Our
Father.[3]

This sharing by all the faithful in the offering is emphasized
again, as we shall see, in the *Orate fratres*, the *gratias agamus* and, still
more forcefully, that phrase which occurs at the ' point where, in
all forms of the liturgy, there is stated in the most solemn manner
precisely what is happening here at the altar—where the " calling
to mind " and offering of sacrifice are formulated in words ' [4]—the
phrase in which the act of offering is attributed not only to the
priest but also to the faithful, the ' holy people ': *nos servi tui sed et
plebs tua sancta.*

Fr Jungmann has pointed out how this idea of the sharing of
the people in the actual offering of the sacrifice was largely lost
sight of in the Middle Ages; how ' an ever increasing emphasis
was placed on the dividing line between clergy and people ' and
' an invisible wall was built up between the people and the altar ';

---

[1] Jungmann: *The Sacrifice of the Church*, p. 33.   [2] The saying of the prayers of the
Canon (apart from the Preface and the words *Nobis quoque peccatoribus*) not aloud but first
in a low voice and finally *tacite*, in a whisper, dates from the eighth century, and seems
to be connected with the growing emphasis in those times on the distinction between
priest and faithful—a distinction which became a marked separation when rood-screens
like solid walls were built between choir or sanctuary and nave—so that the Canon came
to be thought of as itself a ' sanctuary into which the priest alone may penetrate '. Cf.
Jungmann: *Missarum Sollemnia*, t. iii, p. 8; also t. i, p. 116; all quotations from this book
given here are translated from the French translation, Aubier, 1951.   [3] Cf. *infra*, p. 165.
[4] Jungmann: *The Sacrifice of the Church*, p. 12.

and he suggests that this was due to a lack of clear understanding of 'the distinct concepts of offering sacrifice and of consecrating' so that 'there was a fear that any mention of the faithful as co-offerers of the sacrifice might be misunderstood to imply that they were co-consecrators'; but 'the Church of our own day has overcome this bashfulness . . . and Pius XII has now declared explicitly that "the people's offering of the sacrifice pertains to liturgical worship"', for they too share in their own way in the priesthood of Christ.[1]

Thus the paradox, duty-to-offer and inability-to-offer, is resolved: we offer the one, true sacrifice because Christ has empowered us to do so by making us one with himself. But, while no participation of ours can add anything at all to the value of Christ's sacrifice in itself, from our point of view—if 'our sacrifice' is to be 'acceptable'—there must be an identification between ourselves and Christ not only as priest but as victim. As we have seen, sacrifice is essentially self-sacrifice: it is not something that can be done for us in the sense of relieving us of all responsibility, all obligation; and any attempt to shuffle off our obligation can end only in catastrophe and tragedy. Perhaps we may see an illustration of this in the story of David's sin which we considered in an earlier chapter. The ancient animal-sacrifices attempted to express total self-offering through the slaying of an animal with which the offerer had previously identified himself, the value of the sacrifice being thus measured by the preciousness (to the offerer) of the victim and the degree of his identification with it. Thus, for instance, among the primitive Malekulans, for the sacrificer the animal 'fulfils the function of an *alter ego* which . . . he first rears as a woman would rear a child, then consecrates, cherishes and adores it, thereby investing it with his own most secret and cherished desires'; then finally he slays what 'up to this moment has been cherished and cosseted and communed with and . . . has occupied the position of his most cherished companion'[2]. Now Nathan

---

[1] Jungmann: *op. cit.* p. 14.   [2] J. Layard: *Identification with the Sacrificial Animal* (in Eranos Jahrbuch, xxiv, p. 340) quoted White, *op. cit.* p. 544.

the prophet spoke in very similar terms of the ewe-lamb which was the poor man's sole possession and which he had ' reared, letting it grow up in his house like his own children, share his food and drink, sleep in his bosom; it was like a daughter to him '; but here everything is wrong: the lamb, which might have been offered to God, is instead seized by the rich man who had no title to it: David is in revolt against God and therefore, far from sacrificing himself to God, arrogates sacrifice to himself; and his defiance and disorder breed the yet greater disorders of his sons' crimes.

In spiritu humilitatis: we are not to be led, as were the first human beings, into thinking of ourselves ' as gods ', demanding sacrifice instead of offering it; nor on the other hand are we to suppose that our creaturely need of self-offering has been fulfilled for us and that we have nothing further to do. In offering the divine victim in and with the divine priest we are able—and, if the offering is to be efficacious for us, are bound—to offer also ourselves in an act of total self-giving. But it is through that surrender of life that we find life. ' It is characteristic of sacrifices, as opposed to magical rituals, that although (or because) they seek no reward and surrender every claim, they are returned, transmuted and divinized, to the sacrificer. And as God showed his acceptance of the sacrifice on Calvary by raising Christ from the dead, restoring his body glorious and immortal, so now he shows his acceptance of our participation in his sacrifice by giving to us, and transforming us into, the body of him who was slain, but who is now the immortal conqueror of death.' [1]

Let us look now at the general structure of the Mass as we know it today. Historically speaking, it divides at the Creed into two distinct parts, often called the Mass of the Catechumens and the Mass of the Faithful because the as yet unbaptized neophytes were admitted to the first [2] but (a wise precaution in times of persecution) not to the second. For the first part is in fact simply a

[1] White, *op. cit.* p. 548.   [2] In Rome the dismissal of the catechumens seems in fact to have taken place, at one time, *before* the Gospel-reading. Cf. Jungmann: *Missarum Sollemnia*, t. ii, p. 6, n. 1.

development of the ancient Hebrew synagogue service, to which the Jewish christians remained faithful. This meant, first, readings from the Scriptures, which were followed by a homily on what had been read. (The sermon, therefore, though nowadays it is confined to the Mass on Sundays, is historically speaking an integral part of the Mass, and we should so regard it. On the other hand it should indeed be a homily on ' what has been read '; it is a tragedy when, week after week, the inexhaustible truths of epistle or Gospel are brushed aside in favour of exhortations concerning the inadequacy of the collections—or for that matter the inadequacy of bikinis.) Then, secondly, there were prayers, the singing of psalms. This service was continued by the christians as a vigil service, and was not at first always followed by the breaking of bread, the Lord's Supper: but gradually the two came to be regarded as parts of one single act of worship, and so the Mass as such began to develop.

In each of the two parts the universal sacrifice-pattern is revealed: the offering to God, the gift from God. In the first part there is first the offering of prayer to God and then the gift of revealed truth from God; in the second part there is the offering of the bread and wine leading up to the self-offering of the divine Victim, and then the gift of that same Victim in the communion.

The Mass thus contains the two ideas, and realities, of *deipnon* and *thysia*. The word *deipnon* means in general a meal and in particular, as here, a sacred meal at which consecrated food is eaten: a sacrifice therefore, since *sacrificere* means to make holy and therefore to consecrate; *thysia* has in it the meaning of offering sacrifice and therefore of slaughter, but it also means a blazing or flaring up: ' originally the food-offering was intended for the nourishment of the gods; the smoke of the burnt sacrifice carried the food up to their heavenly abode. At a later stage the smoke was conceived as a spiritualized form of food-offering. . . . The dual meaning of *deipnon* and *thysia* is implicitly contained in

139

the words of the sacrament: " the body (which was given) for you ". This may mean either " which was given to you to eat " or, indirectly, " which was given for you to God " '[1]. What is most relevant to our purpose for the moment is simply the idea of fire as being essentially part of the idea of sacrifice.[2]

All through the ages mankind has offered sacrifices to its gods, and the sacrifices have expressed its needs and its longings; and now at last, ' in the fullness of time ', we are given the divine response. We can say that the Mass of the Faithful goes back in essence some two thousand years, and the Mass of the Catechumens yet another thousand or so; but more than that, we can and should see the Mass as something universal: the Church gathering into her arms all history, all humanity, all creation, for the Mass too is in a sense the ' summing up of all things in Christ '.

We can tell the inquiring pagan, then, that in the Mass there are Roman, Greek and Hebrew elements: the clothes the priest wears are in essence simply the clothes ordinarily worn by Roman citizens in the days of the primitive Church; the language used is for the most part Latin though Greek survives here and there as in the *Kyrie*[3] and, on Good Friday, the *Agios ho Theos*; for as in the days of St Paul and the primitive Church Greek was the means of communication between different peoples, so in later times Latin became the common language in the west; as for Hebrew, besides the readings from the Old Testament and the singing of psalms there are such hebraisms as the reply to the greeting, God be with you: And with thy spirit (which simply means, And with you too); and of Jewish origin too are the *Gratias agamus*, and the reply to it, at the beginning of the Preface[4]. But we can also show the pagan how in the Mass the Church speaks with the voice, and voices the needs, of all humanity; and perhaps

---

[1] Cf. Jung: *Transformation Symbolism in the Mass*, pp. 275-6.   [2] Cf. *infra*, p. 183.
[3] Though this prayer is not in fact a survival from days when Greek was the language mainly used by the Church in Rome, but a later borrowing from the Greek liturgy. Cf. Jungmann: *Missarum Sollemnia*, t. ii, p. 88.   [4] Cf. Jungmann: *Missarum Sollemnia*, t. i, p. 39; t. iii, p. 17.

that is even more important than showing him the Mass in its historical setting.

The Mass begins at the foot of the altar: we are, as it goes on, to climb the mountain of vision, to be taken up into the light, but we must begin in darkness, with the confession of sins, the appeal to God for rebirth.

True, the prayers at the foot of the altar were not originally part of the Mass, they were part of the priest's private preparation for it, and were not fixed in their present place until the time of Pius V. But, as Fr Martindale so rightly points out, ' They are there today; and they are so beautiful that it is a thousand pities if we do not join in them, especially as the server, who represents the faithful, does emphatically join in them '[1]. In the ' dialogue Mass ' as it is sometimes carried out the faithful do in fact say what the server says. A plea was recently made by a liturgist that the old order of things should be restored by having again, as of old, two readings (lesson and epistle) instead of the one reading which is nowadays normal, and that these prayers at the foot of the altar should again be relegated to the sacristy: this is surely an example of the *wrong* sort of liturgical-reform thinking. In the long, gradual evolution of the liturgy certain anomalies and confusions have arisen which it is desirable to remove by a return to a more primitive simplicity;[2] but other developments have been either necessary or at least desirable and to the good; and it would be a tragedy if archæological purism were to lead to their removal. The reduction of scriptural readings is only one example of the general process of shortening the Mass which changing circumstances made necessary —and the twentieth century is hardly an apt time to reverse the process. What is quite beyond question is that the Mass as a symbol would be immensely impoverished if this initial confession of sin at the foot of the mountain were to be discarded (and the same is true, as we shall see later, of the last Gospel which originally was also part of the priest's private thanksgiving-prayer but which has

[1] *The Mind of the Missal*, p. 8.   [2] Cf. e.g. p. 146, n. 2, *infra.*

now become an integral part of the Mass and is in fact of the greatest value in understanding and living the Mass as a whole so that it is a tragedy that it should still be mumbled *sotto voce*). As Dr. Jung points out, the offering of a sacrifice ' consists in the first place in giving something which belongs to me '; but what is ' mine ' ' adheres to my ego, because it is part of my personality ' so that there is always bound up with the giving of it 'an unspoken " give that thou mayst receive " '; the giving does not become a true sacrifice unless ' I give up the implied intention of receiving something in return. If it is to be a true sacrifice, the gift must be given as if it were being destroyed '. Without that, the offering would inevitably have the character of a magical act of propitiation, with ' the unavowed purpose and tacit expectation of purchasing the good will of the Diety ', and this would be merely a ' worthless simulacrum of sacrifice '. If I want to avoid this I must recognize my identity with the gift, must admit that ' I am giving myself, forgoing myself, and do not want to be repaid for it '. ' It is therefore quite logical that the confession of sin should come before the rite of transformation in the Mass. The self-examination is intended to make one conscious of the selfish claim bound up with every gift, so that it may be consciously given up; otherwise the gift is no sacrifice.' [1]

When in the Mass, therefore, we offer ourselves to God in union with the self-offering of Christ it must be with at least some faint echo of his own selflessness, his ' Not my will but thine be done ': we hope indeed that through the Mass we may be hallowed—that is its purpose—but we are not driving a bargain, and in fact we shall be hallowed to the extent to which we can give ourselves without the *do ut des*, the giving-to-receive, and can make of ourselves instead a holocaust, a whole-burnt offering.

But the very first thing that takes place at the foot of the altar, before the confession of sins, is the making of the sign of the cross. It is with this sign that the Mass both begins and ends; first because

[1] C. G. Jung: *Transformation Symbolism in the Mass*, pp. 320-2.

it is itself the Sign of the Cross, Calvary represented not physically but mystically, and we must remind ourselves of the fact; secondly because this is a blessing, [1] and we need a blessing when we approach the altar of God; thirdly because in signing ourselves thus we as it were gather the personality together into concentration and strength: we are to give our whole minds and hearts to what is to follow, there must be no wandering of attention or lack of fervour, and so we begin by 'pulling ourselves together' by means of this sacred sign.

Next, in the Roman Mass, [2] there comes the verse of the psalm: 'I will go unto the altar of God, the giver of youth and of joy' (and the verse will be repeated to give it emphasis), and so here at the very beginning we find as a sort of keynote to the Mass the theme we were considering earlier on: we meet again the *puer æternus*, the longing not only for immortality but for immortal youth, youth regained—in the early Church the psalm which includes this verse was used as a baptism song—for if it is the Mass which more than anything else can make us mature personalities, bringing as it does the world of eternity into that of time, the jewel into the lotus, and teaching us to be concerned above all with ultimates, with God and his mercy, with the Word and the pattern, with Calvary, with our own ultimate destinies, at the same time it is the Mass which more than anything else can keep us young (or make us young again) in mind and heart and soul. We grow old in mind if we allow ourselves to become intellectually stale,

---

[1] Cf. Jungmann: *Missarum Sollemnia*, t. ii, p. 45. [2] This book is concerned only with the Mass as it is offered in the Latin Rite; but that Rite includes various different forms or 'uses', and inevitably one has in mind primarily the use with which one is familiar—the Dominican as opposed to the Roman Mass. In fact, the differences are not such as to make the pages which follow puzzling to the reader acquainted only with the Roman Mass: the Dominican Mass, being some three hundred years older than the Roman as we now have it, is considerably shorter, simpler, æsthetically more austere, so that the differences are often a question simply of omission. (It is rather like comparing, say, Durham Cathedral with King's College Chapel.) In the Dominican Mass the prayers at the foot of the altar consist simply of the psalm-verse, 'Praise ye the Lord for he is good, for his mercy endureth for ever'; then the confession of sins and the absolution; and then, 'Our help is in the name of the Lord, who made heaven and earth'. But I have included here the *Introibo*, quoted above, from the Roman Mass because of its obvious relevance to the general theme of the book.

shut in, fixed in certain grooves of thought or prejudice, unreceptive of new ideas; we grow old in heart if we become hard, cynical, unreceptive of new loves and sympathies; we grow old in soul if we become slothful, content with the minimum of religious observance, or unscrupulous and hardened in sin. But the Mass is inexhaustible in its riches and so can constantly renew our sense of wonder, bringing us fresh insights into divine things and our relation to them, showing us ever more clearly and deeply what love means and so deepening thereby our own response to love, and taking us ever more deeply into the ultimate mysteries and so urging us to offer to them more adequately the response they demand. In a moment we shall be confessing our sins and begging God's mercy; but it is joy, so the Mass promises, which is to be the last word, the joy of youth regained, the joy of a new paradise garden, the joy of God.

St Ambrose, commenting on the use of this psalm-verse by the procession of neophytes entering the church after their baptism, links it up with another psalm which sings of the Lord satisfying ' thy desire with good things: thy youth shall be renewed like the eagle's '[1]; and elsewhere he says: ' Thou hast put off the old age of sin and put on instead the youthfulness of grace '[2]. This theme is wonderfully treated in the blessing of the baptismal water during the Easter Vigil service: ' O God, whose Spirit in the very beginning of the world moved over the waters that even then the element of water might receive the power to sanctify; God, who by water didst wash away the crimes of a guilty world and by the outpouring of the deluge didst signify the sacrament of rebirth that one and the same element might, in mystery, be the end of vice and the origin of virtue: look, Lord, upon thy Church and give her increase of those who are reborn in thee, thou who dost gladden thy city with the abundant stream of thy grace and dost open the font of baptism over the whole earth to the renewal of life of the nations.

---

[1] *Ps.* cii, 5 (Douai). [2] *De myst.* viii, 43; *De sacr.* iv, 2, 7; cf. Jungmann, *op. cit.* t. ii, p. 42, n.14.

' At thy majesty's command may the Church receive from the holy Spirit the grace of thy only-begotten Son: may he, through the secret mingling of his divine power, make this water fruitful for the rebirth of mankind, that from the stainless womb of this divine font may come a heavenly offspring, conceived in holiness and born again a new creature, and that all, though differing from one another in age or in sex, may together be brought forth as infants by that divine grace which is their mother.'

The Church goes on to pray that, at God's command, ' all unclean spirits' may be driven away, that ' there be no mingling here of the Alien Power', no insidious encompassing of the water with his snares, no subtle entry by stealth to corrupt it; on the contrary, as the priest touches the water with his hand he prays that ' this holy and innocent creature may be free from every assault of the enemy' so as to become ' a living fountain, a regenerative water, a purifying stream' that ' the stains of every sin may be washed away in it', and those who receive this sacrament may be ' born again into the new childhood of true innocence'.

In the atrium of the ancient christian basilicas there was a fountain for the ritual purification of those about to enter, the external rite being intended to fix the mind on the need for inner purity;[1] in the entrance to our own churches we have the stoup of holy water, and on Sundays the ceremony of the *Asperges* at Mass: as in baptism itself, so in the rites and symbols which remind us of it, the two themes of purifying and new birth go together, the former seen always in the light of the latter for once again it is joy which is the last word. It is, thanks to the waters, as new-born children of the Sun that we enter the church and approach the altar: and in a moment we shall be singing the *Gloria in excelsis*, the great song of praise and joy.

But first there is the moment of darkness: priest and people alike confess their sins, and the priest pronounces the absolution;

---

[1] Cf. Jungmann, *op. cit.* t. ii, p. 355.

only then, having said ' Our help is in the name of the Lord ' does he go up to the altar: the ascent of the mountain can now begin. Bowing down, to express once again our inability to ' do anything ourselves as of ourselves ', he prays God to take away our iniquities that we may be worthy to ' enter with pure minds into the holy of holies '—that sanctuary of the divine presence from which the impassable veil has now been torn; and making the sign of the cross on the altar, he kisses it. This kiss is first of all a mark of veneration and salutation, which the Church took over from pagan antiquity. But also, the altar must be of stone, or at least have a block of stone at the centre, and contain relics of a martyr, for at Mass we look back across the ages to the primitive days of persecution when in the catacombs the sacrifice was offered on the tomb of a martyr; the kiss is the symbol of love, veneration, unity, and so the priest is venerating the relics of the martyrs. But again he is doing more than that: the Roman missal speaks of the altar as Christ; and we recall St Paul's *petra autem erat Christus*, ' the rock was Christ '[1]: this then is a bridal kiss, the Church kissing Christ.

There follows the reading of the *Introit*, usually a verse or two from a psalm or psalms. Originally this was an incessional hymn, to be sung as the ministers approached the altar, as is still done in the Dominican High Mass.[2] The *Kyrie* as we now have it is all that remains of the primitive *Kyrie* litany, in which ' the Invocations were spoken by the clergy or by one cleric, and the people answered with the *Kyrie eleison*'[3]. From the point of view of the pattern it is perhaps a pity that the *Introit* has thus come to interrupt the sequence

---

[1] I *Cor.* x. 4.   [2] It should be remembered, in studying the Mass, that the ' norm ' is the High Mass, offered by celebrant (bishop or priest), deacon and subdeacon as it always was in primitive times. (Choir and congregation also had their active parts to play.) When as time went on it became impracticable for the Mass to be always so offered, the Low Mass, offered by priest alone, was introduced, and it was thought proper that the priest should then himself say the parts which in the High Mass were sung by the choir or by deacon or subdeacon; then it came to be assumed that in the High Mass, when it could be celebrated, the priest should continue to say these parts; and so there are now certain anomalies and ' vain repetitions ' which will perhaps be eliminated by the Church in its contemporary liturgical reforms: the celebrant mumbling the epistle to himself instead of listening to the subdeacon as he sings it, or saying the Gospel to himself and then hearing it sung all over again by the deacon.   [3] Jungmann: *The Eucharistic Prayer*, p. 33.

of confession and cry for mercy; however, these have now been offered to God and we are ready for the *Gloria*.

Though originally it was sung only infrequently in Rome,[1] the *Gloria* has become one of the Church's most frequently used, as it is one of its most beautiful, prayers of wonder. ' We praise thee. We bless thee. We adore thee. We glorify thee. We give thee thanks for thy great glory.' It is of course our duty to thank God for his gifts, but that is not our concern here: human lovers have no need to be taught to say to each other, ' How beautiful, how lovely, how wonderful you are!', but we do need to be taught to say such things to God, and here the Church is teaching us. The whole Mass indeed is a *sacrificium laudis*, a sacrifice of praise: we sometimes forget that if sacrifice in our fallen world is often a sad thing it ought also to be a glad thing, for love loves to give and if we love God enough any offering will be an offering of joy.

Fr Martindale offers an interpretation of the clause ' We give thee thanks for thy great glory ' which we may gladly and thankfully accept without however allowing it to narrow down the application of the words—it is indeed only another example of the rich ' polyvalence ' of symbols. ' I would ask ', he writes, ' whether God's " great glory " may not mean his Son, our Lord. " Glory " has been defined: " A clear knowledge together with praise ". The Son is the perfect Knowledge of the Father, and from him proceeds that holy Spirit who is his perfect love and praise. The Son is the e-radiation, the refulgence, of the Father's glory—he *is* that glory inasmuch as it shines forth from him, Light from a fount of Light. Hence he *is* the Glory that, " in the highest ", in heaven, is ever given to our God, and his perfect praise.'[2]

' Glory to God in high heaven '; the *Gloria* begins by giving glory and praise to God, as the angels did on the first Christmas night; it ends with a reference to glory in a different sense: ' For thou only art holy. Thou only art Lord. Thou only, O Jesus

[1] Cf. Jungmann: *The Eucharistic Prayer*, p. 34.   [2] Martindale, *op. cit.* pp. 16-17.

Christ, art most high, together with the holy Spirit, in the glory of God the Father'. What is this glory? For the Hebrews it meant the *Shekinah*, the visible radiance manifesting the divine presence; christians can think too of the Word-made-flesh, 'sitting at the right hand of the Father' in glory, as *Christos Helios*, the Sun, glorified, glorifying, and calling us to share in the glory.

We are now therefore led nearer to God's presence; and in his presence we shall have to tell him of our needs, our dependence on him. But first of all the priest turns to the people and, holding out his arms, says to them, ' The Lord be with you'. It is a very ancient form of greeting—we find it in the book of *Ruth*—and it has come down through the ages and we still use it, though perhaps unconsciously, whenever we say ' Goodbye'. The gesture too is one of greeting, of welcome, of inclusion: as Fr Martindale so rightly and happily puts it, it is an ' openhanded' gesture: just as Pope Pius XII, when preaching, so often stood with his arms outstretched to embrace the whole world, so here in the Mass the priest is embracing the whole *ecclesia*, the whole congregation, and inviting them all to join in what is now to be done: *Oremus*, Let us all pray together.

So we come to the collects. In ancient times, if the Pope was to celebrate Mass at a given church, the faithful would collect together and await him in another church which thus came to be referred to as the *ecclesia collecta*; when the Pope arrived he would pray for the needs of all, and then they would go in procession to the church where the Mass was to be offered and which in turn came to be referred to as the *statio*.[1] Many liturgists therefore have explained the use of the name ' collect' for this prayer in the Mass by identifying it with the prayer said in the *ecclesia collecta*; but Fr Jungmann argues cogently against this identification, and explains the term, as used in the Mass, as signifying simply an *oratio* or public prayer in which the priest recapitulates or ' collects together' the

[1] This explains the rubric to be found in the missal before the Mass on certain days of the year: Station at St John Lateran, at St Laurence outside the Walls, and so on.

prayers of the people and offers them to God.[1] It is quite clear, at any rate, that the old Roman collects, such as those which we still have today in the Lenten Masses, majestic, concise, rich in meaning,[2] do indeed express the needs of every individual and of the whole world.

The attitude of the priest while singing or saying the collects and other ancient prayers (Secret, Great Prayer, Our Father, Post-communion) in which he is the spokesman of the community, his hands upraised, is not to be confused with the *Dominus vobiscum* gesture: that was greeting, this is supplication, and again it would seem to go back to very ancient times.

So far the Mass has been an offering of prayer *to* God. Now there follows the gift *from* God, the gift of revealed truth in the lesson or epistle and then in the Gospel, the first sung by the sub-deacon, the second by the deacon. In between there come the short chants we call the Gradual and *Alleluia* (or, in Lent, the Tract). The Gradual (*gradus*, a step) is so called because it was sung by soloist and choir, and the soloist stood upon the step of the *ambo* or pulpit. It consisted of a psalm with an antiphon repeated after each verse—we have an example of this form of chant in the *Lumen* of Candlemas—and was evidently regarded as very impor-tant: there was to be no liturgical action during the singing of it, but all were to sit and listen attentively; and indeed, where the proper of a Mass was composed as a whole, the keynote of it can often be found in the Gradual if one reads not just the verse or two which survive today but the whole psalm.

The *Alleluia* is another prayer of praise. When the Mass is sung in plainsong, the word is first sung by the cantor and then repeated by the choir who then carry on the final ' a ' in a long arabesque of sound. In human affairs we often enough say oh! or ah! when we want to express deep admiration, wonder, love, joy; at the same time this final *-ia* is a shortened form of Jahweh, the name of God—and one of our human ways of expressing love

---

[1] Cf. *Missarum Sollemnia*, t. ii, pp. 14, 119–20.　　[2] Nowadays, alas, the writing of collects seems to have become a lost art.

consists in saying, and repeating, the beloved's name. Thus the *Alleluia* echoes the *Gloria in excelsis*; at the same time it leads us on to the Gospel, the vision of glory. (So the cantor stood on the step of the *ambo* because, again, we are climbing the mountain, and the climax is now at hand.)

Meanwhile, in the Dominican High Mass, the chalice has been prepared at the *sedilia*[1]: first the wine is poured in, and we may be reminded of Cana, where our Lord by his miracle blessed the feasting and gaiety just as by his presence he blessed marriage; we can meditate on the prodigality of God, and on the duty of men to be generous to one another; on the other hand we can think of the chalice of our Lord's agony, of the wine-cup that must be drunk to the dregs; then, as the drop of water is added to the wine, symbol of our incorporation into Christ, we can pray to be made worthy, despite our sins, of that incorporation. Dr Jung, having quoted St Justin's remark that the presentation of the cleansed lepers in the temple was an image of the offering of the eucharistic bread, and having linked this up with ' the later alchemical idea of the imperfect or " leprous " substance which is made perfect by the *opus*', goes on to explain the fact that the water which is to be added to the wine in the chalice must first be blessed; for ' as the water is an imperfect or even leprous substance, it has to be blessed and consecrated before being mixed, so that only a purified body may be joined to the wine of the spirit, just as Christ is to be united only with a pure and sanctified congregation. Thus this part of the rite has the special significance of preparing a perfect body—the glorified body of resurrection '[2]. Then the acolytes' candles must be lit, and the incense blessed; and then the deacon, holding the book, begs a blessing from the celebrant,[3] and all rise for the singing of the Gospel.

The lesson or epistle is read for our instruction: it may be

[1] In the Dominican Low Mass this is done at the very beginning, before the prayers at the foot of the altar; in the Roman Mass it is always done after the reading of the Offertory verse. [2] *Transformation Symbolism in the Mass*, pp. 278-9. [3] The form of blessing in the Dominican Mass, slightly shorter than that in the Roman, is: ' May the Lord be in thy heart and on thy lips for the announcing of the holy Gospel of peace '.

St Paul, for instance, telling us how christians ought or ought not to behave. The Gospel is not so much instruction as epiphany: the showing forth of the Word. So, when the deacon has announced the Gospel from which the reading is to be taken, the faithful or choir reply, not ' Glory be to the Lord ', but ' Glory be to thee, O Lord ': the Word dwells amongst us, and in the Gospel we see his glory.[1] Hence the lighted candles, to give glory to the Light of the World; and the incense, that very ancient symbol of honour and veneration—and if we identify our own adoration with the upward-wreathing of the incense we should recall that the sweet-smelling smoke only rises when the incense is put upon the burning coal: our prayer will be of little value unless it springs from the inner fire of love.

The singing or reading of the Gospel usually begins with the words *in illo tempore*, ' at that time '; we may recall how Prof. Eliade constantly uses this term to designate the ' Great Time ', the Golden Age, the sacred, paradisal or mythical time which was *in principio*, in the beginning, as opposed to profane and historical time; primitive man only 'tolerates "history" with difficulty and attempts periodically to abolish it'[2]—to participate instead in the mythical time when deeds were 'exemplary', archetypal, the time which in fact is extra-temporal. For the mystic the *nunc stans*, the abiding moment, of eternity is more real than the incessant flux of the temporal; and for christianity in general life must be seen as involving simultaneously two different dimensions, since the events in the Gospel are both temporal and supra-temporal: it is proper to think of a paradisal Golden Age, before the Fall, and of the second, final Golden Age of eternity when time will have been abolished; meanwhile inescapably we live in history and are involved in the making of it, but at the same time we are to think of the ' kingdom of God ' in terms not just of a remote future but of the here and now, as something which—given *metanoia*, repentance and rebirth—is already within us. The Gospel events are

[1] At the same time, deacon and faithful make the sign of the cross on forehead, lips, and breast, signifying their desire to understand, love and proclaim God's revelation.
[2] Eliade: *The Myth of the Eternal Return*, p. 36.

historical (and therefore for us history is not something to be tolerated, still less abolished, for everything depends on it); at the same time they are ' exemplary ', supra-temporal since in them it is the divine and eternal which acts; and they are ' actual ', present as well as past, inasmuch as they are real and effective for us here and now as they were long ago in Palestine. We may note that Mgr Knox, in his translation of the Sunday Gospels, renders the opening words, *in illo tempore*, not ' at that time ' but ' at this time ', as though to stress this immediacy: we are hearing about events which took place in the past, but we are also hearing about mysteries which are immediately relevant to the present. It may be the story of the widow of Naim: but the Church is the widow and we her children are the dead boy needing Christ to give us life. It may be the feeding of the five thousand with bread and a few fishes: but we are soon to see and receive the Bread of Life, and the Bread is also the *Ichthys*, the Fish which was the ancient symbol of Christ.

The fish is a symbol of rebirth and renewal in general, and of Christ in particular. ' Despite the silence of the Gospels ', writes Dr Julius Baum, ' there can be no doubt that the fish, like the bread, sufficed to symbolize the body of the Lord as administered in the Eucharist. The designation of Christ as fish was familiar by the second century.' He goes on to say that the acrostic formed from the word *Ichthys*, fish, (' Jesus Christ, Son of God, Saviour ') was generally known before Tertullian's time, while Tertullian himself speaks of himself and his fellow christians as ' following after our *Ichthys*, Jesus Christ ', and so of being ' born in water, nor are we saved, except by abiding in the water '. This conception of the ' birth in water ' clearly goes back to the baptism in the Jordan, ' through which Jesus was manifested as the Son of God. '[1] Thus once again baptism and eucharist are united in a single symbol.

The Gospel is sung (in some ancient churches from an ambo higher than the one used by the subdeacon for the epistle) facing

[1] *Symbolic Representations of the Eucharist*, in ' The Mysteries ', pp. 26

the north. Originally the deacon faced the south; and no one seems to have been able to suggest a reason for this except that the men occupied the south side of the church,[1] which might suggest a somewhat misogynist state of mind among early christians. But the change is interesting: in *Isaiah* it is from the north that the destroying angel comes, in *Jeremiah* the north is associated with great calamity,[2] and in folklore generally one thinks of it in connection with vampires and werewolves and witches' sabbats. So, as the Gospel is sung, we can see the Word facing Satan the adversary and driving him back, doing what we pray for in Compline when we say: 'Visit, O Lord, this house, and drive far from it all the wiles of the Enemy'; so also, when the singing of the Gospel is ended, the celebrant, as he kisses the book, says: 'May our sins be blotted out by the words of the Gospel'.

The book is kissed after the Gospel, not after the epistle: for epiphany is more important than statement, moral instruction is obviously essential for us but not as important as personal communion with the Word, and wisdom is of greater value than knowledge: 'Wisdom have I loved, and have sought her out from my youth, and have desired to take her for my spouse, and I became a lover of her beauty.'[3]

Why, in the Low Mass, is the book moved from side to side? Why are some prayers read at the right-hand corner of the altar and others at the left? It is interesting that in the interpretation of dreams the left seems to be associated with the unknown, the unconscious, the mysterious; certainly it is a fact that in the Mass it is on the right that all the practical things are said or done, whilst the left is the side of mystery. At the right-hand corner the priest prepares the chalice, washes his hands, and again takes wine and water for the ablutions after communion; it is there that he reads the 'practical' prayers, the collects, and reads the 'practical' lesson or epistle. But it is at the left-hand corner that he reads the Gospel, the mystery; it is on the left that the book stands during

[1] Cf. *Ordo Romanus* II, n. 8. But for a discussion of the whole question, cf. Jungmann, *op. cit.* t. ii, pp. 178 *sqq.*   [2] Cf. *Isaiah*, xiv, 13; *Jer.* i, 14; iv, 6.   [3] *Wisd.* viii, 2 (Douai).

the Canon, the *mysterium fidei*; and it is interesting that in the Mass as we now know it, while the book is moved back again to the right for the ' practical ' post-communion prayer, the last Gospel is read at the left. As we have seen, this prologue to St John was not originally part of the Mass as such: it was part of the priest's private thanksgiving; but it has come to be part of the Mass now, and perhaps that is the significance of the fact: life is a very practical business, and even the service of God is a very practical business—we have to try to keep the commandments, to pray the prayer of petition, to exercise ourselves in the practice of the virtues and of good works; but, essential though all that is, our deepest need is communion with mystery, is faith not as an assent to a practical proposition but as a personal response to an immediate communication of the divine. If activity, even in the sense of moral striving, is to be sound and wise and fruitful it must be based on contemplation: our deepest need, once again, is to become thoughtful people, prayerful people, aware of the mystery below the surface of things, aware of the eternal within the fabric of time.

But we can never outgrow the practical things, the ten commandments, the practice of the virtues, the good works; and so during the singing or reading of the Gospel we stand: we stand at attention, which here means both being attentive and being ready for action: there is something to be done. The thing that immediately has to be done is the Mass of the Faithful, which begins with the offertory and in early times began with the offertory-procession: the faithful brought to the altar their own offerings, of bread and wine to become part of the sacrifice, but also of gifts for the Church and the poor. While this was being done a psalm was sung; so that the offertory verse as we now have it is simply the remnant of what was once a long processional chant. Nowadays—at least for the most part, in our big churches where the congregations are numbered in hundreds—such a procession would be impracticable; but it may be useful to see the modern ' collection ', which otherwise might seem a rather sordid and commercial business, as simply a development of that lovely, primitive custom.

It is also useful to remind ourselves how and why the custom itself arose: as an antidote, it would seem, to the gnosticism which had grown so wide-spread within the Church in the second century. The gnostic regarded matter, the whole visible creation, as evil, as coming not from God but from the devil. The Church therefore set itself to defend the goodness and value of material things; and so began to stress the fact that, as Fr Jungmann puts it, 'even the christian worship, however spiritual it may be, has its beginnings in matter. Christ himself chose " the bread which comes from creation " and the " chalice which comes from our creation ", and so taught his disciples the new offering '; the christian ritual, then, began to lay strong emphasis, ' both by words and by the external action ' accompanying the words, on the material gifts; the action of bringing the gifts up to the altar and laying them upon it, hitherto informal, now ' assumed the form of a liturgical act, the offertory. . . . In the third century the offertory procession appears, and when the gifts are placed on the altar, a special prayer is said over them before the thanksgiving-prayer, the *oratio super oblata*, the Secret prayer. In this way the offertory was built up into a full liturgical act '[1].

Thus ' the christian sacrifice begins essentially with bread and wine. Therein lies a twofold symbolism (and this on the authority of divine institution). The sacrifice which we offer, however sacred and heavenly it is, does not sway above our heads in the clouds, but the material world is made use of, material creation is reverenced in it, and it is made holy and brought back to God. Secondly, our human life in particular is taken up in these gifts; the work of our hands, the food from which we live and therefore our life itself. Our earthly life on this earth, with all its wants and necessities, is caught up in these earthly gifts; but in gifts the value of which has been raised up to the value of heavenly gifts with which nothing can be compared. They demand from us thanksgiving, adoration and the most interior offering of the heart '[2].

[1] *The Eucharistic Prayer*, pp. 22–3.   [2] Jungmann, *op. cit.* p. 26.

The Mass of the Faithful as we now have it begins with the greeting, ' The Lord be with you ', and then with a ' Let us pray ' which seems to be left standing as it were in mid-air; this is because it formerly introduced prayers for the needs of the Church, for the Pope, bishops, priests, the poor, and so on, and these have now dropped out except on Good Friday; but we can very well apply the words instead to the prayers which are to be said during the action of the offertory.

' What shall I give to the Lord,' the priest says, ' for all that he hath given to me? I will take the chalice of salvation and call upon the name of the Lord.' And in the Dominican Mass, [1] while he says this he raises the chalice with paten and host upon it; and he prays again: ' Accept, holy triune God, this offering which I present to thee in memory of the Passion of our Lord Jesus Christ, and grant that it may ascend to thee pleasing in thy eyes, and may bring about my salvation and that of all the faithful '.

This moment of offering is important. In the universal pattern of sacrifice the victim is identified with, and indeed takes the place of, the offerers; here we have to identify ourselves with the elements which will be changed into Christ; for *Tu mutaberis in Me*, ' Thou shalt be changed into me ': we are to become ' other Christs ', and this is part of the God-given process whereby we do so. As the priest raises the chalice in offering we ought, in mind, to put into it ourselves, our lives, all that goes to make up those lives— work, worries, problems, sorrows, joys, and all the human beings with whom we have some tie of love or responsibility. For every sacrifice is, as St Augustine said, the ' offering of a thing that it may be sanctified '; and here we are offering our lives and person- alities, with all the relationships which they include, in the hope that God, through the Mass, may bless and sanctify them and bring them to fruition.

So we come to the *Lavabo*; which originally no doubt had a more obvious utilitarian purpose than it does now, for after the

---

[1] In the Roman Mass there are two separate offerings, first of the bread and then of the wine; in the Dominican Mass bread and wine are offered together, with these prayers.

celebrant had received the gifts of the faithful and then incensed the altar it is likely that he would be glad to wash his hands. But again and again in studying the Church's symbols we find the same thing (and indeed it is to be expected if we believe that God is the God both of nature and of grace): that some thing or action which had the most matter-of-fact and utilitarian origin proves on examination to be rich in symbolic meaning. In the Dominican Mass the prayers here are short, just two verses, but they are very significant. First: 'I will wash my hands among the innocent, and go about thine altar, O Lord: that I may hear the voice of praise, and tell of all thy wonderful works'. Like the angels 'who stand before the throne' we are meant to be beings of praise; but if we are to praise, to tell of God's wonders, we must first be able to hear, to listen, and if we are to be able to listen we must first be cleansed, baptized, reborn. So once again the Mass, as it moves towards its climax, affirms the essential pattern. Then, 'Lord, I have loved the beauty of thy house and the place where thy *glory* dwelleth'. We sometimes forget that beauty and ugliness are not just a question of æsthetics. One has only to think of the importance of environment in education, in the problem of what is called in contemporary jargon 'juvenile delinquency'; there are saints who were born in a slum, but it is a wonder of God's grace that they became saints for they had everything against them. God made Adam a gardener, to enhance the beauties of Nature with the beauty of art; and that is still, in one way or another, our vocation. The wanton destruction of beauty (physical or otherwise) is a sin; the wanton or unnecessary creation of ugliness is a sin. And is not this indeed one of the most obvious evils of our time? In the service of Mammon the forests are ravaged, the soil eroded, the rivers polluted; flowery meadows are turned into slag heaps, and the humanity of a city, a *polis*, is all too often replaced by the subhumanity of a slum. 'Lord, I have loved the beauty of thy house': how readily we could say it at Chartres, Notre Dame, San Marco, Santa Sabina, or, for that matter, in many of the churches being built today; but what of the pseudo-Gothic monstrosities, the 'repository' statues, the *bondieuseries*, the *objets de piété* (and how felicitous to an English palate that word *objets* is!)? In religion as in life in general we are influenced deeply by our environment; and so we ought to build virile, clean-cut churches, we ought normally to make our statuary as impersonal as Eric Gill's *Stations of the Cross* to ensure that we shall not confuse worship with an emotional wallowing, just as we ought to see to it that when we formally pray together to God, if we cannot achieve the beauty of language of a Cranmer we at least avoid the turgidity of the modern 'manual of devotions'.

The building of a church today involves a double opportunity and challenge: to make—for the glory of God but also for the good of man—a thing of beauty in a world where there is so much ugliness, and to embody and communicate a symbol in a world where symbols are so largely forgotten. The builder's essential task is to make a Mass-house; but the Mass is the Cross in symbol-form; the builder then must show forth that symbol; all other considerations are subordinate to that.

In the earliest christian times, when the Mass was thought of primarily as the thanksgiving-prayer, the *Eucharistia*, there was no fixed altar for it: 'only a table was necessary and this was brought out as required and set up for Mass'[1]; towards the end of the second century there is a shifting of doctrinal emphasis, largely it would seem as an antidote to gnosticism, and greater stress is laid on the idea of sacrifice, of offering and blessing: the very word 'Mass' reminds us of this, for 'in the speech-idiom of the ancient Church, *missa* meant the same as blessing', the dedication and blessing 'of human life and of the earthly world in which it is lived'[2]. The new emphasis affected both actions and words: in the third century the bringing of bread and wine and material gifts to the altar becomes the solemn offertory procession; in the fourth, petitions are introduced into the Great Prayer, the thanksgiving-

[1] Cf. Jungmann: *The Eucharistic Prayer*, p. 23.   [2] Jungmann: *The Sacrifice of the Church*, p. 40.

prayer, itself, and the name *eucharistia* tends to be more and more restricted to the sacrament, the communion, while the sacred action is called rather the *oblatio* or *sacrificium*; at the same time the altar becomes a 'massive structure belonging to the essentials of the church'[1]. With the Peace of the Church in 313 A.D. we enter the age of the great Roman basilicas, modelled it would seem on the plan of the imperial throne-room yet remaining simple and austere, their form 'ruled by strict laws, comparable to those of Gregorian chant'[2]; in England, the little Saxon country-churches have a sweet serenity, and the Norman abbeys and minsters a massive strength, which in their different ways preserve the same quality of simplicity. The Gothic cathedral is more complex; its soaring arches symbolize the upthrust of human aspiration and prayer but it is less obviously built for and about an altar at which clergy and people will offer their common sacrifice. The splendour of baroque is sometimes less sacred than profane; it is easy for eye and mind to be led not to but away from the altar. But it is in the nineteenth century, the 'age of imitations', that 'things become really bad': when, apart from a few noble exceptions, churches no longer express any clear, dominant idea, and when the 'forms of an earlier period', long since thrust aside and therefore no longer a vital idiom, are none the less brought back into use[3].

We have much to be thankful for in this respect today, when all over the world churches are being built in a vital, contemporary idiom, simple, functional, æsthetically austere in accordance with the temper of our times, and making use of the potentialities of modern materials and methods to give the Mass-house once again its full symbol-value. No doubt it was inevitable that when, some years ago in California, a church was built in the shape of a fish, it should be popularly referred to as the church of the holy mackerel (and no great harm in that): the fact remains that it may well have led catholics to inquire into the exact connection between fish and the faith, and perhaps to discover for the first time that it was

[1] Jungmann: *The Eucharistic Prayer*, p. 23.   [2] *op. cit.* p. 45.   [3] *op. cit.* p. 46.

something deeper than a question of Friday dieting; it is good that the vast new underground church at Lourdes has been constructed in the same shape.

The Mass-house should be the creed translated into imagery[1]. Through stone or concrete, through wood and glass, painting and sculpture and fabric, it should tell us of how we are to find life through being re-formed, in and with Christ, into the image of God. To offer our sacrifice we have to go, like Abraham, to the mountain of vision: we must climb up steps to get to the church. So, at the beginning of the Great Prayer or Canon of the Mass, the priest will cry *Sursum corda*, 'Lift up your hearts!', and we may compare too St Paul's admonition, 'Seek the things that are above'[2]. But once up the steps we are not immediately within the church: we find ourselves in the atrium or fore-court, cut off indeed from the 'world' in the Gospel sense but not yet children of the Sun, not yet able to walk carefree into the dazzling light of the mountain-top: we come of a stock and live in a world which are twisted by sin; we must first follow Christ in his dark journey and go down with him into his death, go down into the baptistery: only then, when we are reborn, can we be led up, clothed in white, into the church itself, into the radiance of the Sun.[3] But once there we can stand erect, looking up to the altar, to the east, the sunrise, the *Sol Oriens*: with pride and confidence, not in any strength of ours, but in his: *gloriamur in Deo*, 'we may hold our heads high in the light of God's love because of the reconciliation which Christ has made'[4]; and in thus looking up to the Sun—*Levavi oculos meos*: 'I lift up my eyes to the hills'[5]—we also look forward to the august moment when Christ, through his priest, *elevatis oculis in*

---

[1] The symbols used in the Church's daily life are discussed in detail in *The Water and the Fire*, ch. vi.   [2] *Col.* iii, 1 (Douai).   [3] Most of us do not retain the 'newness of life' which baptism brings to us; we fall again into sin, and so again need renewal; and through God's mercy we find it in the sacrament of repentance, which thus corresponds closely to baptism. It would be a good thing to emphasize this correspondence by building the confessionals in a part of the church opposite, and similar in design to, the baptistery. And if the holy-water stoups at the entrance to the church were of similar design to the font, this would help further to unify in our minds the various ways in which the mystery of the life-giving waters is brought to us.   [4] *Romans*, v, 11; tr. Phillips: *Letters to Young Churches*.   [5] *Ps.* cxx, 1 (Knox).

cælum, raising his eyes to heaven, blesses bread and says ' This is my body ': the supreme moment of the Mass.

The church is built for the Mass. Therefore whatever its shape —whether circular, cruciform, octagonal or anything else—it must be so designed as to make the altar its focal point. And the altar is both communion-table and sacrificial stone, and must be so made as to bring out that dual function. There is no excuse for the kind of altar in which table and stone and all that is done on them are lost sight of in a nightmare riot of spires and niches, of gradines and crocketed ogives and buttresses; on the altar itself it is the cross, flanked by its candles, that must draw the eye, for it is the mystery of the Cross that we are to celebrate—and a mystery is not something which ought to be veiled, but something which, being of its nature essentially veiled, must be made manifest in its outward forms, its symbols. If then there is a rood-screen it should not obscure the altar; if there are choir-stalls they should not have the effect of turning the sanctuary into a lengthy tunnel at the end of which the altar can but dimly be descried. And in the church as a whole, while it is proper to have chapels, statues, shrines, they must never be allowed to break up the unity of the building or distract from its one essential purpose.

But to say that a church should be functional is not to say that it should be stark, unfriendly: on the contrary, the fact that the altar is the communion-table means that the church should be homely and welcoming. (The trouble starts when church-builders confuse the homely with the pretty or even the ' fussy ': a mid-Victorian boudoir is not everyone's idea of home; more important, we must not forget the ambivalence of the symbol and, in our concern for homeliness, lose sight of sublimity, of the fact that this is ' the house of God and gate of heaven '. Nor should simplicity be confused with penury, still less with squalor: it is our duty to make God's house beautiful as well as homely, and it is a sound as well as lovely instinct which makes the poor anxious to embellish their churches, even to make them magnificent, despite the poverty of their own homes and lives, for they know that, as a Russian writer expressed it, a house is ' but a night lodging of a pilgrim ' whereas the church is ' the reflection of eternal life and bliss ' [1], and that the making of beauty in our churches is one of the ways in which we can fulfil the supreme purpose of our lives, the giving of glory to God.

' Lord, I have loved the beauty of thy house ': in the last resort, it is true, it does not matter whether a church and its furnishings, and the prayers that are said or sung in it, are beautiful or ugly provided that people worship and pray; but it remains true that we have a duty to make these things, as also our cities, our villages, our countrysides, our customs, our songs, as beautiful as we can, that they may lead us to God and not away from him. ' St Francis preached to the flowers, and ordered a plot to be set aside for their cultivation when the convent garden was made, " in order that all who saw them might remember the Eternal Sweetness ". So, too, we are told of his spiritual daughter, St Douceline, that " out of doors one day with her sisters, she heard a bird's note. ' What a lovely song! ' she said: and the song drew her straightway to God. Did they bring her a flower, its beauty had a like effect." " To look on trees, water, and flowers," says St Teresa of her own beginnings of contemplation, " helped her to recollect the presence of God ". Here we are reminded of Plato. " The true order of going is to use the beauties of earth as steps along which one mounts upwards for the sake of that other beauty." This, too, is the true order of holy poverty: the selfless use, not the selfish abuse of lovely and natural things.' [2]

So we approach the Canon, the essence of the Mass, in a spirit of joy and selflessness and wonder: ' Lift up your hearts ': there is poetry in morals, as in the ' wind that bloweth where it listeth ', the Gifts of the holy Spirit as opposed to the virtues; there is poetry in doctrine, when the formularies and texts and catechisms are replaced or supplemented by the vital experience of a real world,

---

[1] Gorodetzky: *The Humiliated Christ in Modern Russian Thought*, p. 96 ; quoted in *The Water and the Fire*, p. 158, n.   [2] Evelyn Underhill: *Mysticism*, pp. 215-16.

of the place where the glory dwells; there is poetry in worship, in the giving of thanks, in the giving of praise, as now in the *Sanctus*, and you think of the mounting torrent of praise that is contained in the *Sanctus* of the *B Minor Mass*: this is worship, this is honour, this is glory, this is the *sacrificium laudis*, the sacrifice of praise.

6

The Canon: Preface to Consecration

PRÆFATIO

*Holy, holy, holy, Lord God of hosts; heaven and
earth are full of thy glory. Hosanna in the highest.
Blessed is he that cometh in the name of the Lord.
Hosanna in the highest.*

THE CANON of the Mass should be seen as a single prayer, divided
into thirteen parts and arranged with the Roman love of symmetry.
It begins with the Preface, with its exultant *Sursum corda*, Lift up
your hearts, and *Gratias agamus*, Let us give thanks to the Lord our
God, and its *Sanctus*, the pæan of praise quoted above. The word
' preface ' is the usual translation of *præfatio* and it is therefore used
here; but it must be pointed out that, as Fr Jungmann remarks, it
is ' to say the least a misleading translation ', suggesting as it does
the idea of a foreword or introduction. ' *Præfatio* means a " speech
before something ". But that " before " must not be understood
as referring to time, but to space; as prayer and speech before God
and before the community of the faithful.' [1] In early times the
word seems to have been used to designate the entire Canon or
Eucharistic Prayer. [2] The fact that in the missal as it is printed
nowadays the Canon appears to begin with the *Te igitur* prayer is

---

[1] *op. cit.* p. 8. [2] Cf. Jungmann: *Missarum Sollemnia*, t. iii, p. 12. The author also
gives here (p. 12, n. 37) some examples of the classical use of *præfari* in the above sense—
Vergil's *præfari divos*, Ovid's *præfari Vestam*—and points out that in Suetonius *præfatio* means
precisely ' the prayer accompanying a sacrifice '.

due to an historical accident. In the days before printing was invented, the monks transcribing the missal in their scriptorium took to illuminating the initial letter of the first word of the prayers; the capital T of the *Te igitur* obviously suggested a crucifixion; and as time went by this grew and grew in size until finally it came to occupy a whole page, as in the modern missal, and the Preface was thus elbowed out of the Canon. The modern missal is also misleading inasmuch as it goes on printing *Canon Missæ* at the head of the pages to the very end of the ordinary of the Mass; whereas in fact the Canon ends with the doxology preceding the *Our Father*; [1] what follows is the communion or Sacrifice-Banquet. The Preface is itself a doxology ('Holy, holy, holy, Lord God of hosts') so that when it is restored to its place as part of the Canon the symmetry is clear: you have a doxology, three prayers of remembrance (of the Church, of the living who are specially to be prayed for, and of the saints), then two prayers of offering, and then the central point, the consecration; thereafter there follow two other prayers of offering, three remembrances (of the dead, of the priest and ministers themselves, of all Nature) and then finally there is the Great Doxology: 'By him and with him and in him is to thee, God the Father Almighty, in the unity of the holy Spirit, all honour and glory for ever and ever, Amen'.

We do not know who wrote this Canon or Great Prayer, which goes back some fifteen hundred years. 'The form at present in use', says Duchesne, 'existed already, word for word, at the beginning of the seventh century.' He notes that St Gregory gave to it its final touch, adding to the prayer *Hanc igitur* the words 'dispose our days in thy peace, and bid us to be delivered from eternal damnation and numbered among the flock of thine elect'—the clause praying for temporal peace being, he thinks, possibly occasioned by 'the incessant troubles brought about by the Lombardic invasion'. But, he goes on, the 'author of the *Liber Pontificalis*, which dates from the beginning of the sixth cen-

---

[1] It is absurd to print the *Per omnia saecula saeculorum, Amen*, which concludes the doxology, and therefore the whole Canon, as though it were the beginning of the *Our Father* (cf. *supra* p. 136).

tury, speaks of the Canon as fixed in form, and of known content. He implies also that it had been a long time in existence, for he relates that St Leo (440–461) had added some words to it'. These words are 'a holy sacrifice, a spotless host', phrases which qualify the sacrifice of Melchizedech of which mention is made in the *Supra quæ*: Duchesne thinks that St Leo 'must have intended to introduce by them a protest against the Manicheans who did not allow the use of wine in their liturgy'. Further, the prayer itself can be shown conclusively to have existed in the time of Pope Damasus (d. A.D. 364).[1] Whoever the author was he had a great love of doubling or trebling his nouns and verbs—and it is not empty rhetoric. The second prayer, the *Te igitur*, offers some striking examples of this.

[1] Duchesne: *Christian Worship*, pp. 176–7.

We therefore humbly pray and beseech thee, merciful Father, that thou wouldst deign to accept and bless these gifts, these offerings, these holy, unspotted sacrifices, which in the first place we offer thee for thy holy catholic Church: deign to grant her peace, to protect, unite and govern her throughout the whole world, together with thy servant our Pope, and our bishop, and all orthodox believers and worshippers of the catholic and apostolic faith.

First, we pray and beseech: the second verb intensifies the first and gives the whole prayer a note of urgency it would otherwise lack. Then, we beg God to accept and bless: these verbs give us first of all the pattern of sacrifice we have already studied, the ' offering of a thing that it may be sanctified ' of St Augustine's definition, the victim offered, accepted, divinized; but we might also, here, apply the words to ourselves, for we too have to accept and bless: to accept ourselves as we are, to accept God's will for us, and to bless his name. Humility is truth, is accepting the facts as they are, neither exaggerating nor minimizing. The angel of the Lord came to Mary and told her of her destiny and her glory; and she said first, ' Behold the handmaid, the chattel, of the Lord ', and then later, the greatest boast in human history, ' Behold from henceforth all generations shall call me blessed '—but it was not in reality a boast at all for she was simply stating a fact; and, combining as it were the two sentences, she goes on: ' He that is mighty hath done great things in me, and holy is his name '. She accepts and blesses.

Next the prayer speaks of gifts, offerings, sacrifices: *dona, munera, sacrificia.* Fr Lucas, S.J.. in his book on the Mass suggested that the unconsecrated bread and wine are called *dona* inasmuch as they are God's gifts to us, but *munera* because they are ' still ours to give back to him '; whereas the *Unde et memores* prayer after the consecration speaks of *dona* and *data*, God's gifts and presents to us: ' they are ours indeed, and they are offered once more; but they are no longer ours in the same sense . . . they are no longer in the nature of personal property which might have been otherwise disposed of. They have passed out of our control; in the very act and moment of consecration they have been offered to the eternal Father by our great High Priest, Jesus Christ; and all that we can now do is to unite our intention with his self-offering '[1]. Fr Jungmann sees in the three words an ascending gradation of meaning: *dona* are ' presents ' in the ordinary colloquial sense; *munera* are rather an official ' presentation ' (*munus* being the equivalent of the Greek *leitourgia*, liturgy, a public office or duty whether sacred or profane); *sacrificia* are *holy* gifts or offerings, i.e. consecrated to God.[2]

We all have some gifts, some talents. We are not to pretend they are greater than they are, nor are we to minimize them: we are to use and develop them as best we can; on the other hand we have to accept our limitations, we have to accept and love ourselves as we are, even our ' dark shadow ' (but to love the dark shadow is not to approve of it), and bless the name of the Lord. The temptation is to pretend—to other people, to ourselves—that things are different. In the breviary office for the feast of St Joseph there are readings from *Genesis* about the patriarch Joseph, and at first sight one wonders why, for the two men seem to have nothing in common but their name. The Old Testament Joseph is a glamorous figure: he is ' of a beautiful countenance, and comely to behold ', he wears a ' coat of divers colours ', and we are told that to catch a glimpse of him the maidens ' run to and fro upon the city walls '[3]. His dreams are dreams of greatness, and they are fulfilled: he

---

[1] H. Lucas, S.J.: *Holy Mass*, vol. II, pp. 37-8. [2] Cf. *Missarum Sollemnia*, t. iii, p. 62.
[3] Perhaps the earliest recorded instance of the mass-hysteria of bobby-soxers. Cf. *Gen.* xxxiv, 6; xxxvii, 3; xlix, 22.

becomes second only to Pharaoh in the land of Egypt; and his brothers must do him homage.

St Joseph on the other hand has none of this *panache*: he is the most homely of saints: he is a humble village carpenter; in paintings of the holy family he is usually portrayed wearing rather dun clothes; his dreams are severely practical. But dreams he does have, like his Old Testament predecessor; and it is a commonplace nowadays to say that in dreams we meet our real selves, every mask, every *persona*, stripped away; if St Joseph is the most homely of saints he is also the most ' real ', the most unaffected, the most humble. His is not the glory of Mary his wife; he has a function to perform, a job to do, while the Child is young, and thereafter he fades out of the picture: we do not even know when or where he died.

There is a great deal of misunderstanding about our Lord's injunction, ' Be ye perfect ': it means making the best possible use of the gifts and graces given you, but your graces are not those of a St Paul, a St Francis, a St Teresa of Avila. It is foolish to be discouraged because you cannot pray like St Teresa if you have not been given the graces of St Teresa: be humble, accept and bless, and say your rosary and all will be well. ' Be not solicitous ', our Lord said, and it applies here as elsewhere: do your best, try hard, struggle, but do not fret: your heavenly Father has care of you, and he knows your limitations, he does not expect of you more than you can give. Do you want to be a great poet or painter or actor or philosopher, and then find that you cannot? Never mind; accept and bless: it is more important to be a great person. Do you want to be a great mystic, and find that you cannot? Never mind, it is more important to be a great person. And to be humble, to accept and bless, will make you a great person in the end; so that in the end, however humble and humdrum your life in the world, you will be able to say with the greatest of all human creatures, ' He that is mighty hath done great things in me, and holy is his name '.

Be mindful, O Lord, of thy servants and handmaids,
N. and N., and of all here present whose faith and
devotion are known to thee: for whom we offer, or
who offer up to thee, this sacrifice of praise for them-
selves and theirs; for the redemption of their souls,
for the hope of their safety and salvation, and who
pay their vows to thee, the eternal, living and true
God.

The *Te igitur* evokes for us in its lapidary phrases a picture of the
grand hierarchical structure of the Church; and then immediately,
in the first *Memento*, we are recalled to the homely duty of praying
for those who are dear to us, our relatives and friends, the people
who have asked our prayers. There is the same pattern in the story
of our Lady, who immediately after the immensities of the angel's
coming went with eagerness to visit her cousin Elizabeth, to help
her with the housework until the coming of the baby. So we are
reminded of the importance of the homely, human duties, the
importance of family life, the importance of thinking of the Church
as a family. For a family is something that has to be *made*, by the
painful efforts of those who compose it. People who want to
vilify the Church will talk of the scandals of medieval monasteries,
of the priests' concubinage, and so forth: they do not know the
real scandal, which is the appalling lack of charity, and indeed of
just ordinary human kindness, to be met with among catholics.
'By this shall men know that you are my disciples, that you have
love one for another': but no, X will have an illegitimate baby,
Y will drift away and marry in the registry office, Z will become a
catholic and in fear and trembling come to his or her first Mass

and there find no understanding, no sympathy, no welcome;[1] those who have put the wrong foot forward must be ostracized, the new recruits must learn for themselves, and charity is to be interpreted, not as covering a multitude of sins, but as a substitute for ordinary human decency. 'I love him in the Lord': how often that means in effect, I can't stand the sight of him, and I act accordingly.

Aristotle tells us that one of the 'civic virtues' is affability: being able to live 'pleasantly' with other people: to listen kindly when they talk, to talk oneself with a gay face, to exhibit to all the 'signs of urbanity'; and St Thomas repeats all this, but for him this civic virtue has to be coloured, has to be ensouled, by charity. For Aristotle, the affable man acts as he does, not because of some quality in the people with whom he is dealing, but because of a quality in himself: he could not be other than courteous; he is in fact the 'aristotelean gentleman'. But courtesy in that sense could be compatible with a profound if hidden scorn and superciliousness. The affability which is ensouled by charity is very different. For St Thomas, charity comprises three elements: there must be first a real willing of the good of one's neighbour; then this good-willing must be mutual, which means not only that the other person must reciprocate my goodwill but that I must be humble in receiving help as well as generous in giving it: finally, there must be *communicatio*, a really personal communication, interest, sharing of ideas, ideals, interests, joys, sorrows. Only if our affability or courtesy has all that behind it will it help to build up a family life within the Church. It is true that nowadays the dice are loaded against us in this respect: the impersonality of the modern bureaucratic State and the modern industrial city make it easy for us to assume that it is quite natural not even to know who one's next door neighbour is; and it is difficult to think of a vast modern parish, numbering thousands of souls, as a family. Yet in fact the whole Church is a family; and the *Memento* reminds us of it. In olden times this prayer and the corresponding *Memento* of the dead

<hr/>

[1] Cf. Lucille Hasley: *Reproachfully Yours.*

after the Consecration were called the 'diptychs' because at these points the names of those to be specially prayed for were read out by the deacon from writing-tablets, the word 'diptych' meaning literally a two-leafed, hinged tablet; the diptych of the living would include the names of the Pope, bishops, illustrious members of clergy and laity, benefactors, etc.; the diptych of the dead would follow similar lines. The fact that these diptychs were read out by the deacon explains why, in the Canon as it now stands, they are as it were parenthetical—thus, grammatically, the *Communicantes* follows on from the *Te igitur* which supplies its grammatical subject.

The custom of reading out these diptychs was abolished, it would seem, because of abuses which had crept in through them: thus St Jerome complains bitterly that deacons 'curried favour with the rich by not only reading their names, but proclaiming the amount of their offerings'—*tantum offert illa, tantum ille pollicitus est; placentque sibi ad plausum populi.*[1]

Nowadays this reading out of names has become part of the 'notices' read from the pulpit after the Gospel, so that the appeal for prayers has been wrenched out of its context in the structure of the Mass, but at least we can recall the people then mentioned when we come to each *Memento*. For though the names may mean nothing to us, still we are all members of the same Body, and John X and Mary Y, though we have never heard of them before, have a claim on us because they are our relatives: we all belong to the same family. In some ancient missals the *Memento* begins with a prayer for the priest himself, that God may have mercy on him, who is 'not worthy to invoke thy name; but since these offerings are brought before thee in honour, praise and memory of thy glorious Son, Jesus Christ our Lord, make them to ascend as a sweet-smelling incense into the presence of thy divine majesty'; other MSS have special reference to those who have given alms to the Church; a Palatine missal in the Vatican library begins the prayer thus: 'Be mindful of me, Lord, a miserable and infamous

[1] Cf. Lucas: *op. cit.* vol. ii, p. 28.

sinner, in your eternal life, and of all those from whom I have received alms, those who have confessed their sins to me, those whose hand I have clasped as a pledge of affection, those who are bound to me by the bonds of friendship or of blood, and all those who, having enmity towards me, may yet experience a change of heart '[1].

' By this shall men know that ye are my disciples, that ye have love one for another.' Certainly one of the most important forms of apostolic work, if not quite simply the most important, is this christian friendliness motivated by charity: a going out into the highways and hedges and compelling the lost and the lonely to come into the banquet that the table may be filled. If one were asked, Who are the outstanding apostles of our times? would not one think first of an Abbé Pierre, a Padre Borelli?

People sometimes ask, Is it a sin to dislike someone? The immediate answer is, of course, no: you cannot help being attracted by some people and repelled by others, though there is sin if you take no pains to control your dislike but on the contrary give full expression to it. On the other hand it seems to be true that on a long-term policy, given sufficient charity, dislike can be conquered. Baron von Hügel said that a father will kiss his little son because he loves him, but that he also kisses him in order that he may love him more. Go out of your way to be kind to the people you dislike, to do them small services, and in the end you may discover you have grown fond of them; charity will have turned affability into something more than a superficial, external courtesy.

Memento: ' in the end we shall be judged on love ': your path crosses that of X or Y, perhaps just for a few moments; and perhaps, for all you know, they are in an abyss of loneliness, perhaps near to despair: if you pass by, like the priest and the levite in the parable, you are no christian; but if, like the good Samaritan, you lovingly show them the ' signs of urbanity ', then indeed you are fulfilling the command of our Lord, and surely your charity will cover a multitude of sins.

[1] Cf. Cardinal Bona: *De la Liturgie*, (tr. Lobry, Paris, 1874) tome II, p. 195.

In communion with and venerating first the memory of the glorious Mary, ever a virgin, mother of our God and Lord, Jesus Christ; and then of thy blessed apostles and martyrs, Peter and Paul, Andrew, James, John, Thomas, James, Philip, Bartholomew, Matthew, Simon and Thaddeus, Linus, Cletus, Clement, Xystus, Cornelius, Cyprian, Laurence, Chrysogonus, John and Paul, Cosmas and Damian, and of all thy saints: by whose prayers grant that we may be defended in all things by thy protecting help, through the same Christ our Lord, Amen.

Here we have a cross-section of the christian family, in this reminder of the communion of saints; and again with the typical Roman love of symmetry: twelve apostles and twelve martyrs with our Lady at their head; [1] five Popes and five laymen; men of all sorts, of different races, traditions, temperaments. As Cardinal Bona points out, there is no mention here of any saints other than martyrs: either because the martyrs recall most vividly the Passion and death of our Lord, or because the Canon was composed before the custom was introduced (in the fourth century) of commemorating the confessor-saints. [2] And if one asks why the prayer mentions SS. Linus, Cletus, Clement and the rest rather than other martyrs, the answer would seem to be that these suffered martyrdom in Rome or in places immediately subject to the patriarchate of Rome. But in that case how do Cosmas and Damian come into the list?

[1] The later list of saints, in the *Nobis quoque*, balances this with another symbolic number repeated: seven martyrs of each sex, headed by the Baptist; cf. *infra*, p. 249. [2] It is perhaps for this reason that SS. Luke and Mark are not mentioned in the Canon, since it is not certain that they suffered martyrdom. (Cf. Bona, *op. cit.* p. 204.)

For they were Arabs, who lived and were put to death in Cilicia. In fact there appear to have been three pairs of brothers of the same names: the second pair lived in Asia, the third pair were martyred in Rome. Bona points out that this last pair of brothers were like the first in being doctors and in giving their services free of charge and so meriting the nickname *Anargyri*; and he suggests that the *Acts* of the Roman brothers were lost and those of the Arabs, whose martyrdom was more famous, substituted.[1]

In this list of saints we can all find a patron. There is Peter, impulsive, cowardly, worldly (' Get thee behind me, Satan '), denying his Master but then weeping bitterly and becoming the Rock; there is Paul, so different in temperament, persecuting the Church but then setting the world aflame with the fire of his charity; there is Thomas the sceptic, who will believe only in the palpable; there is James the Less who, as we have seen, was made bishop of Jerusalem mainly, it would seem, because he was the cousin of the Lord, and who is therefore a fit patron for those who find themselves saddled with responsibilities for which they feel inadequate. Simon had been a Zealot: a member of a sect of fanatics ready to use evil means to achieve a patriotic end. These are Jews; but Chrysogonus and Xystus were Greeks; Cosmas and Damian were born in Arabia, Laurence in Spain. Cyprian was a bishop, Laurence a deacon, legend makes John and Paul officials at the imperial court, Cosmas and Damian were doctors.

In the traditional legend, St Laurence, on his gridiron, remarked that he thought one side was now nicely done and that it was time to turn him over. He is far from being unique in that respect: St Thomas More, for instance, similarly joked on the scaffold. What is it that gives the martyrs this fortitude that can express itself in laughter in the midst of torture? One can only suppose that the sense of God's nearness is so vivid to them that physical torture as it were passes them by; but this brings us back to the whole question of the relationship between willing and feeling, for there are presumably martyrs—and one thinks for

[1] Bona, *op. cit.* pp. 202–4.

instance of *The Power and the Glory*—who emotionally are far from welcoming their fate. How much do feelings matter?

The ultimate answer seems to be that feelings do not matter at all: that the essential thing is to do the will of God, regardless of how we feel. But it is not so simple as that, for feelings in fact play a large part in our lives and to a great extent motivate our actions. Unfortunately, we can easily be unaware of our true motives; we rationalize; we persuade ourselves, let us say, that we are acting from a high sense of justice whereas in reality we are pandering to a lust for power. Feelings can be very valuable in so far as they minister to mind and will; they can be lethal when they take over the control of the personality. In education, a child will make great strides in a subject and with a teacher he finds attractive; he will make very little progress in a subject which bores him or with a teacher whom he views with dislike or resentment. So in religion, if for instance God makes prayer emotionally rewarding it is presumably to help us to form a habit of prayer; almost certainly the day will come when it will cease to be a thing of joy and become instead a grinding labour: that does not mean that it has ceased to have value; on the contrary, it probably means that God is asking us to show him that we pray because we love him, not because we love the joy we found in praying. One sometimes comes across the idea, among catholics, that a thing is good in proportion to its unpleasantness; but this is simply not true. To possess a virtue means that acts of that virtue will be 'connatural' to one and therefore congenial. The christian idea of moral behaviour is not duty for duty's sake but St Paul's 'loving what is good': not just loving one or two forms of goodness but loving goodness in itself and therefore having a connaturality with goodness.

We have to avoid living on our emotions; but on the other hand we have to avoid the false and dangerous practice of smothering the emotions lest they lead us astray. We cannot live in an emotional vacuum. It is like our Lord's story of the seven devils: if, playing as we think for safety, we drive out love-feelings and see to it that our hearts are neatly swept and garnished, we shall find other, less attractive, things coming in instead—envy, jealousy, bitterness, perhaps hatred. The christian ideal is not 'emotional detachment': our Lord did not say, Blessed are the detached, he said, Blessed are the poor in spirit, the people who can love without greed, without possessiveness, without being predatory; the christian ideal is emotional attachment, but an attachment which is guided and governed by the spirit, not allowed to dominate or to run loose.

If then we find that prayer, the service of God, the practice of virtue are rewarding, we must thank God for it. But if the joy in these things is taken from us, we must not for a moment think that it means a decline in fervour. It is good to do the thing that God asks of us when the thing in fact brings us joy; it is a much greater gift to him to do his will when on the contrary it is costing and perhaps repellent.

But we do well to give our emotional life an occasional overhaul, a spring-cleaning; and to try to see clearly just what drives are in fact motivating our conduct. It is important to understand our changes of mood, and to be able to cope with them. The temptation is to let our moods dominate us: we feel gay, and so we think all our difficulties are over for ever; we feel pious, and so we think we are ready forthwith for the stigmata; we feel glum, and all is lost in this world and the next. Feelings can after all be controlled: if we feel sad we need not wallow in self-pity, we need not inflict our sadness on other people, we need not whine, we can try to cheer ourselves up by doing something cheerful.

We come back to the essential point: in the service of God feelings are of importance, but only of secondary importance. They are not the criterion of success or failure. Fervour does not mean feeling zealous; love of God's will does not mean an emotional enthusiasm for it; conscience does not mean feeling that this or that is right or wrong; and the test of whether or not we have chosen the right vocation is not whether we always feel happy in it. It is possible to grow up intellectually in the faith while remaining emotionally at an infantile level; and that always leads to trouble. It is worth our while to examine with a clear eye our emotional drives, and to judge them in the light of reason and not be dominated by them; it is well to remember that holiness consists in ' willing at each moment '—willing, not feeling an urge for— ' what comes to us by God's order '.

HANC IGITUR

We therefore beseech thee, Lord, favourably to accept this offering of our service and that of all thy family, and to dispose our days in thy peace, to deliver us from eternal damnation and to cause us to be numbered among the flock of thy elect.

The Church is here referred to as family and as flock: we have already considered it under the first aspect; let us here consider it under the second. There is a sudden roughening of tone in this prayer—'deliver us from eternal damnation'—which dates from times not unlike our own: Rome a prey to floods, famines and plague, and threatened from without by the barbarian hordes. When troubles come upon us and seem to threaten to overwhelm us it is good to think of the good Shepherd: 'The Lord is my Shepherd and I shall want for nothing. He hath set me in a place of pasture; he hath brought me to the waters of refreshment. Though I should walk in the midst of the shadow of death I will fear no evils, for thou art with me, and thy rod [for my defence] and thy staff [for my guidance] have comforted me '[1].

For three thousand years men have found comfort in this psalm and steadied their souls in the praying of it in times of tribulation. Christianity is a religion of joy not because it ignores the sorrows of the world or escapes from them but because it teaches us that sorrow can be turned into joy, that light comes out of darkness and life out of death, and that at the end, after all the struggle, there is the tranquillity of the Sea Pacific. 'Dispose our days in thy peace': that peace which the world cannot give, and cannot take away. But if that inner peace is a gift of God for which we can only pray, the 'bond of peace' which should unite the flock of Christ is some-

[1] *Ps.* xxii, 1-5 (adapted from Douai).

thing we have to strive to create, and which we can all too easily destroy or harm. ' Six things there are which the Lord hateth, and the seventh his soul detesteth: haughty eyes, a lying tongue, hands that shed innocent blood, a heart that deviseth wicked plots, feet that are swift to run upon a mischievous errand, a deceitful witness that uttereth lies, and him that soweth discord among brethren.' [1]

We were thinking just now of unconscious emotional motivations: how relevant they are here, how easily they can lead us to destroy the bond of peace! The obvious things we can deal with more easily, given a little good will, because they are obvious: the quarrels, the fightings, the spiteful talk, the deliberate malice. But in so many ways we can make life a burden to others and destroy their peace without meaning to and without being aware of the fact.

One of these ways is the magnification of the trivial: we are most of us egoists, and so, perhaps quite unconsciously, we tend to magnify what concerns us and to belittle what concerns other people. *My* work is the important thing, and everybody else must adjust his life to its demands; *my* woes are on the scale of Greek tragedy, whereas those of others are negligible; *my* rights and dignities have to be preserved at all costs; a little emotional set-back becomes a world-shaking crisis; and the shortcomings of others become an obsession, a personal affront. Self-pity is a destroying canker: 'Nobody understands me'; 'Poor Mrs X: she enjoys very poor health'; 'Mrs Y is so resigned'—and her too audible resignation is a millstone around the necks of all who have to deal with her.

A retreat from reality into that emotional vacuum we were considering just now can also destroy, at least negatively, the bond of peace: we need to establish healthy emotional relationships with others; we need, if we are to be 'peaceful' people, to have good emotional outlets, creative work, a real interest in others (not inquisitiveness, but that *benevolentia* which is the first of the

---

[1] *Prov.* vi, 16–19 (adapted from Douai).

three elements in St Thomas's definition of charity); we need to find good outlets for instincts which otherwise would be destructive, as for instance the aggressive instinct must be directed to what St Thomas would call *ardua*: climbing Mt Everest, whether literally or metaphorically, is the best way of avoiding riding roughshod over other personalities.

Finally, the bond of peace has to be the criterion where the tongue is concerned: there may come to one's mind the wittiest remark that has ever been made since the days of Petronius, but it will be a legitimate source of deep hurt or grievance to X or Y: are we to hurt them or are we to rob posterity of this jewel of wit? The answer may well be, alas, that posterity must suffer. . . .

For most people life is fraught with difficulties and burdened with sorrows: our concern must be, at whatever cost, to help with the difficulties and lighten the sorrows. 'By this shall men know that ye are my disciples, that ye have love one for another': the test of whether we can say that we are living in the spirit of this prayer is whether we can say sincerely and truly, Lord I have loved the beauty of thy house and the place where thy flock dwelleth.

*Which oblation, we beseech thee, O God, deign to
make blessed, enrolled, established, reasonable and
acceptable, that it may become for us the body and
blood of thy beloved Son, our Lord Jesus Christ.*

It has been suggested that this prayer corresponds, in the Latin Rite,
to the *Epiclesis* in the Greek Rite: the calling upon the holy Spirit
to quicken, to transform, the offerings, to turn the bread and wine
into God.[1]

The five Latin participles in the prayer, *benedictam, adscriptam,
ratam, rationabilem, acceptabilem*, are not easy to translate adequately.
Paschasius Radbertus explains them thus: We beg, he says, that
this offering be blessed, since it is through it that we are to be
blessed; that it be accepted, since through it we are all to be accepted
into heaven; that it be ratified (or authentically established), since
through it we are to be made one with, incorporated into, our Lord
Jesus Christ; that it be reasonable or rational, since through it we
are to be delivered from all that is brutish and carnal in us; and that
it be acceptable, since through it we, in whom there is so much
that is displeasing to God, may become acceptable to him in his
only-begotten Son.[2] There has been a great deal of discussion in
particular about the word *rationabilis*.[3] In the Vulgate, *rationabile*
corresponds to the Greek *logikon*, endowed with spirit; an *oblatio
rationabilis* would thus mean a spiritual, non-material sacrifice: so
the word is used, in the Canon as cited by St Ambrose, with *im-
maculata* and *incruenta* in a prayer after the consecration: the sacrifice,
the *hostia*, is the same as that of the Cross but without the physical
bloodshed, the cruelties and crudities, of Calvary: and therefore

---

[1] Cf. *e.g.* Jungmann: *Missarum Sollemnia*, t. iii, pp. 106, *sqq.*   [2] Cf. Bona, *op. cit.* pp.
208-9.   [3] Cf. Jungmann: *Missarum Sollemnia*, t. iii, pp. 104 *sqq.*

spotless, unbloody, 'spiritualized', *au delà du sang et des souillures terrestres.*[1] By the time of Gregory the Great the meaning of the word had become attenuated: it signified now simply what was 'correct', conformed to reason and good order; and so, in the prayer as we now have it, it seems to share in the juridical tone of the other four words which go with it. Fr Jungmann, it is true, has come to adopt the view that, as 'words in sacred speech often retain their older meaning' though in everyday speech that meaning has changed, [2] we should give the word *rationabilis* in this prayer its original value. However, the five words taken together certainly have a legal, almost a legalistic, colour; as Fr Jungmann himself has pointed out, they contrast sharply with the tenderness of *dilectissimi*, 'thy well-beloved Son'; it is as though we are saying, We have done all the external things in due order, we have carried out the rubrics, more than this we cannot do; the altar is prepared: do you now send the Fire.

As we have already seen, we are fire-worshippers: the saints are portrayed with haloes, which are sun-symbols; the monstrance is fashioned in the shape of a sun with outgoing rays; it is as fire that God manifests his presence in the Old Testament, in the burning bush, the pillar of fire in the desert, the fire on Sinai, the fire in the visions of Ezechiel and Daniel. But are the fire and the law compatible? 'Through Moses the law was given to us; through Jesus Christ grace came to us, and truth.' [3] So St John; and St Paul in his turn talks of the 'bondage of the law'; yet, as we have seen, the law in the last resort is the *lex æterna*: the pattern, the rhythm, of the Godhead.

We must distinguish between the law and legalism. To love the law is, as the hundred and eighteenth psalm makes clear, to love God the lawgiver: the law is *cantabilis*, fit subject for song, it is 'good for me to be humbled so as to learn the law', 'all day long I meditate' the law; it makes me wiser than my masters, wiser than the old, it is what gives me life, what gives me peace.

---

[1] *ibid.* p. 105.   [2] Jungmann: *The Eucharistic Prayer*, p. 21; cf. also the third edition of *Missarum Sollemnia*.   [3] *John*, i. 17 (Knox).

For the law in this sense is not arbitary precept, something weighing down on us from without: the law *is* the fire, is the pattern, is the rhythm of the triune life, is the immortal laughter. Legalism is quite a different matter; legalism is the worship of the letter as against the spirit, as when the letter of some law will be clung to in defiance of a higher law (so people will accuse themselves in confession of missing Mass on a Sunday when, if they are questioned, it turns out that they could not possibly have gone to Mass as they were ministering to a dying mother or father); legalism means forgetting that ethics is not and cannot be an exact science, that the ultimate judgment, whether or not to do this or that, must be an intuitive, prudential judgment based not merely on the type of action involved but on the particular circumstances involved; legalism disregards the fact that law is general whereas the morality of actions is a question always of the particular; legalism ignores the existence of conflicts of duties in which the higher principle must take precedence over the lower; legalism forgets that, as St Augustine says in his *Rule*, we are to be ' not like slaves under the bondage of the law, but like children in the liberty of the grace of God '. The law is in fact the fire; it is for us to internalize what would otherwise be a burden pressing down on us from without: we may, as St Paul says, be free men in the sense of not being another man's slave and still be enslaved by sin; we may be free of that slavery and still be under the bondage of the law; the only way to escape that slavery is either to fall in love with the Lawgiver (for the lover it is no slavery to do the will of the beloved) or to fall in love with the law, to see it as fire, to see it as life, to see it as light, to see it as *cantabilis*, as order and beauty and the pattern of love.

This prayer makes us see how pitiful, and yet how rich, we are: we can do only the external things, the legal things, the rubrics: but we can call upon the Spirit to bring the fire, and bread and wine become God. We can but try to keep the commandments, to do the right things and avoid the wrong things: but we can call upon the Spirit to make us holy in spite of ourselves, to kindle within us the fire of divine love. It is for that that we pray here: for the grace to love the Will in all its forms, for the grace to receive the quickening and transforming fire, that the words of Ruysbroeck may be verified in us: 'Every soul is like a live coal, burned up by God on the heart of his infinite love'[1].

[1] *De Septem Gradibus Amoris, cap.* xiv. Cf. E. Underhill: *Mysticism,* p. 421.

7

The Canon: Consecration to 'Our Father'

Who the day before he suffered took bread into his holy and adorable hands; and with eyes lifted to thee, O God, his almighty Father, giving thanks to thee, did bless, break, and give to his disciples, saying: Take and eat ye all of this, for this is my body.

In like manner after he had supped, taking also this precious chalice into his holy and adorable hands, and giving thanks to thee, he blessed and gave to his disciples, saying: Take and drink ye all of this, for this is the chalice of my blood of the new and eternal testament, the mystery of faith, which shall be shed for you and for many unto the remission of sins.

THIS IS, it would seem, apart from later interpolations like 'the mystery of faith', the earliest written account of the Last Supper ritual;[1] and we might linger a little over that striking phrase, 'this precious chalice', as though the chalice the priest uses this day in A.D. 1958 were indeed the chalice used by our Lord twenty centuries ago. It underlines for us once again that the sacrifice of the Mass *is* the sacrifice of the Cross; there is only a modal difference. If now I sit and now I stand it is always the same I: there is a difference only in the mode of my existence. So it is here in the Mass:

[1] Cf. Jungmann: *Missarum Sollemnia*, t. iii, pp. 111 *sqq.*

we take part in the Passion, though the mode in which it is lived out is different from what it was on Calvary.

But we might think here of the chalice as the symbol of Christ's dereliction: ' My Father, if this chalice may not pass me by, but I must drink it, then thy will be done ' [1]. We are to suppose that our Lord was disappointed even as we are, though in his disappointments there was not the element of surprise that there is in ours. ' He came unto his own, and his own received him not ' [2]; the rich young man whom he loved went away from him because ' he had great possessions ' [3]; he was himself to say to his followers, ' one of you shall betray me ' [4]; Peter was to deny him; again and again the apostles would fail to understand him; at his trial the people who had acclaimed him would turn against him; and alone and in what looks like despair he would cry on the cross, ' My God, my God, why hast thou forsaken me ? ' [5] It is possible also to suppose that on the cross he experienced the bitterness of knowing that the agony he was suffering for men would be, for some men, in vain; had Satan in that respect for once spoken the truth when he urged him to take the easy way, promising that he could thus win the whole world to himself by an adequate display of power ?

Was our Lord's will always in conformity with that of his Father ? St Thomas answers, no: his sense-appetites could not but shrink from pain, his will in its natural instinctive workings could not but recoil from death; it was only in his rational, deliberate will that he chose the path of pain and of death: ' Not my will but thine be done '. We can apply all this to ourselves. What is ' conformity ' with the will of God ? It is not *wanting* to do what God

---

[1] *Matt.* xxvi, 42 (Knox).   [2] *John*, i, 11 (Douai).   [3] *Matt.* xix, 22 (Douai).   [4] *John*, xiii, 21 (Douai).   [5] *Matt.* xxvii, 46. But cf. Sir Edwyn Hoskins: *The Fourth Gospel*: ' It *is finished* (literally, *it has been completed*) announces the victory of the victim. The Christ has accomplished his mission, and the salvation of the world is attained. The word sums up the messianic interpretation of *Ps.* xxii applied to Jesus. The Psalm begins *My God, my God, why hast thou forsaken me?* and, after describing the sufferings of the man of God, breaks out into an almost eschatological cry of victory. . . . The Matthæan-Marcan word, *My God, my God, why hast thou forsaken me?* and the Johannine, *It is finished* have therefore the same significance; the former cites the first words of the psalm, and in so doing involves the whole; the latter sums up its meaning, and is less open to misunderstanding.' (p. 531).

asks of us, it is not *feeling* devout: it is not a question of saying 'Lord, Lord,' but of doing the will of the Father in *fact*. There are times when we know the *tædium vitæ*, a mood of melancholy descends on us, the demon of accidie preys on us: what are we to do? The answer is that we must take what natural means we can to alleviate our distress: if our sloth is due to bodily fatigue we need rest, we should go to bed; if it is due to mental stress we need relaxation, we should read a thriller. There are times when idleness is a duty, there are times when the most meritorious thing we can do is to play a game or watch the television or go to the play or the cinema. Traditionally, sloth is portrayed in two ways: there is the *monachus pigritans* and the *monachus vagans*: the monk who snoozes away the day, the monk who is never in his monastery. We need not take these categories too literally: if, in the time of prayer, the mind is deliberately or at least carelessly allowed to wander, the words floating by unassimilated, *vox et præterea nihil*, then there is sloth, there is the missing of an opportunity, there is accidie. But what are we to do? (For with sloth there is obviously a special difficulty: in dealing with any other vice one brings to bear on the difficulty such will-power as one may have; here it is precisely will-power which is lacking: one lacks the will to give oneself to the things which concern the service of God.) One answer seems to be that if sloth has turned one against the study of divine things it will obviously be stupid to try to plunge straight into the *Summa Theologica* or the works of St John of the Cross, but that one can begin in a humbler sort of way; one can for instance start by reading a novel which in fact is concerned with ultimates, and so perhaps begin almost unwittingly to revive one's interest in those ultimates.

The Church is not unacquainted with the slothful soul, nor lacking in hope for it. In one of the Sunday collects we pray that God will ' force our rebellious wills' into conformity with his own; it is like John Donne begging God to ' batter his heart': when we have no emotional urge whatsoever to do the will of God, when everything in us tugs us away from that will, then is the time to pray for that ' naked intent of the will' the old English mystic wrote of, for, once again, what matters is not what we feel but what we do: what matters is to get on with the job whatever it may be and see it through to the end: it is that which will make us worthy to be told in the end, ' Well done, my good and faithful servant; since thou hast been faithful over little things, I have great things to commit to thy charge; come and share the joy of thy Lord '.

One of the most terrible sentences in the Gospel story of the Passion
is the one with which St Matthew concludes his account of the
soldiers' behaviour at the crucifixion and which, short as it is, stands
by itself, a separate verse, as though to give it emphasis: ' After
they had crucified him they divided his garments, casting lots;
that it might be fulfilled which was spoken by the prophet, saying:
They divided my garments among them, and upon my vesture
they cast losts.

' And they sat and watched him.'[1]

There are different ways of watching torment and agonizing
death. Some torturers gloat over their victims because of the
sadistic pleasure the sight gives them; others, for the satisfaction of
pure cruelty (for cruelty, despite the journalistic *cliché*, is not necessarily sadistic); others again for the sake of savouring revenge or
hatred. We cannot exclude all such emotions from those who
watched on Calvary: there is a mysterious and haunting responsory
in the mattins for Good Friday[2] which tells of how enemies, ' with
terrible eyes have struck me a cruel wound, and given me vinegar
to drink '. And we are told of how high priests and scribes and
others mocked him, by word and gesture, as they passed.

But with the soldiers it is different: they were not emotionally
involved, they were inured to such spectacles, it was part of their
job to see the thing through to the end and so they watched, but
with indifference, perhaps boredom. Perhaps we are not wrong if
we think of them as continuing with their dicing to pass the time.
For indeed they knew not what they had done.[3] There is a poignant

---

[1] *Matt.* xxvii, 35-6 (Douai). [2] *Et terribilibus oculis plaga crudeli percutientes, aceto potabant
me* (Resp. I): this seems to be adapted from *Ps.* lxviii, 22 and *Job* xvi, 10, 15 (' My enemy
hath beheld me with terrible eyes. . . . He hath torn me with wound upon wound.').
[3] *Luke*, xxiii, 34 (Douai).

contrast here with Agar's cry: 'I cannot bear to see my child die '[1].

There is another, quite different, sort of watching: the sort which is a sympathy, a com-passion, the sort in which the three disciples failed in the Gethsemane garden: ' Could you not watch one hour with me? '; and 'he cometh again, and findeth them sleeping: for their eyes were heavy '[2].

The moral we are to draw, the questions we are to ask ourselves, are clear. Every day, all over the world, the Body is raised up at the altar of sacrifice: perhaps there are some who look on it, on ' him whom they pierced '[3], with hatred or scorn, with ' terrible eyes '; there are many who look on with indifference; there are many who do not look on at all, for their eyes are heavy; there are many others who look with adoration and love at the raised Host in the Mass and who watch before the blessed Sacrament when it is placed in a side-chapel on Maundy Thursday or when at other times during the year it is shown forth in the monstrance. ' Philip, he that seeth me seeth the Father also '[4]: it was the insistent desire of the faithful, the people, to *see* God thus made manifest in the sacramental Christ, that brought about the custom of raising the sacred host, and later on the chalice also, after the words of consecration.[5] ' Lord, that I may *see*!': the words of the blind man in the Gospel find a new application here: the faithful in the Middle Ages ' hardly dared to receive ' the sacred body; ' but they wanted at least to gaze on it with their bodily eyes ': this ' need of contemplating the body of the Lord ' was so strongly felt that it was able, ' from the twelfth century onwards, to bring about in the middle of the Canon—though the Canon had for a long time been regarded as an inviolable sanctuary—a very considerable innovation.'[6] True, the innovation can be said to have grown out of the ancient ritual: to stress as thoroughly as possible the identity of the Mass with the Last Supper, the priest not only used (and uses) the words of Christ (This is *my* body) but also accom-

[1] *Gen.* xxi, 16 (Knox); cf. *supra*, p. 85.　　[2] *Matt.* xxvi, 40, 43 (Douai).　　[3] *John*, xix, 37 (Douai).　　[4] *John*, xiv, 9 (Douai).　　[5] Jungmann: *Missarum Sollemnia*, t. iii, p. 124. [6] *ibid*, pp. 123-5.

panied the words, as he still does, with the gestures of Christ, taking the bread into his hands, raising his eyes to heaven, blessing the bread. Now when taking the bread into his hands the priest had also raised it slightly, in offering: it was on this moment and gesture that the attention of the faithful became fixed; and it was to avoid the danger of an adoring of the unconsecrated host that the special elevation, after the words of consecration had been said, was introduced. But considerable innovation it was, none the less, since it meant that henceforth the elevation became the central moment of the Mass: ' to contemplate the divine mystery—this was the climax of the legend of the Grail in which the religious feeling of the high Middle Ages found its poetic expression; and as in the legend, so also here, marvellous results were looked for at the moment of the sacred mystery. . . . Henceforward, for many christians the essence of devotion to the Mass lay in gazing on the sacred host at the moment of consecration '[1].

That certain exaggerations and abuses should grow out of this upsurge of devotion was to be expected: they were remedied not least by the introduction of other acts of worship outside the Mass, such as processions of the blessed Sacrament, the specific purpose of which was the adoration of the body of the Lord. And through the subsequent centuries the same essential need and devotion have continued to be felt and to play a large part in the devotional life of the Church. But the fact remains that, while millions adore Christ's body today in the Mass, while there are religious communities in which the adoration of the blessed Sacrament is kept up continually, and while in the Church at large we keep every year the feast of the body of the Lord and through the

---

[1] Jungmann: *op. cit.* t. i, pp. 158-9. During the consecration and elevation the minister at the altar kneel down; the celebrant genuflects before and after the elevation of host and of chalice. People are sometimes surprised, perhaps shocked, to see ministers at episcopal functions genuflecting before the bishop: it should be remembered that while the genuflection had long been an accustomed way of doing homage to princes it had never been associated with religious worship; it began to be adopted here at the elevation only toward the end of the fourteenth century, though the older gesture, of simply bowing the head still predominated in the fifteenth century and continues even into the sixteenth: it is not until the *Missal* of Pius V, in 1570, that the practice of genuflecting as we now have it was definitely established. (Cf. Jungmann, *op. cit.* t. III, pp. 129-31.)

year adore it constantly not only in the Mass but also in the bene-
diction service, still individually we have to ask ourselves the
question, Am I among the watchers or the sleepers? And if the
former, then do I keep watch with loving adoration, or is my
watching little more in fact than an occasional perfunctory glance?

Video cælos apertos, St Stephen cried as they stoned him: ' I see
the heavens opened '. The elevation is the moment at which the
eternal is made manifest in time, in the ' divine mystery ', the
moment of vision on the Mount of Vision. But we are not meant
to think of the vision as something which, however precious and
sublime, is fugitive, impermanent: essentially it leads on to the
moment of communion, and that in its turn points onward to the
life that is to be led in the world when the Mass is over. The
devotion of the faithful demanded, in the early days, that the
elevation ' should not be a fleeting moment ' but should last for a
space of time ' during which the whole community should do
homage to the body of Christ in songs of adoration '[1]; but the
subsequent reduction of the time taken over the ritual itself should
only make us more conscious of the fact that it ought not to be
fleeting in the other sense: that it ought to abide with us in mind
and heart when we have left the altar. Many an event in our ordinary human experience colours the whole day on which it occurs:
a letter, a meeting, a sight seen, a word spoken, the touch of a hand.
So it should be, above all, with the Mass; and so we may understand the blessing with which the Mass ends (remembering that the
word *missa* itself includes the idea of blessing and therefore referring
this one precisely to the Mass): ' May the blessing of almighty
God, Father, Son and holy Ghost, descend upon you and abide
with you for ever '.

[1] Jungmann: *op. cit.* t. i, p. 160.

As often as ye shall do these things, ye shall do them in remembrance of me.

The Canon is sometimes called the *Actio Missæ*, for obviously here the emphasis is on what is to be done, on the tremendous moment when bread and wine become God, on the self-offering of the incarnate Word, first to his Father in sacrifice and then to his people, his fellow-men, in sacrament. This action is to be continued until the end of time, a daily *anamnesis* or re-presentation of what was done at the Last Supper and on Calvary: not a mere ' calling to mind ' of an event which once took place long ago in the past and is long since over, but a sharing in that same event, for the Mass is one and the same sacrifice as that of the Cross, ' differing only in the mode of its offering '[1].

This emphasis on doing, on positive, re-creative action, which will be repeated at the end of the Mass when the people are told to go back to the everyday world and, empowered by the life they have received, live there their christian lives, doing, working, sharing in the redemptive activity of Christ, is indeed fundamental to the whole christian conception of living. As our Lord said, the night will come when no man can work, but that night is not yet; and meanwhile there is much to be done, to be achieved, to be created. Like the artist who hopes and prays to be allowed the time to finish his masterpiece before death calls him, the christian must hope and pray for the grace to ' make ' his own life and personality as God would have them be, to do his full share according to his individual vocation in saving and healing the world. He may need great zest and energy to do all this if his time in the

[1] Cf. *Concil. Trident. sess.* xxii (Denziger-Bannwart, No. 940).

world is to be short; he will need a dogged perseverance, so as not
to lose heart or courage or enthusiasm, if his time is to be long;
but in either case he must above all see his christian life in that
positive way; a personality, a life, a work, to be fashioned out of
the raw materials with which he must start, as the sculptor's statue
emerges from the shapeless block of marble to become a thing of
integrity, wholeness, beauty.

Jacob, we are told in the Old Testament, ' worked seven years
to win Rachel, and they seemed to him only a few days because
of the greatness of his love '[1]. Let us set beside this two quotations
from St Paul. First, he writes to the Colossians: ' You are God's
chosen people, holy and well-beloved: the livery you wear must
be tender compassion, kindness, humility, gentleness and patience:
you must bear with one another's faults, be generous to each other.
And to crown all this, charity; that is the bond which makes us
perfect '[2]. Then to the Romans he writes: ' Your love must be
a sincere love; you must hold what is evil in abomination, fix all
your desire upon what is good. . . . I would see you unwearied in
activity, aglow with the Spirit, waiting like slaves upon the Lord;
buoyed up by hope, patient in affliction, persevering in prayer;
providing generously for the needs of the saints, giving the stranger
a loving welcome. . . . Do not be disarmed by malice; disarm
malice with kindness '[3].

It seems to be undeniably true that many modern catholics
(at least in some countries) are extremely negativist in the way they
think of the christian life, of christian morality. Determined to
live good lives, they devote all their thought and energy to the
avoidance of wrong-doing. That, obviously, is an essential element
in the christian life; but if there is just that and nothing more there
is every likelihood that a man will end up in a sort of immaculate
moral vacuum; never doing anything that is bad, but on the other
hand never doing anything very much that is good. That is certainly not the ideal presented to us by our Lord when he said ' I

[1] *Gen.* xxix, 20 (Knox).   [2] *Col.* iii, 12–14 (Knox).   [3] *Rom.* xii, 9–21 (Knox). The
rest of this section, down to p. 200, is reprinted from an article in *The Grail Magazine*,
U S.A., (February 1958) by kind permission of the editor.

am come that they may have life, and may have it more abundantly '[1].

True, the majority of the ten commandments tell us what we are not to do; but there are two things to be noted about that: first, they are describing the minimal requirements of the natural law (the commandments would be valid and binding even if they were not revealed to us in the Scriptures) and God in his mercy is content, so to speak, with this minimum: he does not *demand* the maximum of us, though of course he invites it; secondly, our Lord came not to destroy but to fulfil the Old Law, and he fulfilled it by giving us the Golden Rule, the law of love, of God and of our neighbour: again not demanding the maximum of us, but putting these negative rules, the prohibition of murder, adultery and the rest, into the positive framework of charity. ' Above all things, have charity ': we are indeed to struggle against doing evil, but it is even more important that we should struggle to do good. The ' good life ' is primarily a question not of negations however important but of a positive growth in goodness, in love, in ' putting on Christ '.

' You must hold what is evil in abomination, fix all your desire upon what is good'. There can be very few people, one imagines, who do not hold some forms of evil (cruelty to children, for example) in abomination; but that is not enough for St Paul: he wants us to hate *all* forms of evil and love *all* forms of goodness, in other words, to reach the point at which goodness as such is connatural to us and evil in all its forms is alien to us, so that we hold it in revulsion. Again, he would have us ' aglow with the Spirit '—*ferventes*: it means literally ' always on the boil '—and therefore ' unwearied in activity ', in doing good, in being generous, kind, compassionate.

Now being generous obviously involves not being stingy or mean; being kind involves not being cruel; being compassionate involves not being hard, cynical, aloof; but the emphasis is now in the right place: there is nothing very creative about not being mean, there is a great deal that is creative in being generous; there

[1] *John*, x. 10 (Douai).

is nothing very creative about not loving evil; there is a great deal that is creative about hating evil and being aglow with love.

And in fact we shall be most likely to succeed in the essential business of avoiding evil-doing if our motive is a positive love of what is good. The christian life is not to be expressed in the chilly ideal of duty for duty's sake, but in the heart-warming ideal of duty for love's sake. Jacob's laborious years were as but a few days because of the greatness of his love: anyone can be good and do good for a little while, but for most of us the attempt to serve God is a matter of many laborious years, probably at best plodding and pedestrian; and only love will save us from one of two alternative disasters: either becoming disheartened and giving up the struggle, or, on the other hand, by driving ourselves ruthlessly and unlovingly to do our duty, becoming in the end inhuman, cold and arid.

For, as we have seen, law or duty will always seem burdensome to us, something imposed on us, bearing down on us against our will and inclination, unless we 'internalize' it, make it part of ourselves, part of the inner pattern of our personalities, by falling in love either with the law itself or with the lawgiver or with both: just as a command given us by someone we dislike will gall us, while the same command given us by someone we love will on the contrary evoke an eager response, so, equally, the carrying out of an ideal which appears to us hateful will be, if we manage it at all, a very difficult business, whereas if we love the ideal, if it is in fact *our* ideal, we shall find it at least relatively easy to accomplish. Aristotle and St Thomas note the fact that congenial activity is attended by pleasure; and this psychological truth is of great importance in the question of virtue and the moral life. Emotions, once again, are no test of the love of God: you could *feel* very devout and yet be far from any deep love of God or dedication to his service; on the other hand the saints, 'aglow with the Spirit', often have to suffer long periods of complete emotional aridity where God is concerned, clinging to him only with 'naked intent of the will'. But, as we have seen, the emotions are none the less of great importance precisely because they can make the loving and doing of what is good congenial to us.

One of the main points about a child making rapid progress in learning a subject in which he is intensely interested, emotionally engaged, and with a teacher whom he finds congenial, is that that sort of emotional engagement provides the initial impetus, the positive spur, to the formation of a habit (in the aristotelean sense of an acquired skill or facility, as you would say of an accomplished pianist that he has the ' habit ' of playing the piano). So it is that when God gives to those who try to serve him an initial period of emotional delight in that service, it is that they may be encouraged to form *habits*—of prayer, of worship, of the various forms of well-doing—and these habits we call virtues. Now St Thomas points out that there is a world of difference between the way a given good action will be performed by a man possessed of the appropriate virtue and the way the same action will be done by a man who lacks the virtue. The latter must first of all go through an arduous process of reasoning to decide what is in fact the proper action in the circumstances, and then must laboriously school himself to carry it out; the virtuous man on the other hand has, because of his ' skill ', a sort of intuitive sense of what is to be done and will be capable of doing it with eager spontaneity. Thus if for example you love generosity you will instinctively know in any given circumstances what is the generous thing to do, and you will gladly do it.

But St Paul is not content that we should acquire this or that virtue and therefore love this or that form of good: he wants us to hate *all* that is evil, love *all* that is good. And that is where the love of the Lawgiver is of such practical importance in this context; few people if any are naturally and temperamentally predisposed to love all forms of goodness: they may love generosity but be temperamentally cowardly or sensual; they may love chastity but be temperamentally mean or proud; but the man who falls in love with God will come, at least gradually, to love *all* that God loves and wills, and so he will fulfil all St Paul's demands.

There is a famous text in St Augustine: *Ama, et fac quod vis:* Love, and then do what you will. At first sight this might appear to be very rash advice; one might take it as meaning that one can say, Well, I love God, and so now that that's settled I can go off and commit murder, theft, adultery, with a good conscience. An instant's reflection shows the falsity of that interpretation, for to love the lawgiver means to love his law; but there is once again the same emphasis: Love and then go and *do* things, not avoid things. Love will make all that is good connatural, congenial to you, so go and do good. Obviously being generous will involve not being mean, being just will involve not being a thief, being chaste will involve not being a sensualist, and so on. But the accent is on the positive, the creative, not the negative.

All this has a very obvious application to married life. In the beginning of the marriage-relationship emotion and passion normally loom very large; and they make each of the people concerned anxious to please—to do the will of—the other; but these feelings should be used, creatively, to form a habit—a habit not just of emotionally *wanting* the good of the other, but of firmly and deeply *willing* the good of the other. And while that will must of necessity express itself in avoiding what is evil, what is harmful to the marriage, it must express itself still more in doing what is good, in building up the unity and happiness of the marriage and of the family. More, while there is a sense in which one can say of lovers that for each of them what the other wants is 'law', still they must not fall into idolatry: they will in fact love, and do, what is good for their marriage and their family in so far as they make their mutual love part of their shared love of the Lawgiver, who knows better than they what is good for them.

A purely negative concern with avoiding evil could easily turn a man into a sort of nonentity; it is very different with the love and desire and pursuit of the good. A man who is 'unwearied in activity, aglow with the Spirit' must on the contrary be a full, rich, lovable personality: and here the emphasis—and it is the final emphasis—is on the word 'be', for in the last resort that is what all the doing, all the activity, is for, so far as the human personality is concerned: that a man should become, that he should *be*, what God has eternally willed him to be. We do not love other human beings primarily because of the way they avoid faults and failings; on the contrary, we often love them in spite of their failings, and sometimes even because of them. We do tend to love them because of the good they do, as we are predisposed to love someone who is always doing kind and generous things. But above all we love people because of what they *are*: 'I love you because you're you'. And as we are made in God's image we must suppose it to be neither irreverent not irrelevant to see our relationship to God in similar terms. It is important to concern ourselves firmly and doggedly with the avoidance of evil; still more important to concern ourselves with the loving and doing of good; but above all it is important to have charity, the bond which makes us perfect, to live in Love, to *be* what God wills us to be, 'other Christs', till in the end, through his mercy, we may be able to say what St Paul said: 'I live, now not I, but Christ liveth in me'[1].

[1] *Gal.* ii, 20 (Douai).

Wherefore, O Lord, we thy servants, as also thy holy people, calling to mind the blessed Passion of the same Christ thy Son, our Lord, and also his resurrection from hell and glorious ascension into heaven, offer to thy great majesty, of thy presents and gifts, a pure host, a holy host, a spotless host, the holy bread of eternal life and the chalice of everlasting salvation.

We can see this prayer as continuing the theme we have been considering: thanks to the Christ-hero we have something positive to offer to God, our hands are filled with the boon he has brought us, the bread of life, the chalice of eternal salvation. Fr Jungmann notes how ' the title *maiestas tua*, thy majesty, which we have already met in the Preface, evokes in our minds the thought of the greatness of God before which man is lost in his nothingness. Thus the very offerings which we make bold to present to him cannot but be his own gifts: *de tuis donis ac datis* ' [1]. This thought, as the same writer goes on to point out, is a biblical one: we find it in David's prayer to the Lord:

Thine, O Lord, is magnificence and power and glory and victory, and to thee is praise: for all that is in heaven and in earth is thine. . . . Who am I, and what is my people, that we should be able to promise thee all these things? all things are thine: and we have given thee what we received of thy hand.[2]

' Every offering that we might make to God is first of all " a gift, a present " which he has given us; and this is without doubt true in a special sense of the oblation made on our altars. But another

[1] *Missarum Sollemnia*, t. iii, p. 143.   [2] I *Paralip.* xxix, 11, 14 (Douai).

idea is implied in these words, an idea which St Irenæus, thinking of the material element in our offering, stressed so strongly against the gnostics: that our sacrifice is not offered to a Being remote from creation but that on the contrary it is to the Lord of creation that we offer what he himself has created.'[1]

We offer God what we have received; but what we have received enables us to be positive and creative in our approach to God. Often, as we consider the imitation of Christ, what may at first sight have seemed to be something negative turns out on reflection to be thus positive and creative. This prayer makes explicit mention of the Passion of Christ and then of his resurrection and ascension: let us consider first the Passion as the moment of Christ's most complete and abject poverty—stripped of the last shreds of his dignity even as man, as he was stripped of his garments—and then the resurrection and ascension as showing us by implication what the attitude of the christian should be towards matter in general and the flesh in particular in his journey towards eternal life.

Monks and nuns are perhaps almost the only true, practising communists in the world.[2] When they adopt the religious life they take a vow of poverty: its material implications will be different in different Orders and Societies according to their different needs, ideals, the ends they have in view; but in general the vow will mean an abrogation of the right of individual ownership. ' Let all things be held in common amongst you ', St Augustine says in his *Rule*: the moneys earned or otherwise acquired by the religious are at the disposal of the Superior, to be used as he thinks fit for the good of all.

But this material poverty is not an end in itself; it is a means, first to the accomplishment of the end, the work, of the Order; secondly, to the acquiring of poverty of spirit. This latter does not follow automatically from the giving up of worldly possessions, as

[1] Jungmann, *loc. cit.*   [2] The treatment of the three themes of poverty, chastity and obedience in the following pages is largely adapted, by permission of the editor, from articles published in *The Grail Magazine*, U.S.A., in 1958.

Walter Hilton pointed out long ago: ' Thou hast forsaken riches and mickle having of this world, and art shut in a dungeon; but hast thou forsaken the love of all this? I expect not yet; it is less mastery for to forsake worldly good than for to forsake love of it. Peradventure thou hast not changed thy covetise, but thou hast changed it from great things into small, as from a pound into a penny and from a silvern piece into a disc of one half-penny '[1].

If a religious hankers covetously after the riches or the material independence he has given up; if he clings more avariciously to the things of little worth he now has at his disposal than he ever did to his riches in the world; if his material poverty makes him mean-spirited and selfish instead of generous and open-handed, then so far as he is concerned his vow of poverty has failed in its purpose.

Now all this has its application to life in the world. When our Lord said, ' Blessed are the poor in spirit ', he was speaking not just to monks and nuns but to all his listeners, to all humanity.[2]

Let us first of all be clear about just what our Lord meant. St Luke's version of the beatitudes is more stark than St Matthew's, and he explicitly points the contrast between poverty and riches, tears and laughter. But, as Père Lagrange points out, we should be completely wrong if, in reading the Lucan version, we thought of Christ as a ' good revolutionary ', promising the poor ' their revenge upon the rich who looked down upon them '—and a speedy revenge—in this world. What in fact he promises his disciples in this world is ' humiliation and ill-treatment for his name's sake '. No, the whole background to the beatitudes is a complete change of values: from materialist-hedonism to a love of the ' things which are of real worth '; and St Matthew is at pains to make it clear to his Greek readers that our Lord's sayings are to be thus taken in their true spiritual sense.[3]

Christ, then, is not condemning wealth as such, though he

[1] Hilton: *The Scale of Perfection*, ch. lxxi.   [2] For a detailed study of the ' social implications of the beatitudes ' cf. *The Divine Pity*.   [3] Lagrange: *The Gospel of Jesus Christ*, vol. I, p. 151.

points out, here and elsewhere, its dangers; when he says 'Woe upon you who are rich; you have your comfort already' he seems clearly to have in mind those whom wealth has turned into self-centred hedonists, as elsewhere he is perhaps thinking of how easily riches can make a man proud and arrogant, filled with the sense of power and superiority. Wealth has its dangers, but on the other hand there is nothing blessed—and there is plenty of danger —in poverty in the sense of penury. In so far as our Lord is concerned at all with material wealth or poverty we may suppose that it would be the ' poor ' in the sense of those of modest means—such as, for instance, his own family and relatives—whom he would regard as most likely to be carefree in this world and therefore able to give their attention and their energies to that other kingdom which he had come to preach and where true blessedness is to be found.

But while poverty in that sense can make it easier for a man to be poor in spirit, the two things are not necessarily connected. A rich man may be poor in spirit; a poor man may not. Lagrange holds that the poor in spirit are ' those who feel their own powerlessness to satisfy their longing for the kingdom of God '[1]: those, in other words, who are not proud, complacent, self-sufficient, those who resemble not the Pharisee but the Publican in the temple; for the kingdom of heaven is not to be bought with money or power or an arrogant rectitude. They are the humble of heart, who seek glory not for themselves, through worldly grandeur and honours and wealth, but for God.

This in turn means that they will not be possessive or greedy or selfish about such material goods as they may have, or indeed about any God-given possessions, gifts, qualities, abilities: they know that they are only God's stewards in respect of all these things, which have been given them not to be kept locked up in a safe and gloated over in secret but to be used freely, generously, great-heartedly, for the glory of God and the good of man.

[1] *op. cit.* p. 152.

St Dominic, as he lay dying, told his followers, 'Possess poverty'; it is indeed a rich possession since it means a liberation from the cares and fears and vexations of greed, avarice, miserliness, and is the one way to fulfil the Pauline ideal of 'having nothing, yet possessing all things'. It is of the man who is poor in spirit that we can say that 'all things are his to enjoy' precisely because he can love them for what they are in themselves, not for what he can get out of them in terms of pride or profit or power. Just because he is ungrasping he can be contemplative, he can wonder and rejoice at the beauty of things and in his joy give praise to God; he can say of—and to—a leaf or a landscape, a symphony, a poem, a human being, 'How lovely you are!' without wanting to grab these things for his own to be his own 'creatures', and to keep everyone else away from them.

It is in this sense that we must understand the mystics when they tell us that we must love only God and must hate creatures; or the words of Christ himself when he said that unless a man hate 'his father and mother and wife and children and brethren and sisters, yea, and his own life also' he could not be his disciple. [1] Quite obviously Christ is not telling us that we must have hatred in our hearts for our parents, or that husbands and wives must hate each other; and the mystics, far from hating creatures in fact, see them as (to use Erigena's word) a theophany and are led by them to praise God in unison with them.

No, St Thomas explains the matter very simply to us when he tells us that we are to hate (i.e. turn away from) even the most precious things 'in so far as they lead us from God' [2]. Now human beings can quite literally lead one another away from God, as a mother might do all she could to prevent a son or daughter from following a religious vocation, or as one man can lead another into sin. But the same is only metaphorically true of animals and inanimate things: they can be stumbling-blocks, not because of any fault in themselves but because of a fault in us, because of our pride and egoism and greed. It is these things in us which have

[1] *Luke*, xiv, 26 (Douai).   [2] *Sum. Theol.* II. II. xxvi, 7, ad 1; xxxiv, 3, ad 1.

to be ' killed' as the mystics say; and, as M. Maritain has pointed out, we do not have to dilute the mystics' sayings but we do have to understand them; there is all the difference in the world between the ontological language of theology and the mystical language of a John of the Cross. St John is well aware that grace does not destroy nature but perfects it: ' he preaches neither mutilation nor suicide, nor the slightest ontological destruction of the tiniest filament of the wing of the tiniest gnat'; what he does preach is a ' very real death, more subtle and more delicate than any material death or destruction . . . that death which is called the expropriation of self. This death does not destroy sensibility; on the contrary, it refines it, makes it more delicate; it does not harden the fibres of our being but makes them more subtle and spiritualizes them; it transforms us into love'[1]. So it is that in the end we become free, free to love God in all things and all things in God, so that we can cry with St John of the Cross: ' Mine are the heavens and mine is the earth; mine are mankind and the just and the sinners; the angels are mine and the Mother of God, and all things are mine; and God himself is mine and for me: for Christ is mine and all for me. Truly then what seekest thou for, my soul, and what dost thou ask for? All that is is thine and is all for thee '[2].

Now this applies just as much to life in the world as it does to life in the cloister; and it is easy to see how relevant it is to marriage and family life. Our Lord tells us not to be solicitous about material things: that is not to say that we may not plan for the future and try to make provision for the morrow, but only that we are not to be endlessly anxious, fretful, obsessed with the thought of money and material acquisitions. It is the duty of a husband to look to the material well-being of his wife; of parents to provide for the future of their children. They are not to be money-grubbing, but neither are they to be feckless. But, a modest economic stability once achieved, they must be generous, open-handed, with what

---

[1] Cf. Maritain, *Les Degrés du Savoir*, pp. 658-9.   [2] Quoted Maritain: *The Degrees of Knowledge*, pp. 446-7.

they have, always ready to help those in need—and to help them not only with material things but with all their gifts, their 'talents'—for, once again, they are only stewards. They must not be possessive in their attitude to one another: that would make their love sterile, turned in upon itself, till in the end it withered like a plant deprived of light and air. They must not be possessive in regard to their children: they must send them away when the time comes, to live their own lives, to become human persons in their own right: that is real love, whereas possessiveness is self-love.

And as in their relation to God they must be poor in spirit in the sense of being humble, not self-reliant, so in their relation to one another: they have to acknowledge humbly their need of one another, each having something to give which the other needs. The same is true of their attitude to their children: the children need them, depend on them; but they in their turn need their children, who can evoke from them a deeper love and unity, and save them from the danger of being too exclusively wrapped up in one another. And so the horizon expands; for they must teach their children what they have tried to teach themselves: that poverty of spirit which makes them generous to all the world, helping those in need and, as St Paul says, 'giving the stranger a loving welcome'[1], and which at the same time makes the whole world theirs to enjoy.

We cannot love too much the things that God has made, but we can love them in the wrong way; and the wrong way is to love them graspingly, selfishly, apart from God, in defiance of God; if we do that we may destroy them, we shall certainly be in danger of destroying ourselves. The christian attitude to things is ambivalent. On the one hand we are not to forget their transience, their unimportance compared with the immensities of God and his eternity: 'Behold thou hast made my days as the span of a hand, and my substance is as nothing before thee. In truth every man living is but a breath, and passes as a shadow'. But on the

---

[1] *Romans*, xii, 13 (Knox).

other hand we are told of our Father's care for the sparrows—not the peacocks and birds-of-paradise but the little gutter-birds; we are told how the very hairs of our head are numbered; we know of the infinite value of human beings as children of God and co-heirs with Christ. So we have to care, and care passionately, for all God's creatures, and yet at the same time not care: we have to be ready to say if need be—and even of the most precious of God's gifts to us—'The Lord gave, the Lord hath taken away: . . . blessed be the name of the Lord'. What we must do, then, is pray for the grace to care passionately but unselfishly for the least of God's creatures, the grace to love and cherish them all, and, that we may do that, to be made truly poor in spirit and so be given greatness of heart—a heart big enough to encompass the world.

When a man enters the religious life he takes a vow of chastity: he renounces marriage and family life and vows himself to a life of celibacy. But the virtue of chastity means much more than a mere abstention: it is a positive and creative thing, it is, once again, a question not so much of not-doing as of doing and still more of being. The resurrection and ascension of our Lord—and their meaning is reinforced for us by the assumption of our Lady—give us the determining principles of christian sex-morality: we are to think of eternal life and happiness, not in terms of an escape from the body and from matter, but in terms of the glorifying of the body and of matter.

The puritan or manichean streak which is not seldom to be met with among modern catholics runs counter to this. One finds them thinking that the Church gives a somewhat grudging approval to marriage, and therefore to sexual intercourse in so far as its purpose is procreation, but that love-making is not quite right and that even in the sexual act itself pleasure should be held in rigid control or indeed reduced to a minimum. It is sometimes necessary therefore to point out that the Church *blesses* passion when it is really a union of two personalities and not just a selfish pursuit of sexual pleasure. (In the marriage service as we have it in England the man says to the woman ' With my body I thee worship ': the man says it, not the woman, perhaps because, generally speaking, men are less inclined than women to approach physical love-making in a spirit of humility, reverence, worship, more inclined to make it something in the nature of a smash-and-grab raid.)

Chastity comes under the general heading of the cardinal virtue of *temperantia*. (One uses the Latin word because it is so hard to know nowadays how to translate it: ' temperance ' has come to mean merely sobriety in matters of drink, and ' temperateness ' suggests a certain lukewarmness and lack of enthusiasm—though Shakespeare can put us right there when he says,

> *Shall I compare thee to a summer's day?*
> *Thou art more lovely and more temperate—*

for if spring is more temperate than summer it is also more passionate.)

Now *temperantia* is an expression of the humility of the flesh, as prudence is an expression of the humility of the mind or as poverty of spirit (and, in a sense, justice) express humility with regard to possessions, and fortitude expresses humility in strength and courage. In the first case we become lovers of creatures (and in particular of human beings), and of God's dominion over them, in the mode of experience, just as by the other virtues we become lovers in the mode of knowledge, lovers in stewardship, lovers in defence of the rights of God and of his creatures. Just as it is impossible to acquire wisdom, the possession of the mind by Truth, without intellectual humility, so it is impossible for the body-spirit to live in love, to be possessed by love, without the humility of the flesh. The intemperate man is possessive; he dominates and domineers, he is greedy, grasping, selfish; and so he does violence first of all to himself, as creature and lover, secondly to other human beings, since he treats them not as ends but as means, and thirdly to his relationship to God, since he fails to make his human relationships part of the love and worship of God.

Further, *temperantia* is essentially concerned with the creation of beauty in human life and human relationships; so St Thomas, at the beginning of his treatise on the subject, discusses what he calls *honestas* and defines as 'spiritual beauty'. *Temperantia* has of course its negative side: control, continence and so on; but primarily it is humility and creativity. Love-making, when it is indeed loving and therefore humble, helps to create that beauty which St Paul describes as a *magnum mysterium*, that unity of man and wife which he likens to the union between Christ and his Church. For the (supernatural) virtue of chastity, while it restrains from grossness or brutishness, ennobles and sanctifies; it turns what might have been just an animal-coupling into not merely a deeply experienced union of two personalities, body and soul, but, far beyond that, an act of worship and love of God.

The purpose, then, of christian *temperantia* and chastity is not to diminish the intensity of human love or of its physical expression, but simply to govern, deepen, ennoble and sanctify those instincts which, because of the ingrained sinfulness of humanity, tend to separate pleasure from the love which should ensoul it and to seek the former without the latter. Thus St Thomas remarks on the servility or slavishness of *intemperantia*: it reduces us to the level of the brute beasts; and it is in this treatise that he writes of the vice of pride, (for pride would rob human love of its quality of reverence and would prevent it from being an expression of the love of God); on the other hand he links up with *temperantia* the quality of *mansuetudo* or gentleness, for that again is a quality which saves passion from becoming predatory.

Thus there are, on the negative side, two opposite dangers to be avoided. The first is the danger of de-spiritualizing what ought to be a personal relationship, and degrading it to the level of a purely animal—and selfish—satisfaction. Under this heading would come anything that destroys cleanness of heart and indeed clarity of vision: not only brutalities and brutishness and a selfish lack of concern for the other person concerned, but anything which in any way de-personalizes the relationship by allowing the lower levels of the personality to lord it over the higher—or, more accurately, to act autonomously in defiance of the higher. This disorganization is most obvious in the warfare between sense-drives and spirit; but there is also the more subtle—and for that reason perhaps more dangerous—tendency to allow the emotions to take control in defiance of head and heart. No doubt we all at times allow our actions to be dictated by our emotions, without reference either to reason or to the declared will of God: there are moments when (as we accurately say, 'without thinking') we let ourselves be carried away by a gust of anger, jealousy, lust, curiosity. But these momentary aberrations are in themselves relatively unimportant: what is lethal is allowing ourselves, habitually, to live on our emotions: when we should be taking careful thought we act blindly on prejudice; when we should be using emotions creatively within the framework of the psycho-physical unity of the personality we on the contrary allow ourselves to become sentimentalists; our actions are decided not according to what is good, creative, gracious in itself, but according to the mood of the moment; and there is always the danger too that in so far as we allow the mind any say at all in what we do it will be a question not of reasoning but of rationalizing—of finding specious and self-deceptive reasons for doing what, emotionally, we want to do. That is the point, in this context, of clarity of vision: it is usually our emotions—vanity, jealousy, dislike, laziness, the desire of comfort or pleasure—which lead us into the sort of tortuous thinking, the shiftiness, the sometimes ingenious, sometimes puerile, rationalizations, which can wreck not only the unity of the personality but the integrity of a love-relationship. We cannot over-stress the importance of the emotions in the building up of that relationship; but if there is emotion and nothing more, if the two people concerned rely simply on their feelings for one another to overcome every difficulty and to create that deep unity which is love's purpose, then they are doomed to failure just as much as if they rely simply on their physical attraction to one another.

But there is the opposite danger also: that sense-drives and emotions will be repressed or allowed to wither and become atrophied; and this is a danger which besets those in whom the puritan streak is strongly marked. They are tempted to think of the senses, not as valuable—indeed invaluable—friends [1] but as insidious traitors, to be destroyed or disarmed and manacled. For St Thomas, *intemperantia* is a vice, but so is *insensibilitas*: and both of them are equally opposed to *temperantia*. The sort of world we most of us live in today makes it very hard for us to be truly, deeply natural. Cooped up in our vast, amorphous modern cities, remote from the realities of Nature, from field and forest and green growing things: occupied with work that may well be either purely cerebral or purely automatic; surrounded by the sort of commercialized sex which can in the end turn even love into something unnatural because de-personalized; living also in the sort of climate of opinion which views the scientific-rational approach to reality as the only one of any value or validity: it is hardly surprising if in these circumstances we become cut off from our roots, so that many levels of the personality are allowed to wither and become atrophied, and in the end we become impoverished, sick, neurotic, etiolated half-men.[2] Having eyes we see not, because we will not stop to look; having ears we hear not, because we will not stop to listen; and yet, whether we like it or not, we are part-animal: we are dependent on our senses not merely for communication but, what is far more important, for communion. If we want to become again rooted in Nature we must look and listen and feel and smell, till communion is established; look at the blue of the sky and the gold of the sun, at the texture of a leaf or a blade of grass or the breathless transience of a snowflake; listen to roar or ripple of waves, whisper or soughing of leaves; feel and smell the petal of

[1] Cf. Ch.-D. Boulogne, O.P.: *Mes Amis les Sens.* [2] Cf. *The Water and the Fire,* chs. i and ix.

a flower, the fur of a cat. In the same way lovers must use their senses if they are to establish a communion: use them lovingly, as friends; not bully or starve or ignore them, but cherish them. So they will become ' contemplative ' of one another; and if they are really trying to make their love of one another part of their love of God, that natural contemplation of and communion with one another may help them in the work of contemplating and entering into communion with God.

It may well have two other effects of great value. First, their deep and vivid awareness of each other is likely to make deeper and more vivid their awareness of the world about them: it is a commonplace to say that when people fall in love the sky becomes more richly blue, the grass more green: there is in fact a general heightening of sense-awareness, and therefore of appreciation and of love. So, in their worship of God, they will have much more than before to offer him: they will be able to praise him through their love of all his works. The *Laudate* psalms at the end of the psalter, the *Benedicite* which the Church sings daily at Lauds, the *Canticle of the Sun* of St Francis, the apostrophes to Nature of a Rose of Lima, calling on it to join her in praise, the meditations of a Traherne: all these things will become, not some strange echo from an unknown world, but a deeply felt reality which echoes in their own hearts.

Secondly, if chastity does not destroy or chill their ardours but (as it is the nature of the virtue to do) deepens, guides and sanctifies them, it may well bring about in them the effect of the last three fruits of the Spirit—modesty, continence, chastity—which is spiritual beauty, a restoring in some degree of that harmony of the personality which sin disrupted, an expression of that *splendor formæ*, the shining out or radiance of form through and in matter which is St Thomas's definition of beauty, and which in this context is the shining out of spirit in and through the flesh. And so the words of our Lord will be fulfilled in them: ' Thy body has the eye for its lamp; and if thy eye is clear, the whole of thy body will be

213

lit up; when it is diseased, the whole of thy body will be in darkness. Take good care, then, that this principle of light which is in thee is light, not darkness; then, if thy whole body is in the light, with no part of it in darkness, it will all be lit up as if by a bright lamp enlightening thee ' [1].

[1] *Luke*, xi, 34–6 (Knox).

Upon which offerings do thou deign to look with an indulgent smile,[1] and to accept them as thou didst graciously accept the gifts of thy good servant Abel and the sacrifice of our patriarch Abraham and that which thy high priest Melchizedech offered to thee, a holy sacrifice, a spotless host.

This prayer may at first sight seem strange. The ' offerings ' are no longer bread and wine: they have been changed, and are now divine reality: this is the offering of God to God by God: how then can there be any doubt of its acceptance, or point in praying for it? Indeed the Reformers, in their polemic against the Mass, saw here an impertinent attempt on the part of the priest to play the mediator between Christ and God.[2] But the sacrifice of Christ is also the sacrifice of his Church: ' as an act of worship it is essentially committed into the hands of the Church ' and as such remains the ' external sign of the homage paid to God by the Church and more immediately by this or that community '; and this rite can only become a ' truly acceptable act of homage to God if it is animated by at least a minimum of inward self-giving on the part of those who offer it '[3]. The harsh words of the Old Testament prophets, through whom God rejected the ' soulless, merely external sacrifices of his people '[4], may still have their relevance to us if we take no pains to share worthily, inwardly, in the offering of the sacrifice. The Church then recalls here the memory of three great Old Testament figures whose sacrifices were indeed acceptable to God, and prays that our own self-offering may be no less acceptable than theirs.

---

[1] Mgr Knox's translation of *sereno vultu*, in *The Mass in Slow Motion*, ch. xii, p. 151.
[2] Cf. Jungmann: *Missarum Sollemnia*, t. iii, p. 147.   [3] *ibid.*   [4] *ibid.*

Abel, whom our Lord himself called 'the just'[1], offered to God 'of the firstlings of his flock'[2] and became himself 'the victim of his brother's hatred: what we offer is the Lamb of God, the "first-born from the dead"[3], turning the death inflicted on him by his people into a redemptive sacrifice'[4]. Abel is here called God's servant: the Latin word is *puer* which, like the Greek *pais,* conveys also the idea of sonship and, in the framework of this present study, must remind us further of the *puer æternus.*

Next there is Abraham, 'the forbear of all those " who are of faith "[5] and who is therefore called our patriarch': he is the 'example of heroic obedience to God, ready to sacrifice his own son, though in fact the boy was given back to him alive:[6] and our victim too, the most perfect incarnation of obedience unto death, was given back to life through his resurrection. Finally there is Melchizedech who as priest of the most high God offers bread and wine: and it is of bread and wine that our offering also is made'[7]. Thus, as we have seen, this third, symbolical, offering 'ranks even higher than the sacrifice of a son, which is still the sacrifice of somebody else. Melchizedech's offering is thus a configuration of Christ's sacrifice of himself'[8].

Let us then consider our own duty of sacrificing ourselves, in and with Christ, to God: let us, in other words, think of our own duty of obedience to God and his law and to those who have authority in this world to exact obedience of us in his name.

The third vow which the religious takes is that of obedience to his religious superiors. Such obedience is not unlimited (as is the case with man's obedience to God): the religious pledges himself to obey his superiors according to the rule or constitutional laws of his Order or Society; so that if a superior were to command something which was against the divine or natural law the subject would be bound not to obey; if he commanded something which was

---

[1] *Matt.* xxiii, 35.   [2] *Gen.* iv, 4 (Douai).   [3] *Col.* i, 18 (Douai).   [4] Jungmann: *Missarum Sollemnia,* t. iii, p. 148.   [5] *Gal.* iii, 7 (Douai).   [6] Cf. *supra,* pp. 77, 86.   [7] Jungmann, *loc. cit.*   [8] Jung: *Transformation Symbolism in the Mass,* p. 287.

ultra vires but not in itself sinful the subject could obey but would not be obliged to. But if the command is licit and *intra vires*, then the subject fulfils his vow inasmuch as he carries out the task enjoined upon him, but if his action is to be an act of the *virtue* of obedience he must not merely obey externally but obey obediently, i.e. readily, cheerfully, and (whether the command is congenial or not) out of a desire to obey.

It is one of the paradoxes of human nature that while on the one hand we are given free will, on the other we cannot escape obedience. We have to choose between the bondage of the law and the bondage of sin: if we rebel against obedience to the law of God or the natural law we merely subject ourselves to obedience to evil habits and therefore perhaps in the end to the physical laws of disintegration. Obedience to sin is always a bondage; the only way in which obedience to the law can cease to be a bondage is by making it not something external to us but internal, by loving law and lawgiver, in other words by obeying obediently.

The thomist theory of obedience can be said to be based on two principles: first, that for a command to be just it must be ' according to reason '; secondly, that the virtue of obedience is essentially a question of willing, not of thinking. If a superior were to command his subjects to do something irrational (a favourite example is sweeping up leaves against the wind) he would, in fact and objectively speaking, be doing something immoral: his motives might be excellent, for instance he might think such a task would make his subjects humble (though one might suppose it more likely to make them neurotic) but the end does not justify the means: the command in itself would remain an abuse of authority. Again, obedience does not mean that a man must abrogate his integrity or independence of mind. Clearly he will not obey obediently if, even though he carries out the task assigned him, he grumbles about it and criticizes the judgement of his superior, whether externally to others or inwardly in his own heart. And if he is wise and prudent and humble he will reflect that probably his superior knows more about the matter in hand, sees more sides of the question, than he himself can do. But it is not difficult to think of cases in which a subject who without question is an expert in some particular field is given an order concerning something within that field by a superior who is ignorant with regard to it: if the subject knows perfectly well that the order is (not morally wrong of course but) mistaken or ill-advised, he must indeed set aside his *expertise* and cheerfully do what he is told, but he is in no way bound to the unnatural and irrational task of trying to do violence to his own mind, trying to force himself to think that something is correct when he knows perfectly well that it is not. Indeed, while it is an act of the virtue of obedience to carry out devotedly the will of the superior in cases where the task assigned seems to the subject to be wise, valuable, congenial and so forth, it is a specially high and meritorious act of the virtue to obey in cases when this is not so. (As we have seen, God sometimes makes prayer a congenial and joyful thing, and the joy does not of itself detract from the value or merit of the prayer; but sometimes he withdraws the joy, so that prayer becomes arid and unrewarding: and it is then that he gives us the chance to prove that we pray not because we love the joy to be found in our prayer but because we love him.)

Obedience is a question of willing, not of wanting; and here we may note a psychological fact of some importance. Just as men will sometimes rise unexpectedly to the challenge of some great peril, drawing on hitherto unsuspected reserves of courage and endurance, so with obedience: a command which involves a great challenge—a painful uprooting, the giving up of established and congenial work and surroundings for something else which is hard, costing, repellent—may bring out the best in a man, even to the point of a sort of heroism, so that he quietly sets about doing what is required of him without outward grumbling or inner recalcitrance; whereas in the small, ordinary—but often irritating—everyday requirements of obedience, the obedience-aspect may (because the duties are so small and so ordinary) be lost sight of while the irritation-aspect looms large, with the result that, if the duty is carried out at all, it is with a good deal of grumbling and reluctance.

All these ideas and principles have their application to family life. Let us look, first of all, at the relationship between man and wife. There is a tendency nowadays to suggest that the Church has involved itself in a contradiction, asserting on the one hand the equality of man and wife while at the same time clinging to the Pauline idea that the wife must be subject to the husband and obey him. The contradiction is in fact only an apparent one; and will be resolved if we bear in mind the differences of psychological make-up, of function and of ' spheres of influence ', between man and wife.[1]

A great deal of harm, one cannot help thinking, has been done in recent times by a fundamental confusion of thought on the part of some supporters of the ' emancipation of women ' who quite illegitimately identify being equal with being indistinguishable. Thus Mme. de Beauvoir's *The Second Sex*, for all its learning and the many sound and important points it makes, seems to fall into this error: all the differences between men and women are ascribed simply to their different *situations* (to use the existentialist term): give women the same education as men, the same social, economic and political status, and these differences will disappear. But we are psycho-physical beings; and it is therefore reasonable to suppose *a priori* that the undeniable physiological differences between the sexes are paralleled by equally important psychological differentiations. Certainly one must not make glib generalizations; but by and large it seems true to say that the minds of men and women tend to work in different ways—the former more ' rational ', the latter more ' intuitive '—and that this remains true—as indeed why should it not?—no matter how highly educated and socially emancipated the women may be. True, we have witnessed the emergence of the twentieth-century ' virago '; the hard, strident, domineering matriarch-type—and she simply proves the point *a posteriori*: that,

[1] Cf. *The Water and the Fire*, chs. vii. and viii.

normally,[1] if a woman tries to become psychologically speaking a man she becomes in fact a *monstrum naturæ*: she loses the qualities of her own sex and becomes a repellent travesty of the male sex. Men and women should complement each other in mind as in body; and never is it truer than of the 'marriage of true minds' in a deep, loving man-and-wife relationship that two heads are better than one.

Between man and wife, then, there is true equality, of dignity and stature; there is a true meeting of personalities, but of different personalities with different functions, each with its own authority. In the christian tradition the man is the head of the family, the wife (his companion and help-mate, not his servant) is its heart. And as in the sphere of knowledge *le cœur a ses raisons que la raison ne connaît point*, so in the sphere of authority and action: if, normally speaking, it is natural for the man to have the last word in major questions of policy, in economic matters and so forth, it is equally natural for the wife to have the last word in matters concerning her own domain as housewife and mother of her babies; but much deeper than that, the man will not make his decisions (unless he is both stupid and unjust) without hearing and weighing his wife's views, for if the head is self-sufficient in the acquiring of knowledge, it is not so in the acquiring of wisdom: it needs the co-operation of the heart.

Christianity, then, forbids the husband to be despotic and domineering with regard to his wife; similarly it forbids parents to assume absolute power over their children. It is the duty of children to love their parents (both affectively and effectively), to honour them, to be dutiful, to be obedient; but there are limits to the obedience which can rightly be demanded of them. Once they have reached the age at which they should leave home and go out into the world to make their own lives and live their own vocations they become autonomous; and if the parents are possessive and try to hinder them they are acting immorally and have no right to

[1] Perhaps one should again stress the fact that this can be no more than a rough generalization: many women do in fact have predominantly 'masculine' minds.

expect obedience. Similarly in the choice of a career: while boy or girl must give great weight to what the parents have to say and advise, the decision is ultimately theirs, and the parents act wrongly if for frivolous, selfish or unworthy motives they try to force their children into an uncongenial calling or to prevent them from carrying out the vocation on which they have set their hearts.

But in a family which has been built up on love and understanding and sympathy and a common worship of God and his will such major conflicts are not likely to arise; what is likely, if not certain, to arise and to be of practical importance in family life as in that of the cloister is the clash of wills on minor matters. The different generations are not always quick at understanding each other; parents can easily seem rigid, doctrinaire (and, of course, old-fashioned) to their children, while the children can easily seem blind and pig-headed to their parents. In a good christian home it is probably not so much the major issues of vocation and so forth which are likely to cause friction and ill-will as the little everyday issues: and it is here especially therefore that parents have sometimes to remind themselves that they must neither bully their children nor spoil them, while children have to remind themselves that their parents' decisions for them are not just one of the many irritating burdens of life, to be circumvented as far as may be, but a proper exercise of authority which demands of them as a christian duty that they should obey, and obey obediently.

The Pope, exercising greater authority than any man on earth, is the *servus servorum Dei*, the servant of the servants of God; for the more authority a man has over other human beings the more he is subject to law. Children have no authority but are subject to their parents; parents have authority but for that very reason are subject to more laws than are their children—are subject, that is to say, to all the laws which govern parenthood and the exercise of authority. Whatever our state in life we never escape from obedience; but indeed it is not a question of escaping, for obedience is freedom, is a question of free choice. We can if we will choose disobedience to God, but in so doing we choose obedience to

Satan, to what is against God, to sin. But obedience to God and to those who represent him is freedom also in another sense: it is the way to knowledge and vision. So our Lord says that anyone who is prepared to do the will of his Father will know whether his doctrine comes from the Father or not;[1] and the psalmist prays: ' Blithely as one that has found great possessions, I follow thy decrees. . . . Eyes have I none for vain phantoms; let me find life in following thy way. . . . Inspire, instruct me still; all my hope is in thy covenant. . . . Musing still on thy commandments, I have grown more prudent than my enemies. More wisdom have I than all my teachers, so well have I pondered thy decrees. More learning have I than my elders, I that hold true to thy charge. . . . No lamp like thy word to guide my feet, to shew light on my path'[2].

Let us consider further the question of ' conformity to God's will', of ' loving what is good', as illustrated by the men and women who figure in the Passion story and who exhibit every kind of reaction to the demands of God's will, from the utter catastrophe of Judas to the sublime com-passion of the Mother of God.

Judas is the symbol in the human world, as Satan is in the spirit world, of non-being, of self-destruction, of life-refusal. Moved (as seems most probable: we are told in the Gospel that ' he was a thief') by an ignoble greed he commits the most ignoble of sins, betraying his master and friend with a kiss; yet even so all need not have been lost, all would not have been lost, if, when he threw down the silver, the purchase-price of blood, he had had not remorse but repentance in his heart. His darkness might have been creative, as was Peter's; but there is nothing creative about remorse, only the empty, sterile longing that what has been done might be undone; but we cannot rewrite our history, and Judas, unable either to rewrite or to bear what was written, chose the ultimate act of defiance of the Creator, repudiated the boon of life and chose death instead.

Pilate is the weak man who allows his conviction of what is right to be overcome by his cowardice, his fear of Cæsar's disfavour;

[1] *John*, vii, 17.   [2] *Ps.* cxviii (Knox).

he will refuse later on to alter the inscription he has caused to be affixed to the cross, and this is perhaps merely the stubbornness so often associated with weakness: a refusal to give way on some minor point when the essentials have already been surrendered; on the other hand we can see his gesture in a more favourable light, contrasting with Judas's complete despair: he has done an enormous wrong, but at least he will make this small gesture of atonement —and we may often find ourselves in similar case when, having sinned grievously and done great harm, we can at least do some small thing to atone, can salvage some small thing from the wreckage we have made.

Peter stands in sharp contrast to Judas: he too betrays his master, by denying him, but he goes out and weeps bitterly over what he has done, tears not of remorse but of true sorrow; his darkness is indeed creative, the sorrow giving him a deeper love and the deeper love a great strength; so that in the end he becomes the Rock on which the Church stands immovable. His symbol is the cock, which in general is a sun-symbol—the crowing of the cock announces the new dawn, the rebirth of the sun.[1] An early christian tradition tells of how ' God formed Adam with his holy hands, in his own image and likeness, and when the angels saw Adam's glorious appearance they were greatly moved by the beauty thereof. For they saw the image of his face burning with glorious splendour like the orb of the sun, and the image of his body was like unto the sparkling of crystal '[2]. But, owing to his sin, Adam lost his solar nature, to regain it only through the Cross of the Saviour. In the same sort of way we can think of Peter regaining (or, perhaps more accurately, gaining) his solar nature through his creative sorrow: the cockcrow which reminded him of his betrayal was at the same time announcing his new dawn, his new closeness to—and, as

---

[1] The earliest Easter-service we have knowledge of was celebrated at night in such a way as to reach its climax at dawn, at cock-crow, and the Sunday-service must have been, as far as possible, modelled on this; the rising sun was taken, in very early times, as an image of the Risen One, and the words of *Wisdom*, xvi, 28, ' we ought to prevent the sun to bless thee, and adore thee at the dawning of the light ', given a christian application. Cf. Jungmann: *Missarum Sollemnia*, t. i, p. 41. [2] Cf. *The Syrian Cave of Treasures*, quoted Rahner *op. cit.* p. 383.

Solis invicti comes, his identification with—the Sun of salvation.
The weather-cock on church steeples can thus remind us simultaneously of Peter himself, his sin and his sorrow, of Peter as the
Rock, and therefore the Church, and finally of the Sun whose
companion and representative he is.

But the point of Peter's story is not only that strength is born
out of weakness, but that the weakness was born out of a false, an
imaginary strength, out of presumption. 'Methinks he doth
protest too much': Peter begins by an over-vehement assertion of
the strength of his loyalty: whatever others may do he for his
part will never desert his master. We may remind ourselves of
the master's own words: 'Not everyone that saith to me, Lord,
Lord, shall enter the kingdom of heaven'[1]: the love of God is
not a question of fine phrases, of empty rhetoric, of the unreal
emotional outpourings with which our popular hymns and devotions have made us all too familiar; it is better to keep very quiet
about our (problematical) love of God and to content ourselves with
praying that in the end we may indeed come to love him, and to
concentrate in the meantime on trying as best we may to do his
will.

Simon Peter begins with resounding assertions of loyalty but
ends by running away; Simon of Cyrene[2] begins by manifesting
the utmost repugnance to what is demanded of him—they had to
'constrain' him to carry the cross—but it is not unreasonable to
suppose him to have been radically changed by the carrying of
the Tree of life which was thus imposed on him, so that resentment
and anger gave way in the end to faith and love. We have been
considering the difference between wanting and willing: here we
may remind ourselves that often we do not merely not want to do
God's will, we have no will to do it, our wills are firmly set in the
opposite direction; and then we have to pray, in the words of that
Sunday collect already quoted, that God may batter 'our rebellious
wills' till in spite of ourselves they are made conformable to his.

The 'daughters of Jerusalem' who 'bewail and lament' our

[1] *Matt.* vii, 21 (Douai).   [2] Cf. *supra*, p. 57.

Lord can perhaps be seen as symbols of a love of his will which is purely emotional and therefore at best superficial, at worst a form of self-indulgence. It is not Peter's tears that are important but the state of heart and will that lies behind them; here again we have tears, but what lies behind them is less clear; and when we in our turn bewail our sins we have to ask ourselves just how deep our sorrow goes, whether it is a question of a facile emotion or of a real *metanoia* or change of heart: and the answer is to be found in a quite simple, matter-of-fact assessment of the degree to which, if at all, we mend our ways.

In contrast to these women there is the poignant, fugitive figure of Veronica, whose role in the Passion story we considered earlier on.[1] She is not content to stand and weep; she must do something to help our Lord; and, as we saw, her whole life and personality are as it were concentrated, submerged in that one action, so that she becomes the symbol of self-dedication. We are reminded of that equally shadowy figure in the Old Testament, Melchizedech the priest, of whom St Paul says that his name means king of justice and that he was king of Salem, that is, of peace: and ' that is all; no name of father or mother, no pedigree, no date of birth or death; there he stands eternally, a priest, the true figure of the Son of God '[2]. And if this dedication, this ' self-naughting ' in the exercise of a function, applies particularly to the priesthood,[3] it applies in degree to all christians inasmuch as they are called to serve, to represent, to ' put on ' Christ and to minister to the world in his name as Veronica ministered to him.

The two thieves repeat in a way the antithesis between Judas and Peter: the one will not look to the Light and the Life, will not accept them; the other, the ' Good Thief ', does so with ' humble and contrite heart ' and so is promised immediate entry into the kingdom. We are not to read into this promise an impossible

---

[1] Cf. *supra*, p. 57.　　[2] *Hebrews*, vii, 2–3 (Knox).　　[3] Cp: ' The Son of Man had nowhere to lay his head; all day he taught the multitude, at evening he answered the questions propounded by his apostles; sometimes it was only by denying himself sleep that he could find time for prayer. In all this he would be a model for his priests: they were to be, all the time, at everybody's disposal: they were not to keep office hours.' (R. A. Knox: *Retreat for Priests*, p. 48.)

abrogation of divine justice: the thief is not the only example of a
' conversion' as deep as it is instantaneous: he is promised heaven
at once, we are to presume, because his turning to Christ is so complete that he already has heaven in him. But how consoling that
traditional title, the Good Thief, is! And what light it throws on
the theology of sin! Some moralists would doubtless repudiate the
title with horror as an impious contradiction in terms; in fact it
reminds us of two very important truths. First, I may do an action
which in itself, objectively speaking, is wrong, but if in doing it
I am sincerely following my (erroneous) conscience, acting in good
faith and from a desire to do my duty or to serve God, then sub-
jectively speaking my action is a good one, though not a right one,
and may well be an expression of a deep love of God. We can
only speak of ' sinners' in the sense of people given to modes of
behaviour which objectively speaking are wrong; we may speculate
about their inward goodness or wickedness, their guilt or their
merit, but if we do we shall be acting very rashly, for only God
knows the secrets of men's hearts.

Secondly, a man may know quite well that what he is doing is
wrong and yet be unable, because of his human frailty, to resist
doing it: in that case he is certainly not doing a good action but
he may none the less be a good man: he may be among those of
whom it is said that many sins are forgiven them because they have
loved much. It was the Publican not the Pharisee who was a good
man. There are plenty of lovable scamps in the world (and we may
suppose that it is not only to men that they are lovable) just as
there are plenty of pillars of rectitude whom it is impossible or at
least desperately difficult to find lovable. We certainly cannot
minimize the importance of trying to avoid all forms of wrong-
doing; but we can at least console and encourage ourselves in our
frailty by recalling the words of the psalmist: ' A heart that is
humbled and contrite thou, O God, wilt never disdain '[1].

We come next to Mary Magdalen. She is traditionally portrayed as crouching at the foot of the cross, weeping bitterly, while

[1] *Ps.* l, 19 (Knox).

the Mother of God stands rigid, dry-eyed beside the cross. The artists' intuition seems to be justified. There is no question of the depth and intensity of the Magdalen's love of our Lord, whether or not we identify her with the ' woman that was in the city, a sinner ' and of whom our Lord said that many sins were forgiven her because she had loved much.[1] There is no question here, as there may have been in the case of the ' daughters of Jerusalem ', of a love purely emotional and superficial. On the other hand we may be justified in thinking that her love, ardent and profound as it was, was not yet wholly perfect: ' Do not cling to me ', our Lord was to say to her later, in the garden of the resurrection: again she is at the feet of Jesus, ' where she desires to remain so that she may continue to pour out her love. But this was not the time for the sinner to shed tears on the Saviour's feet. Jesus now belonged to the world above, and although he had not yet ascended to his Father, that would take place before long and it was necessary that he should warn his disciples of the fact '[2]. She obeys, of course; but perhaps there is a hint of a gentle rebuke in our Lord's words: it is not yet time for the joys of heaven, there is work to be done, and she must be selfless and go on with that work till her task is done.

That utter selflessness is apparent in the strength and silence of the mother of Jesus. She does not need to be told that her task is not done, her vocation as mother of the Word fulfilled, until the *Consummatum est* has been spoken; she will not give way, yet, to her own grief; she must stand beside him, living out her compassion, trying to comfort, to help . . .

In which of these various figures do we find a resemblance to ourselves? At the two Marys we can but gaze from afar, in awe; they are not of our world; nor, probably, can we claim any likeness

---

[1] We certainly cannot identify the woman who was a sinner with the contemplative Mary of Bethany; nor can Mary of Bethany be the same person as Mary of Magdala. The latter *could* have been the sinful woman, though we are told only that Jesus had cast out seven devils from her, and demoniac possession does not necessarily imply a sinful life. The anointing described in *Luke*, viii, is certainly different from that which took place at Bethany (*Matt.* xxvi, *Mark.* xiv, *John*, xii). Cf. Lagrange: *The Gospel of Jesus Christ*, vol. I, pp. 170–2.   [2] Lagrange: *The Gospel of Jesus Christ*, vol. II, p. 288.

to the self-dedication of Veronica or the utter change of heart of the Good Thief or again to the perfect sorrow of the repentant Peter. But shall we have to confess that our love of God is merely emotional and skin-deep, or that our wills are rebellious? Do Peter's grandiloquent and empty protests of loyalty find an echo in our lives, or are we weak and cowardly like Pilate? At any rate there is one identification which we must not make, which the Mass, as it were, will not *let* us make: we must never confuse sorrow with remorse, never give way to despair; though many times over and in many different ways we are malefactors, still we must go on begging God to look ' with an indulgent smile ' upon our offerings; we must go on hoping one day to hear from the lips of Christ the words the Good Thief heard, the words that can take away the tears of a life-time: ' This day thou shalt be with me in paradise '.

*We humbly beseech thee, almighty God, command
these things to be carried by the hands of thy holy
angel to thine altar on high in the sight of thy divine
majesty; that as many of us as by participation at this
altar shall receive the sacred body and blood of thy
Son may be filled with all heavenly blessing and
grace, through the same Christ our Lord. Amen.*

This is a mysterious prayer, and has given rise to a great deal of
speculation and controversy. What are ' these things '? Who is
the ' angel '? And what is meant by the ' altar on high '?

Dr Jung sees the prayer as deriving from the apocryphal
Epistolæ Apostolorum, ' where there is a legend that Christ, before
he became incarnate, bade the archangels take his place at God's
altar during his absence '; and he goes on to note how this brings
out the idea of the eternal priesthood which links Christ with
Melchizedech.[1] Certainly we are here concerned with the inter-
penetration of eternity and time; and the emphasis in this prayer
is not now on the ' invasion ' of the time-world by the eternal but
on the assumption of the time-world into eternity.

Let us first of all supply a scriptural background to the symbolism
of the prayer. In the Old Testament we are told of how Isaiah had
a vision: ' I saw the Lord sitting on a throne that towered high
above me, the skirts of his robe filling the temple. Above it rose
the figures of the seraphim. . . . And ever the cry passed between
them, Holy, holy, holy, is the Lord God of hosts; all the earth is
full of his glory. The lintels over the doors rang with the sound of
that cry, and smoke went up, filling the temple courts. Alas, said
I, that I must needs keep silence; my lips, and all my neighbours'

---

[1] *Transformation Symbols in the Mass*, p. 287.

lips, are polluted with sin; and yet these eyes are looking upon their King, the Lord of hosts. Whereupon one of the seraphim flew up to me, bearing a coal which he had taken with a pair of tongs from the altar; he touched my mouth with it, and said, Now that this has touched thy lips, thy guilt is swept away, thy sin pardoned.' And so Isaiah was made the messenger and mouthpiece of the Lord[1].

The relevance of this passage to the Mass in general and to the *Supplices* in particular is clear. The imagery of earthly and heavenly praise alike is in these references to heavenly temple and altar; to the angels; the *Sanctus* and the incense; the unworthiness of man remedied by the cleansing and quickening fire, so that he is filled with 'heavenly blessing and grace' and made ready to be an apostle, to obey the command, *Ite*, at the end of the Mass, as Isaiah was made ready to obey the similar command to go and 'give a message to this people of mine'. In the *Supplices* St Augustine's definition of sacrifice as the 'offering of a thing that it may be made holy' is vividly illustrated: 'these things' are to be carried to the heavenly altar, so the Church prays, in order that thence heavenly blessing and grace may come to those who offer them.

We may compare this with a passage from the *Apocalypse*: 'There was another angel that came and took his stand at the altar, with a censer of gold; and incense was given him in plenty, so that he could make an offering on the golden altar before the throne, out of the prayers said by all the saints. So, from the angel's hand, the smoke of the incense went up in God's presence, kindled by the saints' prayer. Then the angel took his censer, filled it up with firebrands from the altar, and threw it down on to the earth '[2].

Fr Loenertz, referring to this passage, links it up with some words of our Lord which are a striking example of those paradoxes we considered earlier on: 'It is fire that I have come to spread over the earth, and what better wish can I have than that it should be kindled? There is a baptism I must be baptized with, and how impatient am I for its accomplishment! Do you think that I have

[1] *Isaiah*, vi, 1-9 (Knox).   [2] *Apoc.* viii, 3-5 (Knox).

come to bring peace on the earth? No, believe me, I have come to bring dissension'[1]. Under the action of the fire ' a sweet scent of religious devotions arises from loving hearts, burning coals are heaped upon the heads of repentant sinners, whilst an eternal fire will torment those who eternally fight against it. . . . It is not by chance that the element which sets burning the incense of the prayers of the saints is the same as that which tortures impenitent sinners '[2]. Is it the will of Christ, then, that he should bring dissension to the world? Is it his will that the fire should be not only creative but destructive as well? Clearly not; we must pay due attention in such passages as this to Semitic idiom and to that sad, almost wistful irony which is so often to be found in God's words and ways in his dealings with men. In the passage from *Isaiah* referred to above, God says to the prophet: ' Thy office is to dull the hearts of this people of mine, deaden their ears, dazzle their eyes, so that they cannot see with those eyes, hear with those ears, understand with that heart, and turn back to me, and win healing '[2]. Compare the comment of Lagrange: In the time of Isaiah as in that of our Lord, ' God willed to save his people, as is shown by the fact that he raised up a preacher and charged him to call the people to repentance, bidding him to call them with words that are impassioned, full of tenderness, yet at the same time threatening, so that every means might be used which would obtain the result desired, namely the people's conversion. That this was God's purpose is evident: it follows from the very language he employs, which is clear, urgent, compelling the Israelites to make their choice. That choice, however, is foreseen, and it will drag them to destruction. Go, then, said the Lord to his envoy, with the angry bitterness of love doomed to disappointment: go and speak to them that they may harden their hearts, and may not be pardoned!'[4] So it is with the fire: Christ is the Sun of salvation ' with healing in his wings '; he comes that his people may have life, and peace: but they are free to reject life and peace if they will, and in his sad heart

[1] *Luke*, xii, 49–52 (Knox).   [2] R. J. Loenertz, O.P.: *The Apocalypse of St John*, p. 71.
[3] *Isaiah*, vi, 10 (Knox).   [4] Lagrange, *op. cit.* vol. I, p. 180.

he knows that that is what in fact so many will do; he will be a 'sign of contradiction' and in the name of the Prince of Peace men who call themselves his followers will hate and tear and rend each other.

But we shall gain further light on Christ's paradoxical words if we read them in the Matthæan version.[1] Here too there is reference to dissensions among members of a family; the sense of the passage is the same; but one essential word is different: for we read in *Matthew* that Christ said, 'Do not imagine that I have come to bring peace to the earth; I have come to bring not peace but a *sword*'. Now the sword is a sun-symbol; in the *Apocalypse* we are told of the vision of the Son of Man, 'his eyes like flaming fire', his face 'like the sun when it shines at its full strength', and 'from his mouth came a sword sharpened at both the edges'[2]: this is the creative fire, the *logos spermatikos*. But the creative fire does not complete its work without struggle. In the passage in *Matthew* already quoted Christ goes on to speak of losing life in order to find it; the sword is two-edged like the sword that guarded the entrance to the lost paradise; it is like the word of which we read in *Hebrews*: 'God's word to us is something alive, full of energy; it can penetrate deeper than any two-edged sword, reaching the very division between soul and spirit, between joints and marrow, quick to distinguish every thought and design in our hearts'[3]. The sun rides the sky till it reaches the glory of the noonday zenith; but having reached it it may not tarry, it must go on. The hero rises 'through battle to his destined heights' and 'always he imagines his worst enemy in front of him, yet he carries the enemy within himself . . . he seeks death, immobility, satiety, rest'; but if in fact he gives way to this longing, if he tarries, he finds that 'this praiseworthy and apparently unavoidable battle with the years leads to stagnation and desiccation of soul'; 'convictions become platitudes ground out on a barrel-organ', 'ideals become starchy habits, enthusiasm stiffens into automatic gestures'. Yet try as we may we cannot remain for ever immobile: 'the dæmon throws us

[1] *Matt.* x, 34–40 (Knox).   [2] *Apoc.* i, 15–17 (Knox).   [3] *Hebr.* iv, 12 (Knox).

down, makes us traitors . . . to the selves we thought we were': and this is catastrophe, for it is an unwilling sacrifice. But if the sacrifice is a willing one, then it becomes a transformation: 'the vanishing shapes are shaped anew, and a truth is valid in the end only if it suffers change and bears new witness in new images, in new tongues, like a new wine that is put into new bottles'[1].

So the Christ of the *Apocalypse*, from whose mouth comes the two-edged sword, is one with the Christ of the Mass, for the sword is that which 'kills and vivifies'[2], and as the body of Christ was physically pierced on Calvary, so in the Mass there is a mystical separation followed, as we have seen, by a mystical resurrection. With us too, therefore, if we are to live out the pattern to the end, the same must be true: no lingering at what may seem to us to be achievement, no blind clinging to what may seem like a zenith, for we are dust, and to dust we must return, the earth which brings us forth must receive us back again, the journey must be finished, consummated. But the hero is not concerned merely with his own renewal, the completion of his own journey: he must bring back the boon to his people; and so, in the passage already quoted from *Matthew*, our Lord having spoken of how a man must lose his life if he would find it goes on to identify his hearers with himself and his Father: 'He who gives you welcome, gives me welcome too; and he who gives me welcome gives welcome to him that sent me'; and so he ends his discourse with the further affirmation of identity between himself and his 'little ones': 'If a man gives so much as a draught of cold water to one of the least of these here, because he is a disciple of mine, I promise you, he shall not miss his reward'.

The christian may not embark on his struggle without any thought for the struggles of others; still less may he allow his own efforts to involve the destruction of others. He must always remain essentially a member of a family, and look to the good of the family. Our Lord foresees the dissensions which in fact will rend his mystical body; but it is unity, not the destruction of unity,

[1] Cf. Jung: *Symbols of Transformation*, pp. 355–7.   [2] Cf. Jung: *Transformation Symbolism in the Mass*, p. 301.

that he desires and prays for; and at the end it is his peace that he leaves with us, his peace that he gives us.[1]

It is against any destruction of Christ's divine purposes in the world that the Church prays in the *Supplices*. As we have seen, there is considerable difference of opinion as to the meaning of 'these things', of the 'angel' and the 'altar'; in fact, a good deal of controversy would have been avoided had it been remembered that we cannot be literal-minded in our approach to symbols: they are to be apprehended not like an algebraic formula but like a poem; they are ambivalent or polyvalent. Let us, with the majority of liturgical scholars, take 'these things' to mean the prayers of the faithful: we need not for that reason wholly exclude the view of writers like Le Brun who see the words as referring to the sacramental gifts, for in the Mass the prayers of the faithful are offered in, with and through the self-offering of the Son. Again, some have interpreted the angel as signifying the ministry of angels in general on man's behalf; so Odo of Cambrai writes: 'Christ needed not the help of angels when, by his own power he ascended into heaven. Why then do we ask that this sacrifice may be carried by the hands of an angel into the presence of God . . .? But what is said is this: that by the translation of the body and blood of Christ we ask that our prayers may be carried [to the throne of grace]. There are, however, angels appointed for us, who daily offer our prayers to God, whence it is written that "their angels do always behold the face of my Father". So in mentioning Christ we ask that our prayers may be carried by the hands of an angel, that under the plea of so great a sacrifice, good angels may bear our prayers to the throne of grace '[2]. Others see in the angel Christ himself who, in the Clementine liturgy is called (in the phrase of the Septuagint *Isaiah*) the 'Angel of Great Counsel '[3]: but again we are not faced with a scientific either-or: it is because of Christ the priest-victim that our prayers are taken up to God, but as the hosts of angels surround the altar as *Sanctus* leads on to

---

[1] *John*, xiv, 27. [2] Cf. Alfred G. Mortimer: *The Eucharistic Sacrifice*, p. 167. [3] Cf. Mortimer, *op. cit.* pp. 167-8.

consecration, so we can visualize the ascent of our prayer as done indeed by Christ but *ministrantibus angelis*, surrounded by those guardian spirits who have been given us.

Similarly we shall see the word ' altar ' in the general setting of the Apocalyptic symbolism of temple, throne, altar, incense, candlesticks. The word ' heavenly ' as used in the liturgies often means simply spiritual as opposed to carnal; the word ' altar ' is used in a variety of figurative senses: by St Ignatius for the arena in which he expected to die; for the unity of the christian body; for Christ himself; for Hermas it is that on which men's offerings are placed to be brought to God; for others it is the faithful themselves.[1] As for the temple, we may recall the vision of the new Jerusalem in the *Apocalypse*: ' I saw no temple in it; its temple is the Lord God almighty, its temple is the Lamb '[2]. As we pray the *Supplices* our minds can be enriched by these various evocations: the main theme of the prayer, once it is taken symbolically, is very clear: that Christ, with his angels, may offer to God our feeble prayers and offerings in union with his infinite self-offering, so that thereby they and we may be blessed and engraced.

In the twelfth century St Ivo of Chartres drew an analogy between the Mass of the Faithful and the Jewish ritual for the Day of Atonement: he recalls how ' the sons of Aaron laid their hands on the head of the scape-goat, and when they had imprecated upon it the sins of the children of Israel, sent it living into the wilderness. Then the high priest returned into the camp, praying for his household and for all the congregation of the people of Israel. He interprets this of the Jews, who in our Lord's Passion laid their hands upon him, and imprecated upon themselves his blood when they cried, " His blood be on us and on our children ". Then he says: " They sent our Lord living into the wilderness, for they could not touch his divinity. They sent him away to ascend, freed by the death of the flesh, to that solitary glory which he had with the Father; ' by a fit man,' that is, by himself; ' carrying the sins of

---

[1] For these and other senses, cf. Mortimer, *op. cit.* pp. 232-3.   [2] *Apoc.* xxi, 22 (Knox).

the children of Israel ', that is, taking away the sins of the world, not retaining them. This our priest commemorates by saying to God the Father: ' Command these gifts to be carried by the hands of thine holy Angel of Great Counsel, who with his own hands, that is, by works endued with peculiar dignity, merited to ascend the heavens and to raise himself upon the altar on high, that is, to intercede for us at the right hand of the Father'. The high priest then returned to the camp; and our Lord said to his disciples, telling them of his ascension, ' I am with you always, unto the end of the world ' " ' [1].

The jewel in the lotus is eternity-in-time; now we have in the Lamb, the altar, the incense, the angels, time being caught up into eternity. The effect of the Christ-achieved at-one-ment with God the Father is the apotheosis, in Christ, of man. In mythological language the end of the hero-story, his triumph, can be represented, as we have seen, either in terms of his *hierosgamos* or sacred union with the goddess-mother, or of his recognition by the father-creator, or again his apotheosis or divinization, or finally his acquisition or theft of the boon he came to gain: and what these things intrinsically signify is ' an expansion of consciousness and therefore of being ' (illumination, transfiguration, freedom).[2] The application of these themes to christian reality is clear. Let us first see how St Thomas, with his usual comprehensiveness, sums up the theme of the *Supplices*: ' The priest,' he writes, ' does not pray that the sacramental species may be borne up to heaven; nor that Christ's true body may be borne thither, for it does not cease to be there; but he offers this prayer for Christ's mystical body, which is signified in this sacrament, that the angel standing by at the divine mysteries may present to God the prayers of both priest and people, according to *Apoc.* viii, 4: " And the smoke of the incense of the prayers of the saints ascended up before God, from the hand of the angel ". But God's " altar on high " means either the Church triumphant, unto which we pray to be translated, or else God himself, in whom we ask to share; because it is said of this altar (*Exod.* xx, 26): " Thou

---

[1] Mortimer, *op. cit.* pp. 295-6. [2] Cf. Joseph Campbell, *op. cit.* pp. 245-6.

shalt not go up by steps unto my altar ", i.e. thou shalt make no steps towards the Trinity. Or else by the angel we are to understand Christ himself, who is the " Angel of Great Counsel " (*Isaiah*, ix, 6: Septuag. version), who unites his mystical body with God the Father and the Church triumphant '[1].

So, through Christ, the sacrifice ends for man in the *hierosgamos* or mystical union of the Church with its divine Bridegroom; in men's at-one-ment with their Father, becoming again as children, God's children and co-heirs with Christ; in the ' divinization ' of man in the sense that he is given divine life through the sacrament, given the boon (*inchoativè*, as St Thomas would say) of eternal life with that ' expansion of consciousness and therefore of being ' which consists of living not only in time but in eternity, not only in this world but in God, illumined by the self-revealing of God, transfigured by the divine fire, and, obedient to the law conceived in terms of love, free—from the bondage of sin and law alike—in the ' liberty of the sons of God '.

As the priest says this prayer he bows low before the altar and then kisses it—the kiss marking the identity of the two altars, in heaven and on earth [2]—for the prayer expresses in terms of supplication what the *Sursum corda* expresses in terms of adjuration and challenge. Being now, as St Paul says, risen with Christ, we must lift our thoughts above, where Christ now sits at the right hand of God; we must be ' heavenly-minded ' not earthly-minded '[3]. There is the same thought in the collect for the feast of the Ascension: ' Grant, we beseech thee, almighty God, that as we believe thine only-begotten Son our redeemer to have ascended this day into heaven, so we too may always dwell among heavenly things '. We cannot here and now see God face to face: we are far indeed, in our sinfulness, from that; but we can try in our earthly way to live in his presence. As lovers are automatically and inescapably aware, habitually, of one another—a ' presence ' at least in the background (when the mind is actually concerned with other things),

---

[1] *Sum. Theol.* III, lxxxiii, 4, ad 9.   [2] Cp. the identification of the two chalices in the words of consecration: ' taking also *this* precious chalice ' . . .   [3] *Col.* iii, 1-3 (Knox).

colouring thought and judgment, aspirations and motivations; so the christian can come to live in the habitual presence of God: not, of course, at every moment actually thinking of him, but habitually; trying to see and judge of things *quasi oculo Dei*, from God's point of view, trying to love things in God, as God loves them.

This awareness he can achieve directly by forming a habit of turning mind and heart momentarily to God from time to time;[1] he can achieve it indirectly also, first by living in the world of symbol which we have been considering, and also by learning to 'associate' things with God—for again what happens automatically in our everyday experience, the power things have to give us joy or sorrow because of their inescapable association with happy or sad events in the past, can be achieved deliberately in regard to God: make the effort constantly, as you see and rejoice in the rose, the corn, the stream, the sky, the gracious frivolity of kitten or puppy, the glory of the lion, the splendour of mountains—make the effort to remember that they are made by God and belong to God and are given you by God; call on them, as the mystics do, to join you in praising God, and then in the end what began as conscious effort will become an effortless habitual enrichment: in your earthly life you will be living 'among heavenly things'.

Finally we must not forget the importance in this context of the angels of whom the *Supplices* speaks. If, in this age, we find it hard to believe in the devil, we also find it hard to believe in any effective sense in angels in general and in our 'guardian angels' in particular. Yet Scriptures, tradition, liturgy, speak to us constantly of them, of their power, their love, their will to serve us and guard us from evil. And what crass folly it is to suppose, in our puny pride of intellect, that we are the sole intelligences in the immensities of the material universe! It is far more logical to suppose that in the gradation of beings from inert matter up to the *actus purus* of infinite Spirit there is no sudden break, no dramatic chasm between man (rational, but still an animal) and God. We are told

[1] Perhaps the most helpful treatise on the subject is the tiny book, *The Practice of the Presence of God*, by the seventeenth-century Carmelite lay-brother, Bro. Lawrence (Nicholas Herman of Lorraine).

about the angels who surround the eternal throne and sing their *Sanctus*; we are told about the angels who surround the altar to join in the *Sanctus* of the Mass; we are told, ' He has given charge to his angels concerning thee, to watch over thee wheresoever thou goest; they will hold thee up with their hands lest thou shouldst chance to trip on a stone '[1]. How stupid we are if we whittle away our world and impoverish our lives by reducing everything to the level of a dull materialism! We are citizens of no mean city: the earth is ours, and its fullness, to contemplate and love and enjoy; the mystery of human beings is ours to contemplate and love and enjoy; and in and about this material world there are the mighty spirits who minister alike to God and to man; and infinitely further our horizon stretches, for all these things dwell in the immensity of God in whom we 'live and move and have our being'[2] and with whom none the less we can walk and talk as Adam did in the garden of Eden, for the Word has been made flesh and dwelt among us, the hero has come home, bringing the boon of life to his people, so that there is a ' new heaven and a new earth '[3], and the heaven is, inchoatively, ours to enjoy here and now upon earth.

[1] *Ps.* xc, 11–12 (Knox).   [2] *Acts*, xvii, 28 (Knox).   [3] *Apoc.* xxi, 1. Cf. *Isaiah*, lxv, 17 (the immediate reference is to the return of the Israelites from the Captivity): ' See where I create new heavens and a new earth; old things shall be remembered no longer, have no place in man's thoughts. Joy of yours, pride of yours, this new creation shall be; joy of mine, pride of mine, Jerusalem and her folk, created anew ' (Knox).

*Be mindful also, Lord, of thy servants and handmaids,
N. and N., who are gone before us marked with the
sign of faith and who sleep in the sleep of peace. To
them, Lord, and to all that rest in Christ grant, we
beseech thee, a place of refreshment, light and peace,
through Christ our Lord. Amen.*

What is the *signum fidei*, the ' sign of faith '? The word *signum*
is rich in meaning because of the importance in the ancient world
of the practice of marking things with a seal (*signatio*). ' Do not
distress God's holy spirit,' says St Paul, ' whose seal you bear until
the day of your redemption comes '[1]. ' The Church is, in biblical
language, a " sealed people ": a people set apart, preserved from
destruction. . . . In the *Apocalypse* we read of the four angels at
the earth's four corners, holding the winds and ready to unleash
them to destroy the earth ', but first there comes ' an angel " ascending from the rising of the sun " who bids them " hurt not the
earth nor the sea nor the trees " till he has signed the " servants of
our God in their foreheads "[2]. This idea of signing or sealing is
suggested by the signet-ring of the oriental monarch, used for the
validation of documents and similar purposes; or again by the
practice of branding slaves and cattle with the owner's mark; so,
in both Testaments, the true followers of God are marked as his
own, to be preserved from catastrophe; St Paul has several references to this divine sealing;[3] and St John speaks of our Lord himself
as sealed by his Father.[4]. . . To have the seal is of immense importance to us, for it is our defence against ultimate catastrophe;

---

[1] *Ephes.* iv, 30 (Knox).   [2] *Apoc.* vii, 1–3 (Douai).   [3] II *Cor.* i, 22; *Ephes.* i, 13; iv,
30.   [4] *John,* vi, 27.

it is an immense privilege, for it marks us as God's own; it is a thing of gladness, for it is by the Spirit of love and joy that we are sealed.' [1]

From the third century onwards in the west the idea of *signatio* was associated especially with the sacrament of confirmation or strengthening: soldiers were marked on hand, forearm or forehead with the sign of their *imperator*, and this suggested a parallel with the *militia Christi*, the mature christian's soldierly loyalty to Christ.[2] But above all the idea applied to baptism: the *signum fidei* is baptism itself: ' to have received baptism is to carry the imprint of the seal, its *character* ' and if the sign is ' preserved intact it is a guarantee of access to eternal life ' [3].

Those for whom we pray in this prayer then are the faithful who have died with the seal of the Spirit upon them. And as in the first *Memento* or diptych, so here in the remembrance of the dead, we think first of all of those who have a special claim on our love and our prayers: those who were nearest to us because of marriage or blood-relationship or friendship or some personal responsibility, or because they belonged to the same parochial *ecclesia* or congregation, the same city or country, as ourselves. But then we go on to include all those who ' rest in Christ ', all the souls in purgatory. And it is noteworthy that we speak of them as ' sleeping in the sleep of peace '. (The word ' cemetery ' means, etymologically, a dormitory.) [4] There seems to be an echo here of our Lord's words, ' The maid is not dead but sleepeth ', and again of his use of the same verb when speaking of Lazarus. Chrysostom suggests that he is telling his followers not to be afraid of death; and perhaps he is contrasting two very different ideas of the after-life: the grey, wraith-like half-existence of Sheol or Hades with the christian idea of heaven as fulfilment, glory, peace. Certainly nowadays we need to be taught not to fear death: in earlier days it was the sex-words which were taboo; now the taboo has been

---

[1] Vann and Meagher: *Stones or Bread?*, pp. 90-1. [2] Cf. Jungmann: *Missarum Sollemnia*, t. iii, p. 163, n.27. [3] Jungmann, *op. cit.* p. 163. [4] The remainder of this section, on purgatory, is reprinted from an article in *The Life of the Spirit*, November 1957, by kind permission of the Editor.

transferred to the death-words, and one must speak not of dying but of passing on or away or even over.

But the ' sleep of peace ' in the *Memento* refers specifically to purgatory; and seems to contrast very oddly with other traditional ideas about the ' suffering souls ', and with the view of St Augustine and St Thomas that ' the least pain of purgatory is greater than the greatest suffering in this world '[1]. On the one hand the flames, the torment; on the other the peace, the beautiful flowered meadow which the seer in Bede's *History* took to be heaven.

In fact, if we are to form a true concept of the state of the holy souls, we need both pictures. On the one hand the earthly struggle is over, and with it the gnawing uncertainty, the fear that we shall fail in the end to save our souls; the infinite bliss and rapture of God can be looked forward to with joy as something assured. So the *Purgatorio* begins with the approach of dawn, and the poet describes how

> *Sweet hue of sapphire, that was spread*
> *O'er the serene aspect of the pure air,*
> *High up as the first circle, to mine eyes*
> *Unwonted joy renew'd.*

In this world we know indeed the keen joy of anticipating joy, but there is always the fleck of fear lest our anticipations be frustrated or at least, as so often happens, that the reality prove less of a delight than we had hoped. In purgatory it is the other way round: there is utter assurance both that heaven is won and that its happiness must infinitely exceed anything that could have been imagined. The words of Gerontius:

> *I went to sleep; and now I am refreshed.*
> *A strange refreshment: for I feel in me*
> *An inexpressive lightness, and a sense*
> *Of freedom, as I were at length myself,*
> *And ne'er had been before,*

[1] *Sum. Theol.* Suppl. lxxii, 1.

are followed by the triumphant song of the angel:

> *My work is done*
> *My task is o'er,*
> *And so I come,*
> *Taking it home,*
> *For the crown is won,*
> *Alleluia*
> *For evermore.*

' I do not believe it would be possible,' writes St Catherine of Genoa, ' to find any joy comparable to that of a soul in purgatory, except the joy of the blessed in paradise—a joy which goes on increasing day by day, as God more and more flows in upon the soul, which he does abundantly in proportion as every hindrance to his entrance is consumed away.' [1]

But this consuming process is itself torment. There is first of all the sense of loss: when Gerontius asks whether he will see his Master when he reaches the throne the angel replies:

> *Yes, for one moment thou shalt see thy Lord.*
> *One moment; but thou knowest not, my child,*
> *What thou dost ask: that sight of the Most Fair*
> *Will gladden thee, but it will pierce thee too.*

That is the first torment: the momentary ecstatic glimpse is vouch-safed but then is of necessity withdrawn since the soul is, in its sinfulness, incompatible with it. And the second torment lies in the blinding recognition of that sinfulness, of its hideousness and horror. So Gerontius cries:

> *Take me away, and in the lowest deep*
> *There let me be:*

for the sinner, however penitent, however much he loves God, knows the terror of God, knows that he cannot approach him

---

[1] Cf. Mother Mary St. Austin: *The Divine Crucible*, p. 61.

till all the sin is consumed away and love and Love are made one.

What exactly are we to understand by the phrase ' purgatorial fire '? Here opinions differ; some think of the fire literally, as material flames, others take it metaphorically; the Church has made no pronouncement on the subject. As Dr Bernhard Bartmann writes: ' We must distinguish between the existence of purgatory and the existence of punishment by fire; the former is defined as a dogma, the latter is not. There is no definition in regard to the nature of the pains of purgatory and there exists no certain dogmatic teaching on the subject. . . . No scholastic asserts that existence of such a fire is revealed truth. Neither is it possible to infer it from some other dogma '[1]. St Thomas takes the literal view, but explains the action of the fire simply in terms of detention or restriction (for obviously flames cannot burn what is immaterial). ' Although, of its nature,' he writes, ' a corporeal thing is able to confine an incorporeal spirit to a place, it is not able of its nature to detain an incorporeal spirit in the place to which it is confined, and so to tie it to that place that it be unable to seek another, since a spirit is not by nature in a place so as to be subject to place. But the corporeal fire is enabled as the instrument of the vengeance of divine justice thus to detain a spirit; and thus it has a penal effect on it, by hindering it from fulfilling its own will, that is by hindering it from acting where it will and as it will.' So, he concludes, the soul ' is tormented by the fire ' by being ' enchained as it were ' by it.[2]

Whatever view one takes, however, of the nature of the fire there is no question about its aptness as a symbol. Baron von Hügel pointed out how, at the basis of all St Catherine of Genoa's teachings about purgatory, there is the assumption of ' the essential unity and continuity of the soul's life here and hereafter '[3], so that she sees purgatory simply as the continuation of the purgatorial

[1] *Purgatory*, p. 126; cf. Mother Mary St. Austin, *op. cit.* pp. 19–20.   [2] *Sum. Theol.* Suppl. lxx, 3.   [3] *The Mystical Element of Religion*, Vol. I, p. 281.

process begun in this life. Now the mystics again and again describe
that process in terms of fire burning away dross or alloy; St Catherine herself speaks of the ' rust of sin ' being burnt away by the
fire so as to lay the soul more and more open to the rays of God
their true Sun.[1]   Here we have that ambivalence which explains
how purgatory can be at the same time both joy and sorrow: to
quote Newman again, the divine effluence scorches and shrivels
the soul so that it lies ' consumed yet quickened by the glance of
God '.

And though the fire ' detains ' the soul, this does not mean
that the soul enters it unwillingly; on the contrary, as St Catherine
says, it ' swiftly and of its own accord casts itself in '[2].   And she
sees the fire too as an inner impetus and impulse: ' When a soul
approaches more and more to that state of original purity and
innocence in which it had been created, the instinct of God, bringing
happiness in its train (*istinto beatifico*), reveals itself and increases on
and on, with such an impetuousness of fire that any obstacle seems
intolerable '[3].   Thus the fire is God adored and God purifying; it
is also the transforming process within the soul. ' The joy of a
soul in purgatory goes on increasing day by day, owing to the
inflowing of God into the soul '; the still imperfect soul is like
a covered object which ' cannot respond to the rays of the sun
which beat upon it . . . because the covering intervenes '.   Now
' sin is the covering of the soul; and in purgatory this covering is
gradually consumed by the fire; and the more it is consumed, the
more does the soul correspond and discover itself to the divine
ray '[4].   So, in the end, it becomes itself fire, in that mysterious
identification with and absorption into the divine life which yet
leaves the created personality intact.

The continuity of the purifying and transforming process in
this life and the next, the thought of the torment-aspect of purgatory
and the helplessness of the holy souls to shorten its duration: all
this underlines for us the importance of the exhortations of the

[1] Cf. E. Underhill, *Mysticism*, p. 202.   [2] Cf. Hügel, *op. cit.* p. 287.   [3] Cf. H ıgel, *op. cit.* p. 288.   [4] *ibid.* p. 290-1.

spiritual writers to do penance and purify ourselves as far as may be in this world. If we could see here and now the horror of sin we should perhaps not sin at all; but we are blind, and can blind ourselves further, and so we not only sin but become connaturalized with sin. We must suppose that the roots of a long-cherished evil habit go very deep—or, to use St Catherine's metaphor, the rust on a soul long neglectful of God must be very thick—and the purifying process will need to be a very lengthy one. The holy souls cannot sin, but neither can they accelerate the process of purgation. With us it would seem to be the other way round: in our weakness we cannot fail to sin, but we can do something to counteract the sin and its effects: we can, through prayer, sorrow, ascetical practices, growth in the virtues, come a little closer to that state of love without which heaven is closed to us.

But the fire-symbolism underlines something else for us: the purifying and transforming process is essentially though not exclusively a passive one. It is God the Fire who purifies; the soul which is purified. Perhaps one should say that the process is *receptive* rather than passive, for of course the process will not go on unless the soul actively wills it; but it is a will to accept the fire—we may recall again de Caussade's definition of holiness as willing what comes to us at each moment by God's order—and all the ascetical and pious practices on which we might be tempted to rely would be of little avail unless above all we were trying to make this our fundamental attitude and praying for the grace to succeed. And indeed how can we hope to achieve even the first step in the ascetical or purgative way, the simplest beginnings of mortification and self-dominance, unless the grace of God works in us to impel us to do so? The holy souls have all the single-minded and intense longing for God which we in our worldliness lack; to have something of that longing must be our first prayer, for otherwise we shall lack the will to accept the fire, we shall fail to see or feel the need to mortify ourselves because we shall fail to see that ' all those self-regarding instincts—so ingrained that they have become auto-

matic—which impel the self to choose the more comfortable part'
are 'gross infringements of the law of love'[1].

If with us the fundamental attitude is the passive or receptive
one, while at the same time we must also be 'busy about many
things' in our attempt to order our lives, with the holy souls, as
we have seen, it is otherwise: they must be wholly passive. Hence
their need of our prayers, and our duty to offer them. We owe
that duty primarily to those who were nearest to us in this life,
for whom we were most responsible or to whom we ought to be
most grateful; but the Church encourages us to pray for all the
souls in purgatory in general, which means a far vaster number
than those who at their death were formally catholics or even
christians; and perhaps there is a special rightness in praying sometimes particularly for those souls who have none to pray for them
personally because their families and friends have no belief in the
efficacy of prayer for the dead.

Gerontius sings of how he must

> The lone night-watches keep,
>   Told out for me.
> There, motionless and happy in my pain,
>   Lone, not forlorn,—
> There will I sing my sad perpetual strain,
>   Until the morn.

'Happy in my pain': we return to the point from which we
began; they sleep in the sleep of peace. The gentleness of Fauré's
Requiem seems closer to the spirit of the *Memento* than do the
majesty and terror of Verdi's *Dies Irae* for all its stupendous beauty;
and Newman's poem too, and Elgar's music, strike at the end the
same note:

> Softly and gently, dearly-ransomed soul,
>   In my most loving arms I now enfold thee
> And o'er the penal waters, as they roll,
>   I poise thee, and I lower thee, and hold thee. . . .

[1] E. Underhill, *op. cit.* p. 220.

The Mystery in the Mass

Angels, to whom the willing task is given
  Shall tend and nurse, and lull thee, as thou liest:
And Masses on the earth, and prayers in heaven,
  Shall aid thee at the throne of the Most Highest.
Farewell, but not for ever, brother dear,
  Be brave and patient on thy bed of sorrow;
Swiftly shall pass the night of trial here,
  And I will come and wake thee on the morrow.

To us sinners also, thy servants, trusting in the
multitude of thy mercies, deign to grant some part
and fellowship with thy holy apostles and martyrs:
with John, Stephen, Matthias, Barnabas, Ignatius,
Alexander, Marcellinus, Peter, Felicity, Perpetua,
Agatha, Lucy, Agnes, Cecily, Anastasia, and with all
thy saints: into whose company we beseech thee to
admit us, not considering our merit but freely pardoning
our offences, through Christ our Lord.

This prayer is usually taken to refer to the priest himself who is
offering the Mass, or to priest and ministers; some writers however
extend it to all those assisting at the sacrifice,[1] that all may be
admitted to the company of the saints and to eternal life. The
saints here mentioned are representative, as Honorius points out,
of the different types of rank or status in the Church: Matthias the
apostle, Barnabas the disciple, Alexander the Pope, Ignatius the
bishop, Marcellinus the priest, Stephen the deacon, Peter the
exorcist (representing therefore the ecclesiastical ' minor orders '),
the married saints Perpetua, Felicity and Anastasia, and the virgin-
saints Agatha, Lucy, Agnes and Cecily.[2]

Now if we think of these saints as having a special significance
for us inasmuch as we are all called to minister, to ' bear witness ',
to the altar, there is a quality about them which we should do well
to notice, a quality which leads them, either directly in their own
lives, or indirectly through the accidents of history, to efface
themselves.

St John the Baptist heads the list. He was clearly a very great
man, a great and powerful personality; he had no need to go

[1] e.g. Bona, *op. cit.* p. 232.   [2] *ibid.*

searching for an audience for his preaching, the multitudes flocked out to the desert to hear him; he could easily have become a national hero and leader. But when Christ is ready to begin his ministry the Baptist sends away his own disciples, to follow the One who is greater than he, the latchet of whose shoes he is not worthy to loose; he is not the bridegroom, only the friend of the bridegroom; he is not the Light but is to give testimony to the Light; and all this he expresses humbly and vividly when he says of Christ, ' He must increase, but I must decrease '. Again when priests and levites ask him, ' Who art thou ? ' he answers simply, ' I am the voice of one crying in the wilderness ': the greatness and power of his personality are absorbed into his function of bearing witness, as the personality and life of Veronica are absorbed in her gesture of wiping the face of our Lord with a towel. If we are to preach Christ and not ourselves, if we are to witness to Christ and not magnify ourselves, it is this self-effacing quality that we need.

St Stephen, too, was a great man: ' full of grace and fortitude ', we are told, he ' did great signs and wonders among the people ': and when he made his great speech before the Council they ' saw his face as if it had been the face of an angel '. But then he was stoned to death; and with a quiet prayer for his murderers he ' fell asleep in the Lord '; and for all his greatness, for all that it was his glory to be the protomartyr of christianity, he figures little enough in subsequent christian history.

It is much the same with St Barnabas: a man of wealth and position, so majestic in appearance that he is taken to be Zeus; it was he who, at Jerusalem, took Saul by the hand ' and brought him to the apostles ' who before had been unable to believe that he was a true disciple;[1] and at the beginning of St Paul's ministry it is of ' Barnabas and Saul ' that we hear;[2] later it becomes ' Paul and Barnabas '[3], till finally, after their disagreement,[4] they separate, and the rest of *Acts* is taken up with the ministry of St Paul: Bar-

[1] *Acts*, ix, 27 (Knox).   [2] *Acts*, xi, 30; xii, 24; xiii, 2 (Knox).   [3] *Acts*, xiii, 43 (Knox).
[4] *Acts*, xv, 36–40 (Knox).

nabas fades out of the picture and nothing certain is known of the latter part of his life.

Again, St Ignatius of Antioch is one of the greatest men of his time; yet in the Butler-Thurston *Lives of the Saints* we read of the ' obscurity which surrounds almost all the details of this great martyr's career '; and we can compare with the self-effacing words of the Baptist: ' A man must be content to receive the gift which is given him from heaven, and nothing more .... I am not the Christ; I have been sent to go before him .... He must become more and more, I must become less and less ' [1], the famous saying of St Ignatius about his coming martyrdom: ' I am the wheat of God, and by the teeth of wild beasts am I milled, that I may be found to be the true bread of Christ '.

Of Pope St Alexander we know nothing; for according to the Butler-Thurston *Lives* the mention of him in the Roman Martyrology is based on a *Passio* which is historically worthless. And the rest of the saints in the list seem to be either wrapped in a similar obscurity (St Anastasia, for instance) or else to have been illustrious or eminent figures in their life-time but to have made little impression on the subsequent devotional history of christianity,[2] while St Lucy for her part, who was martyred at the age of thirteen, may be said to have hidden her life in Christ long before the age at which she could be said to have had a ' life ' at all. Thus it may be said that, apart from the New Testament figures and Ignatius and Perpetua, these are martyrs ' of whom almost nothing is known except their names and the place of their martyrdom ', while even of Matthias, Barnabas and Ignatius it can be said that ' there is no trace of any real *cultus* of them in Rome in the course of the first centuries ' [3].

[1] *John*, iii, 27–30 (Knox).   [2] St Cecily, of patrician birth, and of great fame in the early Church, may indeed be said to impinge on later Church history inasmuch as she is regarded as patroness of music and has often been depicted as playing the organ, but this, unfortunately, seems to bear no relation to reality and to be the result of a medieval mistranslation of some words in her *Office* in the breviary: *Cantantibus organis Caecilia virgo in corde suo soli Deo decantabat,* which means not that Cecily sang in her heart to God alone as she played the organ, but that she did so while organs were being played, or while music was being made.   [3] Cf. Jungmann: *Missarum Sollemnia,* t. iii, pp. 177, 178.

Ignatius was called Theophorus, the God-bearer: an *alter Christus*, absorbed in Christ, he bore witness, selflessly and fearlessly, to the Light, as did all the others in their different ways; and we pray to be of their company, to share in their selflessness, their courage, their love.

Many of these martyrs had to suffer terrible torments terribly prolonged; they remained steadfast. We may not have to face any even remotely comparable suffering; we may be permitted to die quietly in our beds; but we still have to pray for the grace to share in their steadfastness if we are to give testimony to the Light worthily and faithfully to the end. There is always the danger that, having embarked on the christian life, we may for one reason or another abandon it altogether; but there is another danger, more subtle because it can lead us to disaster without our noticing what has happened to us: the danger not of an explicit, total abandonment of Christ but of a gradual declension into sloth; not of a positive denial of our faith but of a gradual withering of faith in any vital sense, of faith as a real conviction governing all our judgments and conduct. It is worth inquiring into the sort of things which can in fact lead from an initial fervour, through a gradual fading of interest and enthusiasm, to some such acquiescence in sloth and so perhaps in the end to a loss of all effective belief and love.

We may consider first of all the warnings of the spiritual writers against what they call worldly pleasures; and let us have in mind here pleasures which are not sinful in themselves but which would come under the heading of profane rather than sacred—going to the play, to films, dances, parties, indulging a taste for games, detective stories, the lighter side of television or wireless, and so on.

The first thing to be clear about is that pleasures of this sort are not wrong in themselves but can be laudable and indeed necessary. For St Thomas, as we have seen, *insensibilitas* is a vice; and it includes treating pleasure as wrong in itself. True, St Thomas points out that pleasures are rightly abstained from for the sake of some good end: for health-reasons, or because of the exigencies of a vocation as athlete or soldier, or again as a mode of penance ' to recover health of soul '; but in general the principle holds good: ' Whatever is contrary to the natural order is vicious. Now nature has introduced pleasure into the operations that are necessary for [our] well-being '; thus: ' the good of reason cannot be in a man who abstains from all pleasures '[1]. And elsewhere he says that ' men need pleasures as a physic to counteract the manifold pains and sorrows of life '[2].

He deals with the same theme at greater length in discussing *modestia* or orderly behaviour. Can playing games be a virtue? he asks; and beginning as usual by arguing against the position he wishes to maintain he quotes Ambrose, ' Our Lord said: " Woe to you who laugh, for you shall weep ". Wherefore I consider that all, and not only excessive, games should be avoided '; and Chrysostom: ' It is not God but the devil that is the author of fun '. But then he goes on to point out that just as man needs bodily rest since ' he cannot always be at work ', so it is with the soul, ' whose power is also finite and equal to a fixed amount of work '; weariness of soul then ' must needs be remedied by resting the soul: and the soul's rest is pleasure '. He goes on to warn us that games should not be ' indecent or injurious ' nor allowed to destroy our sense of balance; they must moreover be conformed to ' persons, time, and place ' and other circumstances; but with these provisos we can accept with approval, as he does, the words of Aristotle, that in this life ' there is a kind of rest that is associated with games ' so that it is sometimes necessary to make use of such things. He then puts the words of Ambrose into their context, for in fact the saint begins by saying that ' jokes are at times fitting and pleasant ', and interprets Chrysostom as meaning the inordinate use of fun. In the next article he remarks that ' excessive play pertains to senseless mirth, which Gregory calls a daughter of gluttony. Wherefore it is written (*Exod.* xxxii, 6): " The people sat down to eat and drink, and they rose up to play " '; but on the other hand he holds, following Aristotle, that to be mirthless is a vice, since it means

[1] *Sum. Theol.* II. II. cxlii, 1, *c. et ad* 2.   [2] *Sum. Theol.* I. II. xxxi, 5 *ad* 1.

being burdensome to others, giving them no pleasure and hindering their enjoyment.[1]

This medicinal character of pleasure we have already considered: what then are the dangers against which the ascetical writers so vehemently warn us? Simply that what begins as a necessary distraction, recreation, relaxation of tension and recovery of energy, may end as an obsession, leading to a neglect of work, of all sorts of duties, of God. From loving the ballet one can become (in the strict sense of the word) a balletomane; one can become ' addicted ' in a wholly uncritical and irresponsible way to the cinema or the television as one can to a drug; there is all the difference in the world between sharing with a friend a bottle of the wine which, as the psalmist says, ' rejoices the heart of man ', and becoming a drunkard; and we are all familiar with the obsessive power which games and gaming, whodunits or westerns, idle gossip (which, incidentally, so often and so easily degenerates into scandal), the tea-party, the cocktail-party, the pub-crawl, can exercise over us. Thus very easily ' worldly pleasures ' (using the adjective in no pejorative sense) can lead us to worldliness, into an absorption in the transient, the superficial, the frivolous, and so into forgetfulness of God and of the deeper levels of life and experience.

That in its turn will probably mean a coarsening of moral fibre in general and of conscience in particular: the lust for pleasure once ingrained in us, we shall begin to find the more innocent forms of it dull, insipid; we shall look for something new, and be less concerned than we should once have been with whether the new forms are morally admissible or not; so, gradually, we may find ourselves indulging without a qualm in pleasures which are definitely sinful; and from that it is a short enough step to a deadening of conscience which will allow us to go untrammelled on our way —and, worse still, to lead others to share the way with us.

But this gradual sinking into forgetfulness of God is not brought about only by pleasure-seeking. A man who sets out (legitimately enough) to make money may find in the end that he can think only

[1] *Sum. Theol.* II. II. clxviii, 2–4.

of money and nothing else; scholar, artist, surgeon, scientist, musician—all may become so wrapped up in their chosen pursuits as to have no time or attention to spare for anything else (for a vocation too can become an obsession); and as such men will be led by their one over-riding interest to neglect wife and family and friends, so they will be led to neglect their religious duties, to neglect prayer and any concern for the moral or spiritual life, to neglect God.

If we allow ourselves to decline gradually into this sort of futility or frivolity or the narrowness of a one-track mind we may one day wake up to the fact that our lives have become hollow and meaningless: that though we may have gained what seems to us so important as to be for us the ' whole world ' we have in the process lost our souls; and perhaps that realization will lead to further tensions within us and further frantic forms of escape. . . .

How are we to guard against all this? Certainly not by trying to eschew pleasure or legitimate interest altogether: that would be not only immoral but crassly stupid; as we have seen, pleasure and relaxation are a necessity and a duty, and to do without them would inevitably lead either to bodily ill-health or to neurosis or both—as also would the brutal atrophying of a gift for this or that skill, vocation, pursuit. What we ought to do is to form as early as possible a habit of relaxing and indulging in pleasurable activities (or, for that matter, inactivities: idleness too can be a duty and a recreation) in reasonable forms and to a reasonable degree, while at the same time being equally reasonable in devoting ourselves to our chosen work, so as to lead a truly balanced life, being neither too ascetical (to the point of becoming neurotic) nor too industrious (to the point of being dour and narrow) nor again too wrapped up in our pleasures (to the point of becoming flabby hedonists).

Secondly, we should be at pains to integrate work and pleasures alike into our life of prayer and worship. The Church encourages us to ' say grace ' before and after meals (and meals should be, at least in most walks of life, not a boring necessity but a pleasure and a joy); why should we not do something of the same sort when it is a question of a job of work on the one hand or, on the other, of a game, a play, a film, a swim, a symphony concert (or, for that matter, for those so disposed, a skiffle-session), a meeting with a friend, a sun-bath or a siesta?

Thirdly, and again as early as possible, we have to try to form a habit of love and devotion to the Mass, to the sacraments, to daily prayer, a habit so deeply engrained in us that the appeal of these other things will not be able to destroy or weaken it; a habit too of faith, faith as a personal relationship to God and as the basis of all moral effort; and finally that habit of living in God's presence which we have already considered.

Thus equipped, and leading a wisely balanced life, firm in our faith and love and service of God, we need have less fear of falling into sloth and disintegration, or of failing in steadfastness: we can hope and pray without presumption to be of the company of these saints whom we commemorate, to share in their self-effacing love of Christ, and so to live our lives and die our deaths—not in their heroic and dramatic ways but in our own pedestrian fashion—bearing witness to the Light of the world.

PER QUEM HÆC OMNIA

*Through whom, Lord, thou dost always create,
sanctify, quicken, bless and give us all these good
things.*

*Through him and with him and in him is to thee,
God the Father almighty, in the unity of the holy
Spirit, all honour and glory for ever and ever. Amen.*

On certain days in the early Church the fruits of the earth were brought to the altar to be blessed, and this prayer concluded the blessing. Thus *hæc omnia*, all these good things, referred not only —if indeed at all—to the sacramental offerings on the altar, but to these fruits of the earth. In the ancient *Sacramentary of the Queen of Sweden* the prayer as we now have it concludes the blessing, thus; 'Bless, Lord, these new fruits of the earth which, through thy dew from heaven and thy beneficent rains, thou hast mercifully caused to grow and ripen, that we might give thanks to thee for them in the name of our Lord Jesus Christ, through whom thou dost always' etc. An ancient Vatican missal places here the Easter blessing of the lamb; elsewhere we find the blessing of milk and honey for the catechumens at the Mass on Holy Saturday: 'Bless, Lord, this water, milk and honey; quench the thirst of thy servants with this living water which is the spirit of truth; nourish them with this milk and honey; for so, Lord, thou didst promise our fathers Abraham, Isaac and Jacob, saying, "I will lead you into a land flowing with milk and honey"; bind together thy servants in the spirit of love and peace, as this milk and honey are united together in our Lord Jesus Christ, through whom' etc.[1] But as Fr Jungmann

---

[1] Cf. Bona, *op. cit.* pp. 233-4; cp. Duchesne *op. cit.* pp. 182-3; Jungmann: *Missarum Sollemnia*, t. iii, pp. 182 *sqq.*

points out, if the word *omnia* (*all* these good things) loses some of its point now that the prayer no longer concludes such blessings, the retention of the prayer in the text of the Canon ' was due to the conviction, which one meets again and again, that the *oblata*, the sacred offerings, even after the consecration preserved their profound solidarity with the world of creatures '[1].

As we say this prayer then we may have in mind the ancient blessings of the ' fruits of the earth ', but we need not take the words too narrowly: we may have in mind all that we mean by the ' good earth ', all that Nature means for us: our daily bread, our daily alphabet, our daily joy; we can think of all the good things of life that God has given us: our own personal gifts and qualities, natural and supernatural, and all the things—the people, the animals, the inanimate things of Nature and of art—which go to make up and enrich our lives. All these God creates; and having created he hallows, through the instrumentality of his Church. In olden days, as Cardinal Bona points out, it was the custom that ' all sacred and ecclesiastical functions, the administration of the sacraments, the various blessings, should always take place during the holy sacrifice of the Mass; for indeed the Eucharist is . . . a consummation, an ultimate, supreme perfection, from which all the sacred functions derive their energy, their power, their holiness; whether therefore it was a question of contracting an alliance, of re-establishing peace, of offering something to God, of excommunicating heretics, of announcing saints' feasts or other solemnities, fasts, processions; or whether it was a question of reconciling the penitent, or of the laying of hands on the catechumens, of consecrating bishops or anointing kings or blessing the holy chrism: all these things and others like them must, it was thought, be placed under the patronage, so to speak, of the Eucharist, so that no sacred ceremony should be performed except during the course of the Mass '[2].

The exorcism of water and of salt, in connection with the rite of baptism, are outstanding examples of a pattern which runs

[1] *op. cit.* p. 187.　　[2] *op. cit.* p. 235.

through the *Rituale*: we must remind ourselves again of the ambivalence of things: the earth and its fullness are the Lord's but at the same time they are infected with evil, they have power to harm us, to corrupt us; even of the most revered and hallowed things and places we must say that *le diable rôde autour*: Satan, who was not afraid to approach Christ, will not be afraid to approach his sanctuaries. All good things are created by God, but then they are attacked, infested, by Satan; so they must be hallowed, and that hallowing is also a quickening: the driving out of their maleficent power is followed by their being hallowed, consecrated, to remedial or (as the blessing of salt says) 'medicinal' uses; water, salt, bread, oil, wine — all the things used in the sacraments —are in a special sense quickened, given a new life and a new function corresponding to it, as the water will now cleanse not merely body but soul, the bread and wine feed not only body but soul. So they are blessed indeed; and we are blessed in our turn when they are given to us; the temple veil is rent, seen and unseen worlds intermingle, eternity 'manifest in the light of day', as Traherne put it, and grace present, powerful, operative in the nerves and muscles and sinews of Nature.

This is the fire which Christ came to cast upon the earth, the transfiguring alike of Nature and of man. St Luke at the end of his Gospel tells us that when our Lord had led the apostles out as far as Bethany 'he lifted up his hands and blessed them; and even as he blessed them he parted from them and was carried up into heaven. So they bowed down to worship him, and went back full of joy to Jerusalem'[1]. He parted from them, was gone from them, and yet they were full of joy, not sorrow; was it perhaps because they had some knowledge or inkling of that fire which was to come upon them at Pentecost and quicken and transform them, to give them the inward wisdom and energy which only the Spirit can give?[2] And the fruits of the Spirit are love, joy, peace . . .

---

[1] *Luke*, xxiv, 50–2 (Knox).   [2] Cf. *The High Green Hill*, ch. vii, 'Man's Response to the Trinity', and *The Water and the Fire*, ch. v, 'The Fire of Life'.

The last word is joy. The latter part of the prayer printed at the head of this section is known as the Great Doxology; and as the priest says it he holds the sacred host in his hand and with it makes the sign of the cross five times, over and in the chalice and its lip and finally at its base. Of the origin and meaning of these crosses—they date only from the Middle Ages and grew gradually in number from two to five—little is known with any certainty; [1] the phrases are very short and therefore everything is done very swiftly, and the movements of the host in and about the chalice remind one, it can be said without irreverence, of the fluttering of a butterfly around a flower; and one liturgical writer has in fact suggested a parallel between these swift movements and those of David dancing before the ark of the Lord.

The parallel is certainly an interesting one. It is especially interesting in view of the English Reformers' sarcasms about the ' dancing God ' of the Roman Mass. [2] ' And David arose and went with all the people that were with him of the men of Juda to fetch the ark of God, upon which the name of the Lord of hosts is invoked, who sitteth over it upon the cherubims. . . . And David danced with all his might before the Lord: and David was girded with a linen ephod. . . . And when the ark of the Lord was come into the city of David, Michol the daughter of Saul, looking out through a window, saw King David leaping and dancing before the Lord: and she despised him in her heart. . . . And David returned to bless his own house: and Michol the daughter of Saul coming out to meet David, said: How glorious was the king of Israel to day, uncovering himself before the handmaids of his servants, and was naked, as if one of the buffoons should be naked. And David said to Michol: Before the Lord, who chose me rather than thy father, and than all his house, and commanded me to be ruler over the people of the Lord in Israel, I will both play and make myself meaner than I have done: and I will be little in my own eyes: and with the handmaids of whom thou speakest, I shall

[1] For a detailed discussion cf. Jungmann: *Missarum Sollemnia*, t. iii, pp. 192 *sqq.*   [2] Cf. Jungmann, *op. cit.* t. iii, p. 195, n. 61.

appear more glorious. Therefore Michol the daughter of Saul had no child to the day of her death.'[1]

David is Christ; he is also the *puer æternus*, as in the statues of Donatello and Michelangelo. ' Donatello's first innovation, which was to be followed many times in the Renaissance, is the trans-formation of the King of Israel into a young Greek god. In his youth David had been comely and, like Apollo, had conquered, by his purity of purpose, an embattled monster. He was also the canonized patron of music and poetry. But the image of David most familiar in medieval art was an old man, bearded and crowned, playing on the harp or on a chime of bells; and although the young David was not unknown in the Middle Ages, it was by a prodigious leap of the imagination that Donatello saw him as a god of anti-quity. Strictly speaking he is not an Apollo but a young Dionysus, with dreamy smile and flexible pose; and the Goliath head at his feet is simply the old satyr head often found at the base of Dionysiac statues.'[2] It is interesting too that for the Florentines Michelangelo's David is *Il Gigante*: the boy is also the hero, more than life-size.

David then is to take the ark of God, which is the Church, into Sion, the eternal city of God, the new Jerusalem; and he will do so with joy, with music and dancing, for ' with the joy of the whole earth is mount Sion founded, on the sides of the north, the city of the great king '[3]. The end is joy, but it is joy born out of sorrow; the end is laughter, but born out of tears. ' The last word is laughter: not the heart-free " sunburnt mirth " of the merry, feckless pagan, but the heartfelt Son-given laughter of the sons of God, who have known sorrow but have seen it turned into joy. They are the ones who, when things go wrong, will not despair or grumble; who really do seek first the kingdom of heaven; who can laugh at their pains because already they have learnt how to laugh for joy; who know deep in their hearts that

---

[1] II *Kings*, vi, 2, 14, 16, 20–3 (Douai).   [2] Sir Kenneth Clark: *The Nude*, pp. 48–9.
[3] *Ps.* xlvii, 2. Knox has ' where it slopes northward ': the new Sion means the vanquish-ing of the powers of darkness for ever (cf. *supra*, p. 153).

in the end " the blessing of the Lord maketh men rich; neither shall affliction be joined to them "[1], and who wait in faith and hope and patient expectancy for the day when laughter shall be no more the fugitive and fragmentary thing it is for most of us on earth, but the abiding laughter which is the sound of the Light Inaccessible, the ripples on the surface of the eternal Sea of peace and joy.'[2]

First then the sorrow: David is mocked by Michol, as Jesus was mocked by the Jews; he is mocked for being naked like a buffoon, as Christ too in his nakedness on the cross was laughed to scorn. ' Blessed are you,' our Lord had said, ' when men revile you, and persecute you, and speak all manner of evil against you falsely, because of me.'[3] So Cornelius à Lapide speaks of how Christ was ' taken by the Jews and hung upon the cross, and was made a laughing-stock; and on the cross he was exposed to them, as it were, naked, hiding from them the power of his divinity and showing them only the infirmity of the flesh'[4]. ' I will be little in my own eyes ', David had said: *ludam et vilior fiam . . . et ero humilis in oculis meis;*[5] *Ludam, inquit, ut illudar,* says St Bernard: ' David says, I will play a game, that I may be made game of. A good game it is that he plays, whereby Michol is angered and God rejoices. A good game, a spectacle which to men is ridiculous but to the angels a thing of beauty. A good game, whereby we become " the scorn of luxury, the derision of the proud "[6]. For indeed what else but a game can it seem to worldly men when we flee from the things they desire in the world, and desire the things from which they flee? . . . This is no childish sport, no theatrical mime: this is a game which is joyful, honourable, serious, noteworthy, fit to rejoice the eyes of its heavenly beholders. It was at this devout and religious game that he played who said, " We are made a spectacle to the world and to angels and to men "[7]. Let us

---

[1] *Proverbs,* x, 22 (Douai).   [2] Quoted from *Stones or Bread?* by Gerald Vann, O.P. and P. K. Meagher, O.P., p. 83.   [3] *Matt.* v, 11 (Knox).   [4] *Comment. in loc. cit.*   [5] In the Knox translation: ' Before his coming play the mountebank I will; humble myself I will in my own esteem.'   [6] *Ps.* cxxii, 4 (Knox).   [7] I *Cor.* iv, 9 (Douai).

then also sometimes play this game that we may be made game of, that we may be put to shame and humbled, till he comes who puts down the proud and exalts the humble, and who will rejoice us and glorify us and exalt us for ever '[1].

We were considering in the first part of this prayer the hallowing, quickening, blessing of all the good things of life: the healing of Nature. To do so is to see the Mass in its 'natural' setting. It was this 'naturalness' of the catholic liturgy which was sensed by D. H. Lawrence: 'The old Church knew that life is here our portion, to be lived, to be lived in fulfilment.... The rhythm of life itself was preserved by the Church hour by hour, day by day, season by season, year by year, epoch by epoch, down among the people.... We feel it in the south, in the country, when we hear the jangle of the bells at dawn, at noon, at sunset, marking the hours with the sound of Mass or prayers. It is the rhythm of the daily sun. We feel it in the festivals, the processions.... This is the wheeling of the year, the movement of the sun through solstice and equinox, the coming of the seasons, the going of the seasons.... Augustine said that God created the universe new every day: and to the living, emotional soul, this is true. Every dawn dawns upon an entirely new universe, every Easter lights up an entirely new glory of a new world opening in utterly new flower '[2].

But if we thus see the Mass (as the supreme moment of the whole liturgy) in its natural setting, we must also and still more see Nature in the setting of the Mass: Nature hallowed and quickened and blessed through the Mass, Nature (including human nature, the body and the soul) made fruitful through the Mass, so that man-in-Nature, being 'loosed from the law of death' need no longer 'bring forth fruit unto death', but can 'bring forth fruit to God '[3], having received that living water which becomes in him a 'fountain of water springing up into life everlasting '[4].

[1] *Epist.* 87 *ad Ogerium.*   [2] *Apropos of Lady Chatterley's Lover*, pp. 60–1.   [3] *Rom.* vii, 4–6 (Douai).   [4] *John*, iv, 14 (Douai); 'fountain': Lat. *fons*, cp. the baptismal font where men are born again of water and the spirit.

Michol, who mocked David, is the symbol of those who mock and reject the fountain of life: her punishment was barrenness: she ' had no child to the day of her death '—and to be barren was then regarded as the greatest shame a woman could suffer; [1] so it is with us if we reject the life-giving water, the *logos spermatikos*. But to accept the life is to join with Christ in the sacred dance, the sacred game which Wisdom played as the world was in the making: ' I was with him forming all things: and was delighted every day, playing before him at all times; playing in the world, with the sons of Adam as my play-fellows '[2] ; for again the last word is laughter, the laughter which is restored to us, as it was to Abraham, when we have reached the mount of vision.

In the apocryphal (and gnostic) *Acts of St John* there is a reference to a ' kind of round dance ' accompanying a hymn of praise: ' Christ stands in the middle, and the apostles, presumably conceived as twelve in number, walk round him in a circle. This strange *chorea mystica*, this ecstatic cult dance, in which the apostles respond with the Hebrew *Amen* (" verily ", " so be it ") is as ancient as the form of the dance mystery itself. In the Mimaut Papyrus we read: " Come to me, thou who art greatest in heaven (in this case, Helios), to whom heaven was given for a dancing ground ". Enraptured by hymn and dance, the mystai circle through the gates of initiation. Such rituals were common throughout antiquity, and they continue to reappear among christians outside of the orthodox church '[3].

There are other parallels in apocryphal literature, and in the writings of christian and non-christian mystics. Thus Plotinus writes of the ' rhythmic dance ' about a divine Corypheus, in which the soul ' beholds the Fountain of Life '; Boehme writes of how the mystic enters ' the Inner Choir, where the soul joineth hands and danceth with Sophia, the Divine Wisdom '[4]; and there is an

---

[1] The Knox translation reads: ' And Michol . . . never bore child again to the day of her death '. It is disputed, in fact, whether the text means that Michol was barren from this moment or whether she never had children at all.   [2] *Prov.* viii, 30-3 (Douai-Knox).
[3] Max Pulver: *Jesus' Round Dance and Crucifixion*, in ' The Mysteries ', Papers from the Eranos Yearbooks, pp. 174-5.   [4] Cf. E. Underhill: *Mysticism*, pp. 231-4.

interesting parallel from the writings of St Mechtild of Magdeburg:
'There will be a glorious dance of praise', she cries out; and, 'in
her poem *Der Minne Weg* (the Way of Love), writes: "Maiden,
dance as deftly as my elect have danced before thee", and the
Virgin replies:

> *I would not dance, Lord, unless thou leadest me.*
> *Wouldst thou that I spring mightily,*
> *Then must thou sing for me.*
> *Thus will I leap into love,*
> *From love into knowledge,*
> *From knowledge into joy,*
> *From joy beyond all human senses . . .'* [1]

We find this same dance theme in an old English carol, *My
Dancing Day:*

> *Tomorrow shall be my dancing day:*
> *I would my true love did so chance*
> *To see the legend of my play,*
> *To call my true love to my dance:*
>
>> *Sing O my love, O my love, my love, my love;*
>> *This have I done for my true love.*
>
> *Then was I born of a virgin pure,*
> *Of her I took fleshly substance;*
> *Thus was I knit to man's nature,*
> *To call my true love to my dance.*
>
>> *Sing,* etc.

The carol then goes on to sing of Christ's birth, baptism, temptation,
betrayal, passion and death, descent into hell ('for my true love's
deliverance') and resurrection ('up to my true love and the dance'),
and ends:

[1] Cf. Pulver: *op. cit.* pp. 175–6.

Then up to heaven I did ascend,
Where now I dwell in sure substance,
On the right hand of God, that man
May come unto the general dance:

> *Sing O my love, O my love, my love, my love;*
> *This have I done for my true love.*[1]

This means first of all, since Christ has ' borne our infirmities and carried our sorrows ' and in so doing has empowered us to embark with hope and courage on our own journey, that we can hope to be in the end of the number of those of whom it is said that God ' will wipe away every tear from their eyes, and there will be no more death, or mourning, or cries of distress, no more sorrow '[2]; but, because of the inter-penetration of eternity and time, of heaven and earth, it can mean more than that, and for the lovers of God does mean more than that, who, being like Stephen full of the holy Spirit and looking up steadfastly to heaven, see as he did the glory of God and can cry out as he cried: ' Behold, I see the heavens opened! '[3]

To see the heavens opened while yet on earth is to see with heightened awareness the beauty of that earth as God made it; it is also to see with horror the ugliness with which men have befouled it. For, to repeat, the making or preserving of beauty, the restoration of it where men have turned it into squalor, is not merely a matter of æsthetic importance, it is of theological importance; the wanton creation of ugliness is an evil, a surrender to the lust for destruction and non-being which derives from Satan the self-destroyer who once was the Lucifer, the light-bearer; it is also of mystical importance, for natural beauty is one of the ways in which men can be drawn to God.

' Closely connected with the sense of the presence of God . . . is the complementary mark of the illuminated consciousness, the

---

[1] Cf. *Oxford Book of Carols*, No. 71.   [2] *Apoc.* xxi, 4 (Knox).   [3] *Acts*, vii, 55 (Douai).

vision of "a new heaven and a new earth", or an added significance and reality in the phenomenal world.'[1] To see ' all creatures in God and God in all creatures ' is to become aware of ' the living reality of that World of Becoming, the vast arena of the divine creativity, in which the little individual life is immersed. Alike in howling gale and singing cricket [the self] hears the crying aloud of that " Word which is through all things everlastingly ". It participates, actively and open-eyed, in the mighty journey of the Son towards the Father's heart: and seeing with purged sight all things and creatures as they are in that transcendent order, detects in them too that striving of creation to return to its centre which is the secret of the universe '. Thus ' all things are perceived in the light of charity, and hence under the aspect of beauty: for beauty is simply Reality seen with the eyes of love. As in the case of another and more beatific Vision, *essere in caritate è qui necesse.* . . . The true mystic, so often taunted with " a denial of the world ", does but deny the narrow and artificial world of self: and finds in exchange the secrets of that mighty universe which he shares with Nature and with God. Strange contacts, unknown to those who only lead the life of sense, are set up between his being and the being of all other beings. In that remaking of his consciousness which follows upon the " mystical awakening ", the deep and primal life which he shares with all creation has been roused from its sleep. Hence the barrier between human and non-human life, which makes a man a stranger on earth as well as in heaven, is done away. Life now whispers to his life: all things are his intimates, and respond to his fraternal sympathy '[2].

All this explains the mystic's sympathy with and power over God's lesser creatures; it also underlines for us the duty of doing what we can to prevent Nature's ' intimations of immortality ' from being smothered by the predatory and destructive hands of man. But this ' illumination ', this enhanced awareness of things, with its accompanying joy in them and in God, is not the end

---

[1] E. Underhill: *Mysticism*, p. 254.   [2] Underhill, *op. cit.* pp. 258–60.

of the mystic's journey: he must press on, to find through new and deeper sorrows a deeper joy, a more complete freedom. Now ' that fruition of joy of which Ruysbroeck speaks in majestic phrases, as constituting the interior life of souls immersed in the Absolute—the translation of the Beatific Vision into the terms of a supernal feeling-state—is often realized in the secret experience of those same mystics as the perennial possession of a childlike gaiety, an inextinguishable gladness of heart. The transfigured souls move to the measures of a " love dance " which persists in mirth without comparison, through every outward hardship and tribulation. They enjoy the high spirits peculiar to high spirituality: and shock the world by a delicate playfulness, instead of exhibiting the morose resignation which it feels to be proper to the " spiritual life ". . . . Moreover, the most clear-sighted among the mystics declare such joy to be an implicit of Reality. Thus Dante, initiated into Paradise, sees the whole universe laugh with delight as it glorifies God:[1] and the awful countenance of Perfect Love adorned with smiles.[2] Thus the souls of the great theologians dance to music and laughter in the Heaven of the Sun;[3] the loving seraphs, in their ecstatic joy, whirl about the Being of God.[4] *O luce eterna che . . . ami ed arridi*, exclaims the pilgrim, as the Divine Essence is at last revealed to him,[5] and he perceives love and joy as the final attributes of the Triune God. Thus Beatrice with *suoi occhi ridenti*—so different from the world's idea of a suitable demeanour for the soul's supreme instructress—laughs as she mounts with him the ladder to the stars. So, if the deified soul has indeed run ahead of humanity and " according to his fruition dwells in heaven ", he too, like Francis, will run, rejoice and make merry: join the eager dance of the Universe about the One. " If ", says Patmore, " we may credit certain hints contained in the lives of the saints, love raises the spirit above the sphere of reverence and worship into one of laughter and dalliance; a sphere in which the soul says:

[1] *Paradiso*, xxvii, 4. [2] *ibid*, xx, 13. [3] *ibid*. x, 76, 118. [4] *ibid*. xxviii, 100. [5] *ibid*. xxxiii, 124–6.

> *Shall I, a gnat which dances in thy ray,*
> *Dare to be reverent? " '* [1]

Certainly we who are so earthbound, while we may sense what Patmore means, and understand the humility behind his words, may for our part be more concerned with the unhappy consequences of our *lack* of reverence, of the cavalier way we treat God and those ' heavenly things ' in which we ought to live. But it is important that we should understand him, and the light his words throw not only on humanity but on divinity as well. The idea of the eternal Wisdom playing, with the sons of Adam for his play-fellows, finds an echo in what some of the mystics have to tell us of the divine ' Game of Love '. St Teresa speaks of it as a game of chess, ' in which game humility is the Queen without whom none can checkmate the divine King '[2] ; Bl. Henry Suso saw in a vision an angel who said to him: ' Cast a joyous glance into thyself, and see how God plays his game of love with thy loving soul '; the game seems to consist in the alternation in the soul of a joyous awareness of the indwelling God and the arid sense of an apparent abandonment: so St Catherine of Siena is told in ecstasy, ' With the souls who have arrived at perfection I no longer play the game of love, which consists in leaving and returning again to the soul; though thou must understand that it is not, properly speaking, I, the immovable God, who thus elude them, but rather the sentiment that my charity gives them of me '[3].

It is the eternal Wisdom who plays this game; and it is important to notice that while Wisdom is the Word who became man, the Old Testament speaks of ' her ', in the feminine, so that we read, ' She, from my youth up, has been my heart's true love, my heart's true quest; she was the bride I longed for, enamoured of her beauty '[4]. And of Suso we are told that sometimes he saw her as a beautiful maiden, at other times as a noble youth.[5] And indeed it is important for us to remember that if God is our Father, he is

---

[1] Underhill, *op. cit.* pp. 437-8.   [2] Cf. Underhill, *op. cit.* p. 227.   [3] *ibid.* p. 228.
[4] *Wisd.* viii, 2 (Knox).   [5] Cf. *Henry Suso*, by S. M. C., p. 15.

not lacking, in his merciful dealings with us, in the qualities of a mother. Androgynous deities are not uncommon in the world of myth; according to the Midrash, Adam was created androgynous (and we can compare the myth in Plato's *Symposium*), and androgynous symbolism is to be found in the medieval Cabbala and among the gnostic christians.[1] In the Greek festival of the Soteria the deity of the day is, in Aetolia, the male Zeus Soter, in Cyzicus the female Kore Soteira or Maiden-Saviour;[2] in the *Tao-te-king* we read, of Tao: 'I do not know whose son it is', but also: 'It would seem to be the mother of all things', and according to the Taoist religion, Tao is divided into the pair of opposites, Yang and Yin, of which the former is warmth, light, masculinity and the latter is cold, darkness, femininity;[3] in the Mass symbolism, 'the combination of offering and offerer in the single figure of Christ is implicit in the doctrine that just as bread is composed of many grains of wheat, and wine of many grapes, so the mystical body of the Church is made up of a multitude of believers. The mystical body, moreover, includes both sexes, represented by the bread and wine. Thus the two substances—the masculine wine and the feminine bread—also signify the androgynous nature of the mystical Christ'[4]. We may compare also, in the apocryphal *Acts of Thomas*, the identification of holy Spirit with Mother.[5] And, as we have seen, the ringing of the bell during Mass has more than a utilitarian significance: reminding us of how the androgynous deity is portrayed with thunderbolt in the right hand, symbol of the power and authority of fatherhood, but with bell in the left, for the tenderness and compassion of motherhood.

It would be great folly to exaggerate the element of truth in the androgynous symbolisms to be found in non-christian or heterodox-christian religious thought: first, we have to bear constantly in mind that it is the soul, the creature, that is ' feminine to

---

[1] Cf. Campbell, *op. cit.* pp. 152–3.   [2] Cf. C. Kerenyi: *The Mysteries of the Kabeiroi* (in 'The Mysteries', p. 34).   [3] Cf. Jung: *Psychological Types*, pp. 265, 267.   [4] Cf. Jung: *Transformation Symbolism in the Mass* (in 'The Mysteries', p. 290).   [5] Cf. Jung: *Symbols of Transformation*, p. 359.

God '; secondly, if we bring together the two ideas of Mother and Spirit as in some way identified in the Godhead we are wise to think of Spirit, not in any trinitarian sense but simply as the term ' Spirit of God ' is used in the Old Testament; thirdly, we must be on our guard against the danger of allowing the idea of the ' motherly ' in God to weaken in any way our concept of divinity, our awe in face of the *mysterium tremendum*, our humility and sense of nothingness in face of the infinite creative power of God.

But with those ideas clearly in mind we can find a rich reward in the thought of the divine motherhood; and indeed it is to that thought that we are inevitably led by all the symbolism of baptism, sorrow, rebirth—the Son returning to his mother for renewal; and it is in that same light of tenderness that we must see the divine game of love. We are at the opposite pole to Lear's despairing cry,

As flies to wanton boys, so are we to the gods.

The end is joy and laughter: it is on this note that the Canon draws to its close. From the sublimities of the mystics' union with God, from the joy and laughter of the saints in paradise, from the ecstatic dance of the seraphs, we are of course, most of us, immeasurably removed; from the dark plains where we plod and stumble and grope and fall we can but look as from an infinite distance to the mountain of vision. Yet we can at least treasure the thought of these things and ponder over them with hope in our hearts; we can try our best to dwell at least in some degree among heavenly things: if we cannot see the heavens opened we can at least try to catch a fugitive glimpse, can try to live in the presence of God, and to see him in all creatures and all creatures in him; if we cannot know the ecstatic joy of the saints we can at least try to be cheerful enough and mirthful enough not to be burdensome to others, joyful enough not to sink into despondency and thence perhaps into sloth; and always and every day we can come back to the Mass and to the glory it reveals dwelling among us and bringing us life and light and zest and power, and so we can go on clambering as best we may up the mountain of vision, telling ourselves — and without the sad irony of Abraham — that God will provide, till one day we come to that fullness of vision and love and life and liberty and laughter for which God made us.

8

'Our Father' to 'Agnus Dei'

THE CANON now ended, we are concerned with the sacrifice-banquet, the prayers leading up to and including the communion. And we begin with the *Our Father*. Cardinal Bona points out that it is right that this prayer, taught us by our Lord himself, should follow the most sacred *action* in the Mass, that 'God may be disposed to show himself more attentive to the prayers of the faithful who have just recalled to him the memory of the cruel Passion of his Son'[1]. From St Gregory, St Jerome and others we learn that this inclusion of the Lord's Prayer in the Mass goes back to the time of the apostles; it was St Gregory who ordained that it should be said immediately after the Canon,[2] thus bringing the Roman usage into line with the Byzantine.

But before the priest begins the words of the *Our Father* itself he recites a very short preface: 'Taught by thy saving precepts and following thy divine directions, we presume to say: Our Father,' etc. It is as though he would say that as he is a sinner, an unworthy son of God, he would not dare to address God as Father if our Lord had not bade him do so.[3] In various liturgies there are variants on this theme: in the Greek rite: 'Make us worthy, Lord, to invoke thee confidently and without temerity as our Father, and to say to thee, Our Father,' etc.; the Maronite: 'Open, Lord, our mouths and our lips, sanctify us, body and soul, purify our spirits and our hearts, so that we may be able to cry with suppliant voice

[1] Bona, *op. cit.* p. 236.   [2] *ibid.* p. 237.   [3] *ibid.* p. 238.

273

to thee, our God, the Father of mercies, to pray to thee and to say, Our Father,' etc.

In the early Church only the faithful were allowed to recite the prayer; those about to become initiates were taught it together with a short explanation which is to be found in the Roman *Ordo* and other ancient MSS:

' *Our Father who art in heaven:* this is a confident cry of freedom; we must live then in such a way as to be able to be the children of God, the brothers of Christ: for how can a man dare to call God his Father if he turns away from his divine will? That is why, beloved children, we must show ourselves worthy of this divine adoption, for it is written, To all who believed in him, he gave them power to become the sons of God.

' *Hallowed be thy name:* we ask, not that God should be sanctified by our prayers, he who is ever holy, but that his name should be sanctified in us, so that we, hallowed already by baptism, may persevere, and may continue as we have begun.

' *Thy kingdom come:* God, whose empire is undying, reigns always and supremely; but we pray for the coming of that kingdom which he has promised us and which was won for us by the blood and Passion of our Lord.

' *Thy will be done on earth as in heaven:* i.e. may we who are on earth faithfully carry out what God in heaven wills to be done.

' *Give us this day our daily bread:* we must understand here a spiritual food,[1] for Christ is our bread, he who said of himself,

---

[1] We certainly need not take this phrase in a restrictive sense, as though we were not also to pray about our natural needs and material necessities; but it should be remembered that the *Our Father* here in the Mass is a direct preparation for the holy communion. ' The first generations of christians felt a close—and not exclusively liturgical—connection between the *Our Father* and the communion. . . . The Latin Fathers, following Tertullian, commonly apply the phrase "our daily bread" to the Eucharist, and the same is true of some of the Greek Fathers. Considering that the literal sense of the text is obviously concerned with material bread, this fact is remarkable, and implies the use of this prayer by the faithful in receiving communion even before the date at which there is documentary evidence of its incorporation into the liturgy. . . . From the very earliest times the *Our Father* was, it would seem, the first prayer said by neophytes on their reception into the christian community and before receiving their first communion, and at least on such occasions it was certainly said aloud and in common. The earliest commentaries on the Mass which mention the *Our Father*, the mystagogical catecheses of Jerusalem and those of Milan, make a point of explaining the *Panem nostrum* in a sacramental sense, which shows that it was in fact said

I am the living bread that has come down from heaven; we call it our daily bread because he commands us to live a life so remote from sin that we may always be worthy to partake of this heavenly food.

' *Forgive us our trespasses as we forgive them that trespass against us:* this is said to show us that we cannot hope to be forgiven our sins unless we first forgive all those who have in some way offended us; for so our Lord teaches us in the Gospel: If you will not forgive men, neither will your Father forgive you your offences.

' *And lead us not into temptation:* i.e. let us not be overcome by the tempter, the spirit of evil. Scripture tells us that it is not God who tempts us to do evil, but the devil; and that we may escape his snares our Lord tells us: Watch and pray that you enter not into temptation.

' *But deliver us from evil:* the Apostle tells us that we know not what we should ask in our prayers: therefore we must pray that everything which the frailty of human nature would prevent us from foreseeing and asking may be freely granted us by our Lord Christ, who lives and reigns with Father and holy Spirit for ever and ever, Amen.' [1].

Fr Jungmann points out how the first part of the *Our Father* forms ' a sort of summary of the Great Prayer: with " hallowed be thy name " we take up again the threefold acclamation of the *Sanctus*; " thy kingdom come " is in a sense a resumption of the two epicleses, the *Quam oblationem* and the *Supplices;*[2] while " thy will be done " expresses the spirit of obedience and self-giving which must animate every true sacrifice ' [3].

Lagrange comments on the structure of the prayer: the opening invocation, then three expressions of the soul's desire for the accom-

---

[1] Bona, *op. cit.* pp. 240-2.   [2] A variant reading of *Luke* xi, 2, has, instead of ' thy kingdom come ', a prayer for the coming of ' thy holy spirit '; cf. Jungmann: *Missarum Sollemnia,* t. iii, p. 203, n. 14.   [3] Jungmann, *op. cit.* p. 203.

---

in this spirit, and in his instructions on this point St Ambrose develops the theme at length in order to exhort the faithful to go daily to communion.' (Jungmann: *Missarum Sollemnia,* t. iii, pp. 203-4.)

plishment of God's will, and finally three prayers expressing our indigence and the weakness which finds strength in him: in all, seven parts, seven the sacred number, symbol of completion.[1]

This use of the number seven to signify completeness or sacredness or both is, as we saw before, very ancient and widespread. One thinks of the seven heavens, seas, planets, days of creation, the seven parables of the kingdom, seven sacraments, beatitudes, gifts of the holy Spirit, the seven loaves and baskets in the feeding of the four thousand and the seven disciples who ate with the risen Christ at the lake-side. In the *Apocalypse* there are the seven churches, candlesticks, stars, angels, seals, eyes and so on. Sometimes the number seems to suggest a process leading up to completeness; so the Sūfi poet 'Attar describes the mystical journey to the palace of the King as passing through seven valleys;[2] perhaps we may think again in the same way of the ' seven words ' on the cross, leading up as they do to the final *consummatum est*, as also of the ' seven swords ' which mean, at the end, the com-passion of Mary. There is the same idea in the fact that the work of creation, and the work-a-day week, end in the peace and completeness of the sabbath.

We have seen how the idea of the sabbath as a day of rest means more than just a relaxation from labour—and how this is of particular relevance and value to christians living in the world of today. 'Rest' is essentially a state of ' peace ' between man and Nature, and the weekly day of rest in this sense is paralleled by the Jewish ' sabbatical year ' or ' year of rest ' during which the land was to lie fallow, at peace. We have noted also the contrast between the holiness of the Lord's sabbath and the unholiness of the devil's sabbat: if the former means the establishment of unity between man and his natural setting, man ' at peace with the world ' and consequently on the way to establishing his own inner harmony and a harmony between himself and the God who created both nature and the sabbath, the witches' sabbat on the other hand is a symbol of the satanic quest for destruction and disunity and

---

[1] Lagrange, *op. cit.* vol. II, pp. 15–16.   [2] Cf. Underhill, *op. cit.* p. 131.

debasement. For the christian, the sabbath day is kept holy primarily by his church-going: his recalling of the meaning for him of water and wood and bread; his participation in the Mass-offering, his communion; in the worship of Satan these life-giving rites are travestied—the brackish water, the black draperies, the defiled host, the substitution of erotic orgy for *agape*. Thus the Incarnation is reversed: whereas the Word made flesh restores goodness to matter, harnessing it to the service of love, Satan defiles matter and harnesses it to the service of hate. Satanism leaves man at war with himself, with the world, with God; it is the spirit of the sabbath that alone can give him peace.

We begin the *Our Father*, then, on a note of childlike confidence and simplicity; we pray the prayer of praise, and beg for the fulfilling of God's plan, the coming of his kingdom, and then in general for the accomplishment of his will, making that *fiat* which must be at least implicitly at the heart of every prayer of petition; only then do we go on to pray for our bread, the necessities of natural and supernatural life for which, as creatures, we are wholly dependent upon God; and for the forgiveness of our sins since we for our part forgive others the wrongs they have done us—an awesome thought for us, who in fact are so often reluctant to forgive, tenacious of resentment, lustful for vengeance (and the Gospel story of the king and the two debtors [1] drives home the lesson for us); and so finally we beg God to deliver us from all evil.

---

[1] *Matt.* xviii, 23-35. There is no comparison between our offences against God and any offence committed against us by other men, since the former, precisely because they are against God, have a certain infinity about them; so the first servant owed his king an immense sum of money, but was owed only a paltry hundred pieces of silver by his fellow-servant. We may note that the punishment of the King's minister was that he should be given over to the torturers until he had paid the debt—which, since he clearly could not hope to do so, must mean to be tortured indefinitely. But against this terrifying conclusion to our Lord's story we can set the words which immediately precede it, when he tells Peter that he is to forgive not seven but seventy times seven times, which is to say, always. ' God's mercy is infinite; he never wearies of forgiving. Therefore Peter must forgive . . . always. Can he who is always in need of mercy refuse it to others? One might almost say that such a one ought to be more disposed to pardon even than God himself, since he has so often received pardon for his own offences.' (Lagrange, *op. cit.* vol. I, p. 286). The ultimate emphasis is indeed on how abominable it is for one man to refuse to forgive another; but we can recall with gratitude and hope the fact of the infinite mercy of God on which it is based.

This last request is taken up again in the next prayer, which therefore is called the Embolism or development (as a musical theme is developed in sonata or symphony): 'Deliver us, Lord, from all evils, past, present and to come; and by the intercession of the blessed and glorious virgin Mary, Mother of God, together with the blessed apostles Peter and Paul and Andrew and all the saints, graciously grant peace in our days, that through thy mercy we may always be free from sin and secure from all anxiety'.

It is not clear why St Andrew receives special mention in this prayer: Bona suggests that it is because he was the first of the apostles to be called; Fr Martindale, more significantly, reminds us that it was Andrew who pointed out the boy who had the few loaves and fishes which were to feed the multitude.[1] We are in fact concerned from now on, as we have seen, with the sacrifice-banquet, with the communion; and the keynote of all the prayers which now follow is the idea of peace. The Embolism makes a vivid contrast between the evil from which we would be delivered and the peace for which we pray: and few prayers could seem of more actual and contemporary significance to us, for we live in an age of fear. Over us all hangs the fear of a war which might well destroy the world; fear of the power of a science which may become a Frankenstein's monster; for christians in many places there is a fear of persecution, perhaps of torture and death; and if what we fear is the destruction of external peace among men, the anxieties these fears foster are themselves destructive of inner peace of soul. Moreover, to these anxieties we must add the unhappiness and restlessness of the sin-laden soul, sadly and fearfully aware of its sinfulness but unable or unwilling to turn from its sin and find its rest in God. But it was peace that our Lord, as he himself said, left us as a legacy; and it is in and through the Mass especially that we receive that legacy.

[1] Cf. Bona, *op. cit.* p. 242; Martindale: *The Mind of the Missal*, p. 44; for another historical explanation, cf. Jungmann, *op. cit.* t. iii, p. 209.

During the concluding words of the Embolism the priest first breaks the host into two parts and then, breaking off a small fragment, makes the sign of the cross with it three times over the chalice, saying, ' The peace of the Lord be with you always '. To understand the significance of this we must go back in mind to the primitive ' breaking of bread ' when all present who wished to communicate did so by receiving a particle of a single consecrated loaf, as happened, we are to suppose, at the Last Supper, when Jesus ' blessed and broke and gave to his disciples '. The putting of the fragment into the chalice, i.e. the mystical mingling of body and blood, is a symbol of the risen Christ and therefore looks towards eternal life as the effect of communion; so the priest, as he carries out this ritual, says,[1] ' May this sacred mingling of the body and blood of our Lord Jesus Christ be to me, and to all who partake of them, health of mind and body and a wholesome preparation for the meriting and obtaining of everlasting life '. But again we should see the action in its historical setting. In the early days in Rome it was the custom to preserve a fragment of the host to be solemnly carried next day to the church where the Pope was to say Mass. So, at this point in the Mass, the fragment was presented to him by the deacon, and placed by him in the chalice, while he set aside a fragment of the host he had just consecrated, to be used in the same way in the Mass of the morrow. So the unity of the Mass was made clear: ' in a true sense there is but one Mass in all the world; and by inserting thus yesterday's Mass into today's, and today's into tomorrow's, this unity was vigorously proclaimed '[2]. This explains also why the deacon at High Mass holds the paten shrouded in the humeral veil during the Canon: ' why all this mystery about an empty plate? Because, at first, it was *not* empty. It had on it the blessed sacrament from yesterday, and that is what the minister held studiously covered, until he handed it to the priest to be placed in today's chalice '[3]. But this moment of the Mass emphasized, through another ancient ceremony, not only the unity

---

[1] In the Dominican Mass.   [2] Martindale, *op. cit.* p. 44.   [3] *ibid.* p. 45.

279

of the Mass but the unity of the Church. This was the custom of the *fermentum*: by the hands of duly ordained acolytes, fragments of the host of the Pope's Mass were carried to bishops in the city who were celebrating at the same time; similarly bishops sent the *fermentum* to their priests. The word *fermentum* means leaven, and the symbolism is obvious: the Eucharist is that which binds the faithful together in communion, in unity, as the leaven is that which binds together the loaf.[1]

The prayer of 'mingling' is preceded[2] by the *Agnus Dei*, which, originally a choral chant only, seems to date in its present form and position from the time of Pope Sergius I, the ending of the third invocation, 'give us peace', being substituted for 'have mercy on us' to bring the prayer into line with the main theme of this part of the Mass. We may see the various prayers for peace as begging God to free us, first from war, violence, international discord, secondly from inward trouble of soul, and thirdly from discord within the christian family. For nothing is clearer in this part of the Mass than that it is a family feast; and this idea is given emphasis by the giving of the kiss of peace. In the Dominican High Mass the priest kisses first the chalice at the end of the 'mingling' prayer, and then the *pax*—a silver image, symbolical of peace —which the deacon holds out first to him and then to the subdeacon, saying 'Peace be to thee and to the holy Church of God', after which the subdeacon takes it to each of the community in turn. (Some families, when they return home after being at Mass and holy communion together, give each other the 'holy kiss', which is clearly an extension of the *pax* ceremony, and a very lovely way of emphasizing the immediate relevance of the 'sacrament of peace' to the life of the family.) The kissing of the chalice is a *stylisation* of the earlier practice of kissing the sacred host itself: the purpose is to emphasize the *source* from which the peace comes which is then transmitted by the celebrant, through his ministers, to the community; in the same way the use of the *pax* (also called *instru-*

[1] Cf. e.g. Duchesne: *Christian Worship*, p. 185; Lucas, S. J. *Holy Mass*, vol. II, pp. 76–8; Martindale, *op. cit.* p. 45.   [2] In the Dominican Mass; in the Roman Mass the order is reversed.

mentum pacis or *osculatorium*) is a formalized way of giving the kiss of peace. (According to Fr Jungmann, both these formalizations are of English origin.[1])

Meanwhile the priest is saying the pre-communion prayer, addressed to Christ himself: 'Lord Jesus Christ, Son of the living God, who in accordance with the will of the Father and with the co-operation of the holy Spirit hast through thy death given life to the world: deliver me by this holy body and blood of thine from all my iniquities and from all evils; make me always cleave to thy commandments and never let me be separated from thee, who with the same Father and Spirit livest and reignest God for ever and ever'.

In the Roman Mass this prayer is preceded by another, also addressed to Christ: 'Lord Jesus Christ, who didst say to thy apostles, "Peace I leave to you, my peace I give unto you", look not upon my sins but upon the faith of thy church, and deign to give her peace and perfect unity according to thy will'; and then a third prayer follows: 'Lord Jesus Christ, may thy body, which I, unworthy, presume to receive, be for me not a cause for judgment and condemnation but, for thy kindness' sake, a safeguarding of mind and body and the source of my healing'. Rightly indeed Fr Martindale comments: 'Can more comprehensive, more rich, more humble and more trustful, more personal prayers anywhere be found? Observe the rare approach, now, to our Lord in person; and the "I" used by the loving, yet trembling priest'[2]. For these prayers lead on to the communion of the priest himself: in the Dominican Mass immediately, for the *Domine Jesu Christe* is immediately followed by: 'May the body and blood of our Lord Jesus Christ keep me unto eternal life'; in the Roman Mass, after the triple prayer quoted above, the priest adds: 'I will receive the bread of heaven, and call upon the name of the Lord', and then, beating his breast, he says three times: 'Lord, I am not worthy that thou shouldst enter under my roof,

---

[1] Cf. *Missarum Sollemnia*, t. iii, pp. 254–6.   [2] *op. cit.* p. 46.

yet say but a word and my soul shall be healed '[1]. Then, having himself received the divine bread, he proceeds to take it to the people.

Peace in the sense of freedom from war or the threat of war and from discord among the nations is something that most of us can only hope and pray for. Peace in the sense of freedom from discord within the christian family is something for which indeed we must pray but which also we must labour to achieve: we need to remind ourselves sometimes of the true scale of moral values, of the supreme importance of the sins against *caritas*—we can recall the fact that if there are ' six things the Lord hateth ' (and they are all anti-social sins) there is a seventh which his ' soul detesteth ', and it is sowing discord among the brethren; [2] we can remember that ' he who hateth his brother is a murderer ' and therefore cannot have ' eternal life dwelling in him '[3]; our Lord himself tells us: ' Love your enemies, do good to those who hate you; bless those who curse you, and pray for those who treat you insultingly '[4]. And in this context of the sacrifice-banquet, the common table, the breaking of bread, we cannot but remember those other words of Christ: ' If thou art bringing thy gift, then, before the altar, and rememberest there that thy brother has some ground of complaint against thee, leave thy gift lying there before the altar, and go home; be reconciled with thy brother first, and then come back to offer thy gift '[5].

There is the third sort of peace, the freedom from the burden of sin; and this again is not merely something we can pray for but, through his mercy, something we can achieve by approaching the sacrament of repentance, and achieve not just once but ' seventy times seven times '. In thinking of the *Memento* of the dead we dwelt on the idea of death being but the ' sleep of peace ': a transient stage, not a final extinction. Through God's unending mercy something of the same sort is true of spiritual

---

[1] In the Dominican Mass the priest says this last prayer only as he faces the people, repeating it three times as he holds the ciborium and lifts up a host in his right hand, immediately before giving the communion. [2] *Prov.* vi, 16-19 (Douai). [3] I *John*, iii, 15 (Knox). [4] *Luke*, vi, 27 (Knox). [5] *Matt.* v, 23-4 (Knox).

death: to be plunged into grave sin need not be the end of every-thing, will not be if we accept his mercy. Confession means for the sinner a constant rebirth, re-awakening, a renewal of courage and strength to start off again on the journey to life everlasting.

From baptism, from confession, or from the prayers of sorrow at the beginning of the Mass, we approach the Lord's table humbly but with hope and joy and determination. 'Never let me be separated from you': there is something particularly moving in this prayer, which was incorporated into the well-known *Anima Christi*. We are praying that Christ will keep us close at his side despite our sinfulness, and keep us there till the end, doggedly trying to love him and to do our duty because we love him. It is a good thing sometimes to meditate on dogs.[1] They have not perhaps—*pace* the more extreme cynophiles—the beauty and grace, the wisdom, the mystery of the cat—or the ' stealthy terror of the sinuous pard '—but they have their own fine and important qualities which we do well to imitate. They are intelligent, but humble and obedient; they have a way of gazing, patiently and devotedly, at their master that reminds one of the verse of the psalm: ' See how the eyes of servants are fixed on the hands of their masters, the eyes of a maid on the hand of her mistress '[2]; they wait for the word of command; they obey it when given; and they follow it through to the end—and sometimes even beyond, as in the case of Greyfriars Bobby in Edinburgh, who would not be moved from his master's grave. They are good and faithful servants; and those are qualities of which we all stand in need; and sometimes when, like Simon of Cyrene, we are reluctant to do what is demanded of us even though we know quite well that it is our duty to do it and to do it cheerfully, it may help us to say to ourselves, I will be a dog, and indeed a gay dog: I will try to do the job given me, thoughtfully, humbly, cheerfully, faithfully, to the end, for indeed I have been given the power to do so if only I will accept and use it,

[1] This may be said to apply more especially to Dominicans because of the ancient pun on their name, *Domini canes*, the dogs of the Lord; but it has its general application. [2] *Ps.* cxxii, 2 (Knox).

the power that comes to us in the bread of life and which, even though we may still have a long way to go, perhaps the *grandis via*, the symbolical forty days' and forty nights' journey, of Elias, will enable us to complete it, till we come like him to the mountain of God.

9

Communion

In the Roman Mass, communion is given to the faithful with the words, ' May the body of our Lord Jesus Christ keep thy soul unto life everlasting '; in the Dominican Mass [1] the formula substitutes ' thee ' for ' thy soul '. The essential meaning of the two formulas is of course the same; but perhaps one may linger a little over the theological implications which the Dominican form brings out more clearly.

In the Creed we declare our belief in the resurrection of the body; we hope for a heaven in which the whole man, the psycho-physical entity, will enjoy eternal bliss. True, we have no means of knowing what a glorified body looks like, or what it feels like to have one; and modern science, with its equation of matter and energy, gives us plenty of scope for speculation. But St Paul gives us certain clues in his first letter to the Corinthians: first, when you sow a seed in the ground it must die before it can be brought to life, and what you sow is ' not the full body that is one day to be '; secondly, ' Nature is not all one; men have one nature, the beasts another, the birds another, the fishes another; so, too, there are bodies that belong to earth and bodies that belong to heaven; and heavenly bodies have one kind of beauty, earthly bodies another. The sun has its own beauty, the moon has hers,

---

[1] As also in the ordination service for the diaconate and subdiaconate, and in the liturgy of the Carthusian Order; cf. Jungmann: *Missarum Sollemnia*, t. iii, p. 325.

the stars have theirs, one star even differs from another in its beauty. So it is with the resurrection of the dead. What is sown corruptible, rises incorruptible; what is sown unhonoured, rises in glory; what is sown in weakness, is raised in power; what is sown a natural body, rises a spiritual body '[1].

Thus St Thomas regards the glorified body as being impassible, immune from hurt or pain; agile, having the power to move effortlessly and as though instantaneously where and as the soul may desire; subtle or 'spiritual', as having the 'most complete bodily perfection' and therefore the power to obey, to 'express' perfectly, every motivation of the soul; finally, radiant, shining, because of the overflowing into the flesh of the glory of the spirit: so the book of *Wisdom* speaks of the just as shining out, 'unconquerable as the sparks that break out, now here, now there, among the stubble '[2], and in *Matthew* we read that ' the just will shine out, clear as the sun, in their Father's kingdom '[3].

St Thomas offers a further elucidation of these ideas of agility, subtlety, clarity when he tells us that the blessed will rise again in *juvenili ætate*, with 'youthful' bodies. He is not thinking of childhood: the christian paradise is no Peter Pan existence, and if there is here an echo of the theme of the *puer æternus* it is of that theme as transfigured by the theology of the Cross, and we are to think of paradise as peopled by human beings in ' the flower of their age ' who combine in themselves the physical qualities—the agility and grace—of youth and the psychological qualities—the maturity, experience, wisdom—of age.

The application of all this to our present circumstances is clear enough: it is as psycho-physical beings that we must serve God, must grow, must try to do good and to be what God wants us to be. We cannot adhere to the platonist doctrine of the body as the prison of the spirit; we cannot accept manicheism, that *pessima hæresis*, worst of heresies, in any of its forms: we are, as christians, committed to a definite view regarding the relationship between matter and spirit, as also between nature and grace. The christian

---

[1] *I Cor.* xv, 35–44 (Knox).   [2] *Wisd.* iii, 7 (Knox).   [3] *Matt.* xiii, 43 (Knox).

life is an engraced (or ' graceful ') way of being natural, or a natural way of responding to grace; for grace is not at a tangent to nature, the supernatural is not a world totally distinct and cut off from the world of natural realities, experiences, activities. If grace is active in us it is active in and through the mind, the heart, the will, the body; if we become holy we do so because God's grace transforms indeed but does not destroy our natural personalities. If, like St Paul, we are to beat our bodies into subjection it must be done with love, not hate; the purgative and transforming process involves, as we have seen, not the slightest ontological destruction; and the killing of egoism, the passage from the egocentric to the theocentric life means not a rejection of life at any of its levels but an acceptance, for it is evil, not good, that is non-being. We are not forbidden to long for happiness: on the contrary, our Lord is at pains repeatedly to promise eternal happiness to his faithful followers; we are not to suppose that the most perfect course of action is necessarily the most painful (though it may be), or that virtue consists in always sternly denying ourselves all that we desire: we have to accept, and use as best we can, the raw materials of living which God has given us: this body, these senses, this imagination, this mind, and so on, and to love them because they are God-given, because they are good, because through them we can worship and serve God, because they are destined for heaven. Communion means the receiving of Christ's flesh and blood into our own: how then can we fail to love what that divine flesh and blood have come to hallow and make his own?

The communion once given, the Mass draws very swiftly to its close. The psalm-with-antiphon which originally was sung by the choir during the communion of the faithful is now reduced simply to the antiphon; this is followed by the post-communion prayer, a prayer of thanksgiving, and then, after a final *Dominus vobiscum*, the deacon (or at Low Mass the priest) gives the dismissal: *Ite, missa est*, Go, the Mass is completed.

We may notice here a striking parallelism between Collect, Secret and Postcommunion, as also in the general framework in which these prayers are set, the introductory part of the Mass, the Offertory, and the Communion. In each case there is external action which includes a procession—the Introit, Offertory and Communion processions; in each case (and in the primitive liturgy only at these three moments) there is antiphonal psalmody sung by the choir; finally, in each case, the *oratio* follows various prayers which are said in a low voice, while the *oratio* itself, composed each time according to the same rules of style, is preceded, more or less immediately, by the ritual greeting, ' The Lord be with you ', and the exhortation, ' Let us pray '[1].

The *Ite, missa est* is first of all quite simply a formula of dismissal, of a kind very commonly used in ancient Rome for declaring a meeting closed or other similar purposes. It might then seem strange that of all the names used at various times for the christian sacrifice this one, the Mass, should have become the most common. But it must be remembered that *missa* came to have also the meaning of ' blessing ' because of the Church's custom of blessing her children before dismissing them.[2] More than that, the Mass is not a ritual which bears no relation to daily life in the world: it is the rite which empowers the christian to live his daily life in a Christ-like way. The swiftness with which, after the communion, the Mass draws to its close may be interpreted as showing the Church's desire to leave the faithful who have received Christ to speak to him in their own individual way: but it may also be linked up with the idea of the *Ite, missa est* as not merely a statement of fact but a challenge to action: the official ' action ' of the Church is over, and now it is for the faithful to go back to the everyday world, to turn away from the altar in the east and set their faces to the west, to the journeyings which the day will bring with it, the attacks of Satan—in some churches the *Ite* was at one time said facing the north, as the Gospel is [3]—and the opportunities it will provide for helping, in the divine power which has been received, in the healing and hallowing of the world. They have seen the Light, they have

---

[1] Cf. Jungmann: *Missarum Sollemnia*, t. iii, p. 358.   [2] Cf. Jungmann: *op. cit.* t. i, p. 219.
[3] Cf. Jungmann, *op. cit.* t. iii, p. 374, n. 39; cf. *supra*, p. 153.

received the Light: now they must go forth to give testimony to the Light.

The Last Gospel, the prologue to the fourth Gospel, was originally, as we have seen, not part of the Mass but of the priest's private thanksgiving; in the Mass as we now have it the priest, after the *Ite*, bows down before the altar and quietly says the *Placeat*, praying that through God's mercy the sacrifice he, though unworthy, has offered may be a propitiation for him and for all who have offered it with him; then he kisses the altar and (except in the Mass for the Dead) turns round and blesses the people, after which he goes to the left-hand corner of the altar to read the last Gospel.

The kissing of the altar is a farewell salutation and mark of veneration, corresponding to that given at the beginning of the Mass. Fr Jungmann quotes a beautiful accompanying prayer from the Syrian-Jacobite liturgy: ' Dwell in peace, holy and divine altar of the Lord! I know not if it will be given me to approach thee again, but may the Lord grant me to see thee in " the church of the first-born whose names are written in the heavens " ' [1].

The same writer points out also that the prologue to *St John* came in the course of the centuries to be regarded as an instrument of blessing, and that in many places at the end of the Middle Ages it was the custom for the people to say it with the priest ' with the evident intention of accentuating its value as such '; he also notes how the order, of blessing, *Placeat* and the kissing of the altar, varied until the Missal of Pius V established it definitively, and logically put the blessing (itself in olden days sometimes called *missa*) at the end; and he goes on to record that at the end of the Middle Ages the same sentiment led the Church at Rouen to defer this blessing until after the Gospel of St John. [2]

If there were to be question of any re-arranging of these last moments of the Mass it would indeed seem both desirable and logical for the Gospel to precede the *Ite* and the blessing, and to be said aloud either by the priest or, better still, by the whole assembly. Certainly it is difficult, and painful, to imagine the

[1] *Missarum Sollemnia*, t. iii, p. 374.   [2] *op. cit.* t. iii, pp. 385, 389, 383-4.

Mass now without this Gospel: for how richly and perfectly it concludes and summarizes all that has been said and done! We are reminded first of all of the eternal aspect of the events which have just taken place in time: reminded that the sacrifice of Christ is the sacrifice of the eternal Word, God offering himself to God. This is the creative Word, through whom all things were made, and in whom all things are summed up—*omnia in ipso constant:* it was God's 'loving design, centred in Christ, to give history its fulfilment by resuming everything in him, all that is in heaven, all that is on earth, summed up in him'[1]. He is the *Logos* in whom the Godhead knows itself, the 'radiance of his Father's splendour, and the full expression of his being'[2]; an expression, a self-revealing, communicated to us, first through the unfolding of the total cosmological process in which the 'living God' is ever active, then, within that process, through the shadowy perceptions vouchsafed to mankind as a whole and enshrined by mankind in its mythology; then, more directly, through the mouths of the prophets of the chosen people; and finally and perfectly, through the coming of the Word himself to dwell among us and, by his living and dying among us, to give us life, that 'more abundant' life which is life eternal.

The creative Word is also the enabling Word: all creation, we are told, depends for its support upon him;[3] he is also the mandatory Word, dwelling among us to show us the Way which is himself but at the same time giving us his command to follow the Way which is himself. For the Word is the pattern, and the pattern is the *lex æterna*, the eternal law, and that law is light and life for us; and, as his supreme commandment makes clear to us, law and light and life alike are love, and it is to love that we have to give testimony as we go through our journey in the world.[4]

'The Word was made flesh . . . and we had sight of his glory.' The last Gospel, like the first, is said at the left-hand corner of the altar: we are to give testimony, but before we can give testimony,

[1] *Ephes.* i, 9–10 (Knox).   [2] *Hebrews*, i, 3 (Knox).   [3] *ibid.*   [4] Cf. *Prov.* vi, 23:
'The commandment is a lamp to guide thee, and the law a light to beckon thee, and the warnings correction gave thee are a road leading to life.'

before we can act, we must have sight, we must enter into mystery, we must enter, so far as is possible in *huius sæculi nocte*, in the darkness of this world, into the glory.

In the Old Testament the glory of God is the light (sometimes the lightning) which manifests the divine presence: ' The whole of mount Sinai was by now wreathed in smoke, where the Lord had come down with fire about him, so that smoke went up as if from a furnace '[1]; ' all about him are clouds and darkness; and from his throne, on right and justice pillared, a fire goes out in his presence, burning up his enemies on every side '[2]; it is the Lord's voice, ' thundering over swollen waters ', that ' kindles flashing fire '[3]; when Moses asks him, ' Give me the sight of thy glory ', the Lord replies, ' All my splendour shall pass before thy eyes, and I will pronounce, in thy presence, my own name of Javé. . . . But my face, he said, thou canst not see; mortal man cannot see me and live to tell of it '[4]; even the reflection of that splendour is unbearable to the eyes of men, so that when Moses comes down from mount Sinai, his face ' all radiant after the meeting at which he had held speech with God ', the glory causes the sons of Israel to ' shrink from all near approach to him '[5]

In later times the Hebrews distinguished between the majesty of God (*Shekinah*) and the light accompanying it (*Kabod*): as we have seen, in the Sapiential books of the Old Testament it is Wisdom which (or rather, who) is ' pure effluence of his glory who is God all-powerful ', the ' glow that radiates from eternal light ', the ' untarnished mirror of God's majesty ', the ' faithful echo of his goodness '. ' Alone, with none to aid her, she is all-powerful; herself ever unchanged, she makes all things new; age after age she finds her way into holy men's hearts, turning them into friends and spokesmen of God. . . .'[6] Brightness is hers beyond the bright-

[1] *Exod.* xix, 20 (Knox). [2] *Ps.* xcvi, 2 (Knox). [3] *Ps.* xxviii, 3, 7 (Douai). [4] *Exod.* xxxiii, 18–20 (Knox). [5] *Exod.* xxxiv, 29–30 (Knox). [6] Cp. ' You yourselves sent a message to John, and he testified to the truth. . . . He, after all, was the lamp lit to show you the way. . . . But the testimony I have is greater than John's.' (*John,* v, 35.) Only the *Logos* is Light; those who give testimony to the Light, like the Baptist, receive their luminosity

ness of the sun, and all the starry host; match her with light itself, and she out-vies it; light must still alternate with darkness, but where is the conspiracy can pull down wisdom from her throne?'[1]

All glory, then, 'belongs to our Lord Jesus Christ'[2] who is eternal Wisdom, creative Word, incarnate *Logos*; he is the 'radiance of his Father's splendour'[3]: his manifestation it was that shone about the shepherds[4] and that broke forth from heaven and shone about Saul of Tarsus so that he fell to the ground and cried, 'Who art thou, Lord?'[5] It is of him that we are told that he will 'come hereafter in his Father's glory with his angels about him, and he will recompense everyone, then, according to his works'[6]. This is the splendour on which no mortal man can look and yet live; and at the same time it is the ineffable humility and self-emptying of the incarnate Word; this is at once the Lion of Juda and the Lamb of God; the Judge coming in majesty on the clouds of heaven, and the Baby wrapped in swaddling clothes. And the splendour lies not on one side or the other of these paradoxes but in the fusion of both: there are the thunder and lightning, the mouth breathing forth fire, the voice that breaks the cedars, that kindles flashing fire, that makes the wilderness rock;[7] there is also the 'still, small voice' in which Elias recognized his God, there is the Man of Sorrows, acquainted with infirmity; there is the God who did not reject the woman in the city who was a sinner, who was gentle with the woman taken in adultery, who said 'Come to me, all you that labour and are burdened, and I will give you rest'[8]; and again all these are one. We have to remember the

[1] *Wisd.* vii, 25-30 (Knox). [2] *James*, ii, 1 (Knox). [3] *Hebrews*, i, 3 (Knox). [4] *Luke*, ii, 9. [5] *Acts*, ix, 3-5 (Knox). [6] *Matt.* xvi, 27 (Knox). [7] *Ps.* xxviii, 5-8. [8] *Matt.* xi, 28 (Knox).

from him that they may become 'spokesmen of God'. Cp. *Ps.* xvii, 29: 'Thou lightest my lamp, O Lord: O my God, enlighten my darkness'. The saints have their aureoles; but it is because the *Sol invictus* has set them aflame. To give glory to God is the ultimate end of all creatures; to give formal (i.e. conscious and explicit) glory to God is the ultimate end of all intelligent creatures, and this they do, first by becoming themselves aflame, and then by sending forth flame, the flame which is their participation in the Light. There is the same idea in the vision of the City in the *Apocalypse* (xxii, 5) where there will be 'no more need of light from lamp or sun; the Lord God will shed his light on them'.

terror of the Judge coming in thunder and cloud amidst a myriad of angels and announcing the doom of the accursed; on the other hand we have to remember the love, the light, the laughter, the dance, the divine comedy, the everlasting mercy. How shall we reconcile these irreconcilables? Perhaps best by remembering, learning, living the Mass, which is glory in high heaven and, on earth, peace. Perhaps by recalling such words as those that Claudel has written somewhere: 'Have pity on every man, Lord, in that hour when he has finished his tasks and stands before thee like a child whose hands are being examined'.

The business of the Mass is transacted now on the right hand of the altar, now on the left: now on the side of fatherhood, of law, of instruction, of action which is according to the law, *adscriptus, ratus, rationabilis*, now on the side of mystery, of motherhood. The law-giving *Logos* is also the 'hen, gathering her chickens under her wings'[1]; the Eternal Wisdom is both God and bride; the soul is feminine to God, and yet in some incomprehensible fashion, because of his love-impelled *kenosis*, his self-emptying, it is also the other way round, it is the Word who, being himself the Door, yet stands at the door, knocking, and must wait for someone to listen to his voice and open the door.[2] ' " God *needs* man ", says Eckhart. It is Love calling to love: and the journey, though in one sense a hard pilgrimage, up and out, by the terraced mount and the ten heavens to God, in another is the inevitable rush of the roving comet, caught at last, to the Central Sun. " My weight is my love ", said St Augustine. Like gravitation, it inevitably compels, for good or evil, every spirit to its own place. According to another range of symbols, that love flings open a door, in order that the larger Life may rush in, and it and the soul be " one thing ". . . . " In the book of Hidden Things it is written," says Eckhart, " ' I stand at the door and knock and wait '. . . thou needst not seek him here or there: he is no farther off than the door of the heart. There he stands and waits and waits until he finds thee ready to open and let him in. Thou needst not call him from a distance; to

---

[1] *Matt.* xxiii, 37 (Douai).   [2] *Apoc.* iii, 20.

wait until thou openest is harder for him than for thee. He needs
thee a thousand times more than thou canst need him. Thy opening
and his entering are but one moment ".' [1]

' A knock on the door, and then my true love's voice: Let me
in, my true love, so gentle, my bride, so pure! See, how bedewed
is this head of mine, how the night rains have drenched my hair ! ' [2]
But this again is the *ludus amoris*, for, as we read on: ' Then my
true love thrust his hand through the lattice, and I trembled inwardly
at his touch. I rose up to let him in; but my hands dripped ever
with myrrh; still with the choicest myrrh my fingers were slippery,
as I caught the latch. When I opened, my true love was gone; he
had passed me by. How my heart had melted at the sound of his
voice! And now I searched for him in vain; there was no answer
when I called out to him '[3]. But the end is not tragedy: we are
concerned with the divine comedy: ' I searched for my heart's
love, and searched in vain. . . . I met the watchmen who go the
city rounds, and asked them whether they had seen my love; then,
when I had scarce left them, I found him, so tenderly loved; and
now that he is mine I will never leave him, never let him go '[4].

We may return here to a point which we considered at the
beginning of this book: that the comedies of redemption are of
a higher rank, a deeper truth, and offer a more complete revelation
than tragedy; and that the ' happy ending ' is to be read not as a
contradiction but as a transcendence of the universal tragedy of
man. And what brings that tragedy to its happy ending is the
everlasting mercy, the motherhood of God. It is in that motherhood
that for us, ' poor, banished children of Eve ' as we say in the *Salve
Regina*, the divine glory is supremely revealed and brought close to
us. The greatest purely human expression of the *Logos*-pattern is
to be found of course in Mary, the mother of God and of man;
and as her whole life was given to her Son and the fulfilling of his
vocation, so her whole being is given to reflecting, through her
own motherhood, the mystery of the motherhood of God. The

[1] Underhill: *Mysticism*, p. 133.   [2] *Song of Songs*, v, 2 (Knox).   [3] *ibid.* v, 4–6.
[4] *Song of Songs*, iii, 1–4 (Knox).

' living God', ever active in and through the creative and re-creative cosmological process, is also the power and the glory, the *Shekinah*, brooding over that process; and as in the beginning the Spirit brooded over the waters of chaos and darkness that light and life and form might be, so in the fullness of time the ' power of the most High' overshadowed the girl in Nazareth who, bringing forth the Glory into the world, herself reflected that Glory: it has been pointed out that ' blue, which is for christian art the special colour of the blessed Virgin, was and is for Jewish thought the colour of the *Shekinah* '[1]. We all know the joy of lying on grass or sand and letting the hot sun, the ' purring lion ', penetrate and vitalize us while we gaze up at the blue sky which seems to cover our world as with a protective mantle: that sky can remind us of the blue mantle of Mary, encompassing and protecting the children of men; but that in its turn must remind us of the divine reality to which it owes its being, and to which its whole purpose is to lead us.

We were thinking earlier on of the self-effacingness of the saints: here we have the most self-effacing of them all. She began by saying, ' Behold the handmaid of the Lord '; and her words summarize not only her life upon earth but the history of her *cultus* as well.[2] Those who accuse the catholic Church of mariolatry would do well to study the history of mariology. Of her more truly than of any other creature it can be said that she had greatness thrust upon her: true, she foresaw it, and humbly stated it when she sang, 'Behold from henceforth all generations shall call me blessed '; but the honour, the glory, the veneration were not of her seeking, and when they came to her it was first of all as the result of defending the truth about her Son, and as they grew and grew through the ages their effect was, as she would wish, to increase men's love and understanding of her Son, while on the other hand attempts to destroy her *cultus* and deny her greatness have ended in a denial of the divinity of her Son.

If one were to ask, for instance, whether the apostles believed

[1] Cf. Underhill: *Worship*, p. 201, n. 2.   [2] The next few pages are adapted by kind permission of the Editor, from an article in *The Life of the Spirit*, May, 1958.

in what is commonly called the immaculate conception—the doctrine that Mary was preserved from all taint of original sin—or thought of and revered her as Queen of Angels, the answer would presumably be no, since they had had no occasion to think of her in such terms. Obviously they held her in deep veneration as the mother of their Lord; but she was still Mary of Nazareth: she became known and revered as Queen of Heaven not suddenly and *per saltum* but as a result of a long and gradual development, and a development which was at first not devotional but theological.

The folly of confusing sacredness of office with personal holiness seems to be quite a recent phenomenon: many modern catholics seem to think—in bland defiance of the facts of history—that a Pope must *ipso facto* be a saint, or, for that matter, that a man who writes ' spiritual ' books must be a spiritual man. Earlier ages suffered from no such delusions; no one ever had a deeper or more vivid veneration for the papal office than Catherine of Siena, for instance, yet no one could be more outspoken and scorching in denouncing the moral shortcomings of the holders of that office. In the same way the early christians saw no immediate connection between the immensity of Mary's vocation and her own personal glory: in what is sometimes called the ' official ' gospel—that of Christ's ministry, from baptism to ascension—Mary is not specially exalted; on the contrary, when she and her relatives come to claim our Lord's attention he seems to ignore her; St Paul in *Galatians* speaks of the incarnate Word simply as ' made of a woman '[1]; the attitude of some of the early Fathers can be seen in their reading of the story of Cana, in which they see Christ as rebuking his mother, either because she doubted (Tertullian) or because she sought glory through his power (Chrysostom). (Misunderstanding of our Lord's reply to his mother has often been due to a misreading of the sense of his words: ' Woman ' is, in the original idiom, a term not of rebuke but of honour; the rest of the phrase can mean simply ' leave it to me '[2].) But the first chapters of *Luke* underline her unique dignity: ' The holy Spirit will come upon thee, and the power of

---

[1] *Gal.* iv, 4 (Douai).　　[2] Cf. Lagrange: *Evang. s. S. Jean* in ch. ii, 4.

the most High will overshadow thee'; 'How have I deserved to be thus visited by the mother of my Lord?'; 'From this day forward all generations will count me blessed';[1] and one can say that the germ of all that will follow through the ages is contained in the threefold idea of Mary as overshadowed by the Spirit, as mediating (at Cana) between men and Christ, and (at the cross, according to an age-old application of Christ's words to John) by being made the mother of all mankind.

In the first centuries the Church had to safeguard the truth about Christ from two opposing errors: that of denying the reality of his humanity, and that of denying his divinity. It was to counter the first of these heresies that the phrase *natus ex Maria* was formulated: the Christ-man was really formed in the womb of Mary; on the other hand it was to assert Christ's divinity that the Council of Ephesus (A.D. 431) declared Mary to be *Theotokos parthenos*, the Virgin Mother of God. The Council of Chalcedon (A.D. 451) reiterates this definition, and in so doing closes this stage of mariological development, the stage of precise doctrinal definitions; and there will be no further official development until 1854. But meanwhile the theological interest in and discussion of the personality, the attributes, the status of Mary continue: Anselm explores the question of her close relationship with the Trinity; her greatness (greater than that of the angels) is elucidated; the idea of her sinlessness becomes clearer until it develops into the controversies concerning the immaculate conception—if she was sinless she was not in need of redemption by Christ, which cannot be true since she is a member of the human race and the human race as a whole was under the bondage of sin; if on the other hand she was redeemed she cannot have been sinless, which derogates against the dignity of the Word born of her flesh—controversies which were finally settled by the recognition that she was indeed redeemed but by preservation, not by liberation, from original sin.

In the Middle Ages a new approach is discernible, no longer so predominantly intellectual but now more affective. The cult of

[1] *Luke*, i, 35, 43, 48 (Knox).

the *Theotokos* had had a great centre in Rome since the dedication of S. Mary Major in the fifth century; but in the age of chivalry, of courtly love, of the exaltation of woman, we find a marked development in the *cultus* of Mary in, so to speak, her own right: she had always been venerated, she had been portrayed in christian art, but always with her Son: gradually she begins to be portrayed also alone, she becomes Our Lady, *Notre Dame*, a Sovereign, a Queen; at the same time she becomes also the refuge of sinners, interceding for them: there is in other words a simultaneous development of interest in and devotion towards her as Queen of glory and as the mother of men, of sinners, praying for them to her Son. This latter aspect of her place in the Church and the world's history was the subject of renewed theological speculation about her exact rôle in the work of redemption: her *fiat* was recognized as a free act of acceptance of that rôle and therefore as the beginning of a true co-operation; it was seen moreover as given, as St Thomas says, *loco totius humanæ naturæ*, speaking for mankind as a whole; the Passion of Christ is linked with her freely given and suffered compassion, and his universal love and redemptive will are linked with her universal motherhood. The attacks on her cult in the Reformation period again produced a renewal of study and a greater precision of definition regarding her graces, her knowledge, her sufferings, her glory, her power, her mediating intercession at the throne of God; at the same time the precise nature of the *cultus* due to her was further explored, that *hyperdulia* which is a veneration much greater than the *dulia* given to all the saints, yet infinitely removed from the adoration which is due to God alone. The development in the seventeenth century, largely under French influence, was not entirely felicitous, tending as it did to the florid, the rhetorical, the unctuous, to a devotion in which can be discerned the germs of modern *bondieuseries* and repository art.

What a heart-felt relief it is to turn, from the turgid sentimentality of modern ' devotions ' to the mother of God, to such splendid things as the prayer which Villon, the rascal-poet, wrote for his old mother:

Dame du ciel, regente terrienne,
Emperiere des infernaux palus—

and which was so beautifully paraphrased by Synge:

' Mother of God, that's Lady of the Heavens, take myself the poor sinner, the way I'll be along with them that's chosen.

' Let you say to your Son that he'd have a right to forgive my share of sins, when it's the like he's done, many's the day, with big and famous sinners. I'm a poor aged woman was never at school and is no scholar with letters, but I've seen pictures in the chapel with Paradise on one side, and harps and pipes in it, and the place on the other side, where sinners do be boiled in torment; the one gave me great joy, the other a great fright and scaring; let me have the good place, Mother of God, and it's in your faith I'll live always.

' It's yourself that bore Jesus, that has no end or death, and he the Lord Almighty, that took our weakness and gave himself to sorrows, a young and gentle man. It's himself is our Lord surely, and it's in that faith I'll live always.'[1]

With the nineteenth century we come to the great age of ' mariophanies ', of Lourdes and the rest; and these in turn led, or helped to lead, to that greater concentration on the power and importance of Mary, her loving activity within the redemptive plan, which is characteristic of our own century. Yet always these accretions of glory seem to flow back from her to her Son: it is as when Dante, looking into the eyes of Beatrice, sees reflected in them not his own image but that of Christ. Her greatest glory is, as it always was, to give glory to him. To think of Lourdes as a purely personal glorification of Mary would be entirely wrong: its affirmation of her divine motherhood is an implicit affirmation of the divinity of her Son; there is an implicit affirmation, moreover, of the legitimacy of religious development, of ' popular ' forms of piety:[2] the emphasis here, as in other shrines, on the rosary is

---

[1] Cf. D. B. Wyndham Lewis: *Villon*, pp. 305-7, 335.　　[2] ' Popular ' is not at all the same thing as ' debased ': valuable developments of theology and ultimately of defined doc-trine have come from the devotional life of the people; but popular devotion can ' go

after all a recall to the 'mysteries' of Christ's life and passion; and the 'message' of all these appearances, the call to a *metanoia*, to a change of heart, to repentance and prayer, is a call to accept, acknowledge and serve the sovereignty of Christ and to live within the framework of his redemptive plan.

Thus we can see the essential office of Mary as being not only to bring grace *from* Christ, but to lead us back *to* Christ, just as we can see the essential purpose of her motherhood of men as revealing to us, and leading us back to, the motherhood of God. At the same time, she, who is so often liturgically identified with Wisdom and with the Church, leads us back to the essentially *motherly* nature of the Church.

We think of the Church as 'summed up' in the person of our father the Pope; and we are right; so too every parish is in a sense summed up in the person of the priest, the father, who is its pastor, though to be accurate we should think here of the *ecclesia docens*: it is the teaching, authoritative, jurisdictional aspects of the Church which are summed up in the papacy. Even so, the personal infallibility of the Pope derives from and expresses the infallibility of the Church: it is the Church, in the last resort, that 'has the mind of Christ'. And we think of the Church not as father but as mother. Too often nowadays the aspect of the Church as life-giving or life-renewing mother is overlaid and obscured by an exaggerated preoccupation with its paternal aspects—with the legal, the canonical, the penal aspects of authority. True, law and life are one, as we have seen; but it is possible to separate them, so that law is devitalized into legalism. Dr Erich Fromm defines a patriarchal society in terms of an authoritarian, hierarchical, legal, social system; a matriarchal society as one in which the moving force is to be found in the laws of blood, love, and the solidarity of all

---

wrong' just as on another level theological speculation can go wrong; to approve of popular forms of prayer or worship (e.g. the rosary) is certainly not to approve of such disastrous phenomena as the 'Lourdes hymn' or the *objets de piété* which pullulate at Lourdes and other shrines; nor can we deny the undeniable fact of a good deal of naïve superstition masquerading as religion within the christian family.

humanity;[1] the Church can be seen as a matriarchy, not in the sense of being ' run by women ' but inasmuch as the paternal-legal aspects of its life must always be ensouled by the maternal aspects, the endless torrent of life-giving waters, the laws of blood and love and solidarity, the all-embracing cross, the font-womb which is the comfort of the afflicted and the refuge of sinners.

All this is vividly illustrated for us in the rosary. In the first place, we tend to think of it as a prayer to our Lady, and the bulk of the words we say are indeed addressed to her; but the *Hail Mary* is in fact bracketed between the prayer to our heavenly Father and the praise of the Trinity; and the events and truths recalled in the mysteries are concerned primarily not with Mary—from some of the events she is physically absent—but with Christ, and then with his mother precisely as his mother-to-be or mother-in-being and, finally, as queen and mother of all men. During her Son's earthly life she is with him when (and only when) she is needed, to serve and help him; when he is gone she mothers for a time the *pusillus grex*, the little flock which is the infant Church; and when, her Son's glory accomplished, it is time for her to be glorified in her turn, her triumph does but underline for us, bring home to us, the love and mercy, the nearness, the motherhood, of God.

Some catholics find it difficult to pray the rosary; and sometimes no doubt the reason is that despite its all but universal appeal it is not ' their ' prayer, they are temperamentally unsuited to it; but perhaps more often it is because they set about it in the wrong way. There are the words to be said, the beads to be told, the events to be considered, and underneath all this there is the essence of all prayer, the awareness of God; and they find this multiplicity confusing, distracting, and they scold themselves for being unable to concentrate on all these things at one and the same time. But why should they? There are various ways of praying the rosary, and we can pick and choose according to our different temperaments or the needs and moods of the moment. We can, if we will, concentrate on the words we are saying (' Mother of God, pray for us,

---

[1] *The Forgotten Language*, pp. 190–1.

sinners '); or, knowing what we are saying, we can turn our immediate attention away from the individual words and phrases and concentrate on the scene with which we are concerned and with the ideas it suggests, its relevance to our own lives; or again, while retaining a vague awareness of the scene (whether as mental image or as idea) we can give all our attention to the divine love which lies behind it and is expressed through it: we can rest in the immobility of the divine reality which is mediated to us through the moving panorama of the temporal events. We can do now one now another of these things, free and tranquil of mind; we can also do them all simultaneously if we remember that the essence of prayer is the awareness of God and that all the other activities comprised in the saying of the rosary can be of great help in stilling the other levels of the personality and so making this deep awareness possible. Women often find it easier to concentrate on a lecture if they can do some knitting during it; in the same way the telling of beads can tranquillize the body and help the mind to concentrate; the vague awareness of a picture in the imagination (vague because quiet, unstrained) can similarly help to keep that faculty stilled; words too, if they are used in the same effortless sort of way, can occupy and still the body, the imagination, the surface of the mind, and so allow the essential process to take place in the deeper levels of the soul, in the ' fund of the spirit '.

It seems reasonable then to suppose that the praying of the rosary should involve not great mental strain and effort but on the contrary a feeling of freedom and tranquillity. Indeed for those who have made themselves familiar with it, and who love God and his mother, this must surely be the case unless they put unreasonable demands upon themselves. The rosary is a unity; its various mysteries are all part of a single pattern, so that the words or events of one scene may well lead the mind to think of another or of the total pattern or again of some parallel between them and something —whether realized or hoped for—in our own lives. As we begin the joyful mysteries the ' Behold the handmaid ' of the first mystery may remind us of the ' Behold from henceforth ' of the second, or of the ' Behold the Man ' of a later mystery, or again of how that initial humility, the humble acceptance of things, whether great or lowly, as they are, is the key to the fulfilling of the pattern in our own lives as in these others', the key to the creative living of our lives, to learning from and being reborn through the experience, the joys and sorrows, of which our lives are made up and out of which the final glory is to be fashioned. There is no harm in allowing ideas and images to float thus to and fro in mind and imagination provided that they do not stray too far from the pattern or some point in it or some application of it or from the reality behind it, and provided also, once again, that this gentle activity has a quietening effect on the personality as a whole and so enables the deeper levels to be tranquil, attentive, receptive.

It is in fact soothing to allow the fingers to play with well-worn, well-loved beads, the lips to murmur again and again a well-loved phrase, the imagination to linger over a well-loved scene, the mind to consider a familiar but always evocative story or idea; on the other hand we know how quickly, when we make an effort to recollect ourselves, to concentrate, the body begins to fidget, the mind to wander, the imagination to lead us off into endless irre-levancies; we know that if we attempt to pray we shall almost certainly be distracted after the first few moments, our attention will wander and perhaps we shall fail for quite some time to advert to the fact that it is wandering. But the solution to our difficulties does not seem to lie in tremendous effort and stress and strain, for these can never bring about in us that tranquillity which is the condition of awareness. The solution must lie rather in learning to be humble and patient and gentle. If at the beginning of our time of prayer we have made an initial act of adoring awareness of God we need not be discouraged by the fact that our attention to him is so short-lived, so piecemeal. If for some part of the allotted time we can keep our surface-consciousness occupied with divine things as the rosary can help us to do we should rejoice: we are doing well, and our inability to do more must be taken as part of those human limitations which we have humbly to accept as part of ourselves; but even if we fail to achieve this much we need not think our time is wasted: our initial attention and intention have laid open to God's impulse and influence the 'fund of the spirit'.

But in the fund of the spirit what matters most is not what we do but what is done in us. 'He that is mighty hath done great things in me, and holy is his name.' In the Mass (explicitly in the *epiclesis* of the Greek rite but equivalently in the Roman Canon too) we pray that when we have fulfilled all the external requirements of the rubrics, and when the earthly offerings of bread and wine have been brought to the altar and duly prepared, the quickening Spirit may come, the fire may descend upon the altar, so that the offerings ' may become for us the body and blood ' of the incarnate Word. The rosary too gives us ' external ' things to occupy—and enrich—the periphery of consciousness: the beads, the words, the images; but these things will best fulfil their purpose if they make all things quiet in us. so that then, our ' house being now at rest ', we can allow unimpeded entry to the quickening Spirit. We pray to and think of our Lady, but it is essentially in order that she may lead us to her Son; we think of the human events in the life of that Son, but it is essentially that we may be led *per humanitatem ad divinitatem*, through those human things to the divine reality they express and reveal. We say ' Mother of God, pray for us, sinners '; but it is essentially in order that through growing in love and understanding of the motherhood of Mary we may be led to know and love and adore, to accept and so be renewed by, the creative motherhood of God.

In the polyvalent language of symbol, then, though not of course in the ontological language of theology, wisdom and spirit and mother, water, wood and fire are all one: wisdom is ' a tree of life to them that lay hold on her ' [1]; there are three things that ' give testimony on earth: the spirit, and the water, and the blood: and these three are one ' [2]; and the cross is ' tree of life and bearer of light in one, and both symbols stand for Christ himself, who " hallowed the water, by his suffering ", endowing it with the

---

[1] *Prov.* iii, 18 (Douai). [2] I *John*, v, 8 (Douai).

doxa that he earned on the cross, the power of the holy Ghost '[1] ; and all these things are mother-symbols because all of them signify rebirth, renewal, the coming out from the darkness into light.

We live in an ' age of Mary '. If this is of immense psychological importance inasmuch as it may mean for us a redressing of the balance between masculine and feminine elements in our psychological life in days when the former have become so dangerously hypertrophied at the expense of the latter, it is also of extreme theological importance in reminding us of the danger of allowing our religious thinking to be coloured by this prevailing climate of opinion in the world of today.

Christ is born of the Well, the Source, the *fons amoris*, the *fons signatus*; and if we are to imitate him we must be similarly born, or reborn, of water and the Spirit. For us, the well or *fons amoris* is the font of baptism, made fruitful to life everlasting through the generative power of the cross;[2] it is the ' mystery of wood and water ' therefore: the ' water of life springs up at the foot of the tree of life '[3]; and the tree, once again, is a mother-symbol: in the Old Testament, Elias laid himself down under the juniper tree and prayed to have done with life, for, he said, he was no better than his fathers; but there he was renewed, and in his renewal of strength went his forty days' journey to the mount of God;[4] in myth, Hiawatha similarly lies down to rest under the pine-tree; perhaps we should see an echo of the same theme in Christ's words to Nathanael, who passed from scepticism to belief when Jesus told him, ' I saw thee when thou wast under the fig-tree '[5]. Fr Rahner quotes a ' wonderful pæan of praise to the cosmic and biblical mystery of the cross ' from a sermon of the pseudo-Chrysostom:

' This tree as broad as the heavens has grown up from earth to heaven. Immortal tree, it extends from heaven to earth. It is the fixed pivot of the universe, the fulcrum of all things, the foundation of the world, the cardinal point of the cosmos. It

---

[1] Rahner, *op. cit.* pp. 396–7. [2] Rahner, *op. cit.* p. 394. [3] *ibid.* p. 387. [4] III *Kings,* xix, 4. [5] *John,* i, 48 (Knox).

binds together all the multiplicity of human nature. It is held together by invisible nails of the spirit in order to retain its bond with the Godhead. It touches the highest summits of heaven and with its feet holds fast the earth, and it encompasses the vast middle atmosphere in between with its immeasurable arms.

' O crucified one, thou leader of the mystical dance! O spiritual marriage feast! O divine Pascha, passing from the heavens to the earth and rising again to the heavens! O new feast of all things, O cosmic festive gathering, O joy of the universe. . . . The people which was in the depths arises from the dead and proclaims to the hosts above: the chorus of the earth returns!' [1]

So we come back to the dance, the music, the radiance, the song of the spheres, the song of the seraphim, the ' snow-white rose ' espoused by Christ, the smile of the eternal Light. We do not, we cannot, forget the burden of our sin, the weight of the murky pall of evil lying over the world; we do not neglect the Woes of the *Apocalypse* or the anguish of the *Dies Irae*; we know the fear of death, the fear of judgement, the terror of the *mysterium tremendum;* and yet we look—and yet we must look—beyond these to the love and the mercy and the motherhood, must look in faith and hope and love to an ending which, because of the Tree and the Cup, is joy and music and laughter and the cessation of all sorrow for ever:

> *I looked;*
> *And, in the likeness of a river, saw*
> *Light flowing, from whose amber-seeming waves*
> *Flash'd up effulgence, as they glided on*
> *'Twixt banks, on either side, painted with spring,*
> *Incredible how fair; and, from the tide,*
> *There ever and anon, outstarting, flew*
> *Sparkles instinct with life; and in the flowers*
> *Did set them, like to rubies chased in gold.* [2]

[1] Cf. Rahner, *op. cit.* pp. 386-7.   [2] Dante: *Paradiso* (tr.Cary), xxx, 59-67.

So Dante describes the beginning of his ultimate vision; but Beatrice told him how the stream, ' with all this laughter on its bloomy shores ' is but a preface, ' shadowy of the truth '; and so he went on to view the vast circle which ' spreads so far that the circumference were too loose a zone to girdle in the sun ', the circle of the snow-white rose which is the multitude of the saints; and as he gazed, his eyes

> *Coursed up and down along the living light,*
> *Now low, and now aloft, and now around,*
> *Visiting every step.   Looks I beheld,*
> *Where charity in soft persuasion sat;*
> *Smiles from within, and radiance from above;*
> *And, in each gesture, grace and honour high.*[1]

And then at the bidding of St Bernard he raised his eyes higher till they saw the burning of the ' peaceful oriflamb ',

> *And in that midst their sportive pennants waved*
> *Thousands of Angels; in resplendence each*
> *Distinct, and quaint adornment.   At their glee,*
> *And carol, smiled the Lovely One of heaven,*
> *That joy was in the eyes of all the blest.*[2]

Then Bernard begged the Lovely One, Mary, that Dante might be given to gaze on the Godhead itself, the ' abyss of radiance ', the ' three orbs of triple hue, clipt in one bound '; and so he gazed, till he could gaze no more, *tanto che la veduta vi consunsi*, on the ' everlasting splendour '[3].

The consciousness of sin may make us turn away from this splendour, as sorrow may make us turn away from laughter, but it should not, for we have known the wood and the water and the wine; provided we repent of our sins we remain, in spite of them, the ' children of the promise '; and in the power of that promise we can listen with awe and exultation to the words of Clement of Alexandria: ' Thou shalt dance with angels around

[1] *op. cit.* xxxi, 43–8.   [2] *op. cit.* xxxi, 119, 121–5.   [3] *op. cit.* xxxiii, 107–9, 79–80.

the unbegotten and imperishable and only true God, and God's *Logos* shall join with us in our hymns of praise '; and in the joy of that promise we can recall the words of the psalmist: ' For a moment lasts his anger, for a life-time his love; sorrow is but the guest of a night, and joy comes in the morning '[1].

[1] *Ps.* xxix, 6 (Knox).

ACKNOWLEDGMENTS

The Author wishes to acknowledge his indebtedness to the following, who have kindly given permission for the use of copyright material contained in this volume: Messrs. George Allen & Unwin Ltd. from *Poems and Translations* by J. M. Synge; Blackfriars Publications from an article appearing in *The Life of the Spirit* entitled *The All-Sufficient Sacrifice* by Victor White, O.P.; Messrs. Burns Oates & Washbourne Ltd. from *The Gospel of Jesus Christ* by M.-J. Lagrange, O.P.; Challoner Publications (Liturgy) Ltd., from *The Eucharistic Prayer* and *The Sacrifice of the Church* by J. A. Jungmann; and Aubier of Paris from the same author's *Missarum Sollemnia*; The Guild of Pastoral Psychology from *A Map of the Psyche* by K. F. Lander, *The Old Testament and Analytical Psychology* by H. Westmann, and *Walter Hilton* by Victor White, O.P.; Messrs. William Heinemann Ltd. from *East of Eden* by John Steinbeck; The Estate of the Late Mrs. Frieda Lawrence and Messrs. William Heinemann Ltd. from *Apropos of Lady Chatterley's Lover* by D. H. Lawrence; Messrs. Methuen & Co. Ltd. from *Mysticism* by Evelyn Underhill; Messrs. John Murray Ltd. from *The Nude* by Sir Kenneth Clark; Librairie Gallimard of Paris from *Images et Symboles* by Mircéa Eliade; Messrs. Routledge & Kegan Paul Ltd. from *Symbols of Transformation* and *Practice of Psychotherapy* by C. G. Jung, and *The Mysteries: Papers from the Eranos Yearbooks*; Messrs. Sheed & Ward Ltd. from *The Mythic Dimension in Christian Sacramentalism* by Beirnaert.

In addition to the works referred to in the text, the Author wishes to acknowledge his indebtedness (in preparing the section on the Mass especially) to such books as: *The Holy Sacrifice of the Mass* by Nicholas Gihr; *Sacred Signs* by Romano Guardini; *Interpreting the Sunday Mass* by W. R. Bonniwell, O.P.; *The Meaning of the Mass* by Paul Bussard; *The Great Prayer* by Hugh Ross Williamson; *The Holy Sacrifice of the Mass* by Martin B. Hellriegel.

INDEX

310

Index

311

Index

313

Index

Index

315

Index

Index

Index

Index